THE PLACE OF HOOKER
IN THE HISTORY OF THOUGHT

THE PLACE OF HOOKER
IN THE HISTORY OF
THOUGHT

by

PETER MUNZ
M.A., Ph.D.

Senior Lecturer in History, Victoria University College
Wellington, New Zealand

GREENWOOD PRESS, PUBLISHERS
WESTPORT, CONNECTICUT

Originally published in 1952
by Routledge & Kegan Paul Ltd., London

Reprinted with the permission
of the author, Peter Munz

First Greenwood Reprinting 1971

Library of Congress Catalogue Card Number 71-137085

SBN 8371-5548-7

Printed in the United States of America

To My Mother

CONTENTS

PREFACE

MY attention was first drawn to Richard Hooker by the remark that Hooker's political thought was much like Burke's, in that it was based upon the realization of the importance of tradition and upon the rejection of the individual's private judgement. As I was interested in the philosophy of conservatism, I read Hooker. But before I had progressed very far I was forcibly impressed by the fact that Hooker was a Thomist and an Aristotelian and that he condemned the Puritans on grounds altogether different from those which led Burke to condemn the Revolutionaries. It is true that both men defended the political constitution of England in their time. But it is equally true that they did so for very different reasons. I have, therefore, endeavoured to unravel the historical background to some of Hooker's leading ideas. By thus determining his place in the history of thought I hope to have made also a contribution to the understanding of Hooker himself; for much light is thrown on his thought by a clear appreciation of the philosophical issues he raised and the difficulties he had to face when he embraced the cause of Thomism in Elizabethan England. I have therefore not attempted an exhaustive study of Hooker's thought and in particular have not discussed his theology and his relation to contemporary political ideas. The latter subject has been treated recently by the Reverend F. J. Shirley, in his *Richard Hooker and Contemporary Political Ideas* (London, 1949). Unfortunately this book reached me too late for me to avail myself of its scholarship.

The present study was originally a Ph.D. thesis presented in the University of Cambridge. I have recorded my indebtedness to other scholars in the footnotes. But I would like to take this opportunity of thanking Professor M. C. Knowles for the kind encouragement and friendly criticism he has given me, and

Professor A. P. d'Entrèves for the stimulus I have received from many conversations with him. I also owe a very special debt of gratitude to Professor F. L. W. Wood for helping me to revise my English and for making it more consistent with common usage, and to Dr. W. Strich for the inspiration I have received from his profound philosophical understanding. I also wish to thank Professor N. Sykes for much valuable criticism, Dr. J. C. Beaglehole and Dr. H. O. Pappe for many good suggestions and my wife for her help in reading the proofs. It is entirely my own fault that, in spite of so much kind help and advice, I have not been able to write a better book.

Finally, and gladly, I thank Victoria University College for the subsidy from its Publications Fund which has made possible the appearance of the book.

P. M.

September 1951
Victoria University College
Wellington
New Zealand

CHAPTER ONE

INTRODUCTION

'THE State exists not only in order to enable people to live; but in order to enable people to live well.' It is hardly an exaggeration to say that the whole of Christian political philosophy during the Middle Ages was a commentary on this famous quotation from Aristotle. To Aristotle himself these words had meant something entirely different from what they came to mean to the medieval Christian philosopher. But it is just this transformation of their meaning that illustrates so pointedly the transition from pagan political philosophy to Christian political philosophy and the institutional problems peculiar to it.

It all turns on the meaning of the phrase 'to live well'. To the pagan Aristotle the good life was the life which enabled man to reach happiness in this world. Happiness meant success, personal, social and economic. And no matter what one meant exactly by success, there was no doubt that it was to be measured entirely in terms of this present natural life. The degree of adjustment and harmony a human being attained between birth and death was the ultimate standard of judgement: the end of human life, to the pagan philosopher, was immanent in life itself. But the gospel brought a new conception of life: and its profound and world-shaking message lay just in its assertion that the end of life lay in God, i.e. transcended all earthly and human existence. Henceforth no philosopher who had accepted the gospel could hold that the degree of harmony attained in this life could be the ultimate standard of judgement whether a life was good or not. From now on 'to live well' received an entirely new meaning. To live well, meant to save one's soul or to find the divinely appointed end of

human existence, the beatific vision. The result of man's earthly
existence could no longer be judged by purely earthly, and hence
immanent, criteria; but had to be scrutinized from the point of view
as to whether it would enable a man to reach the beatific vision
and the salvation of his soul or not. The standards of measurement
of human conduct were no longer to be derived exclusively from
human existence in this world. Life in this world, limited by birth
and death, could and was generally held to be, conducted success—
fully in the light of human or natural reason. But the message of
the gospel transcended the sphere where human reason was appli-
cable: the requirements and standards of conduct for the salvation
of the human soul were revealed to man by God; they could
neither be formulated nor proven by human reason. And thus was
added to the body of rules that governed personal as well as social
life, to the body of natural law, a body of super-natural or divine
law. Both kinds of law came to be known through St. Augustine
as part of the eternal law which God had set down to Himself
for the government of the world.

Here then, there arose a political problem which had been
completely unknown to pre-Christian political philosophy: the
State had been considered a function of natural law; and natural
law itself had been taken to be discoverable by human reason.
No other institution for the regulation of social affairs had been
needed, for there was no other kind of law. Now, however, people
found that social and personal life had to be subjected to the requirements of divine as well as of natural law: it was obvious that
the State, no matter what kind of views one had as to its origin,
purpose or nature, could not be regarded as the source or expression or function of divine law. The State was an institution
governed by reason and administering rules that had been agreed
upon by rational discussion. But divine law could neither be
found nor be discussed by human reason. Its canons had been
revealed to man by God; and through the Incarnation of the Word
and the foundation of the Church which continued and extended
this Incarnation in the World, there had been created a depository
of divine law. From the Christian point of view then, social
organization was no longer a matter for the State alone, but for
the State and the Church. Natural law had to be supplemented

by super-natural law; the State, as an administrative organ, had to be supplemented by the Church. This need created a set of political problems and frictions with which the pre-Christian world had been unacquainted.

The kind of relationship which one believes ought to exist between State and Church, between the institutions representing the two types of rules that are to guide human conduct, depends of course on the kind of relationship one believes to exist between natural and divine law. Ultimately therefore, the problem is an epistemological problem: by what methods do we attain to the knowledge of natural and divine law respectively? There can be no question, of course, that the solutions that were actually given to that epistemological problem were rarely determined by purely philosophical considerations. Emotional and psychological factors as well as purely political and practical circumstances became the basis of proposed solutions. But that need not blind us to the fact that the problem was essentially a philosophical one, even though the disputants should have allowed themselves to be swayed by philosophically irrelevant considerations. On the answer to the epistemological question then, depends the kind of Christian political philosophy one had to adopt.

Logically there are three possible views as to the relationship between natural and divine law or between reason and revelation, the two respective sources of the two sets of law. And in fact it is possible to show empirically that each of the three possible views has had its representatives.[1]

One can hold that through the Fall human reason has become so weakened that it has become a most unreliable guide; that therefore all natural law which we may think to have discovered is an unreliable guide for human conduct and that man must therefore rely exclusively on the commands of divine law. According to this first view the State, in so far as it may exist at all, must become the servant or handmaid of the Church. Human nature is in fact so depraved that it cannot hope for salvation

---

[1] I am indebted for the outlines of this classification to M. Grabmann, *Studien über den Einfluss der aristotelischen Philosophie auf die mittelalterlichen Theorien über das Verhältnis von Kirche zu Staat; Sitzungsberichte der bayrischen Akad. der Wissenschaften, Philos.—Phil. Klasse, München, 1934.*

except through the complete rejection of all purely natural standards and dictates and by an exclusive trust in the commands of the revealed word of God.

One can secondly hold that human nature, though weakened by the Fall, has not been entirely corrupted and can therefore, within the order of nature itself, recognize through reason those rules of conduct which are known as natural law. Having been weakened, however, reason does not suffice to find those laws that define the supernatural end of man. In the order of supernature therefore reason has to be supplemented by revelation. But reason and revelation are two independent sources of law, each of which is competent to guide man in the order to which it respectively belongs. There can be no question here of the Church supplanting the State; but merely of the Church supplementing the State.

The third and last view makes a rigid distinction between the order of nature and that of supernature. It recognizes the competence of reason and revelation in each order respectively; but it refuses to admit that the two orders are in any way supplementary. The material, natural world, i.e. human life between birth and death with its problems, is one complete and self-contained order; and human life as it transcends this order is another order purely spiritual and self-contained. The law or reason, therefore, is omni-competent. It can neither add to nor subtract from the law of revelation. Nor can the latter in any way influence the former. The two are, like the orders which they govern, completely independent of one another. And how absolutely that independence came finally to be conceived can be gauged from the fact that it was not considered to be absurd for the two sets of laws actually to contradict one another. According to this view, the State as an institution could have no traffic or relationship with the Church as a purely spiritual factor. But in so far as the Church was also a social institution with social commitments it was to be the servant of the State, controlled by the latter in exactly the same way as it controlled other political organs of which it availed itself for the implementing of its policy.

In each case, the crucial question is the theory of human nature which one believes to be the correct one. And it appears that the theory of human nature to which one yields one's assent depends on the kind of consciousness one has of one's own nature. In this sense it is certain that all political philosophy is by its very nature existentialist philosophy *par excellence*. To each of the above views there corresponds, again logically, a type of theory of human nature. And here too one can empirically verify that such correspondence has actually manifested itself historically.

To the first view there corresponds the idea that human nature is depraved and that man, if left to himself, is essentially wicked. Psychologically there seems to be at the bottom of such a negative view, the fact of conversion; and the philosophy resulting from it has aptly been described as a 'metaphysic of conversion'. Its defenders are more often than not reacting against the inclinations and propensities of their earlier life and in order to make doubly sure that they are now following the right path they exhibit an enormous distrust of all those manifestations of human life that took place before they partook of divine grace. Hence their suspicious attitude towards reason and a law that had been found independently of divine grace. In the specifically Christian context such men are usually prone to base their devotion to the next world on a hatred of this world rather than on pure love for the object of their devotion. Such an attitude will in general be marked by a fervent hatred of all half-measures and compromises which will always appear as concessions to the powers of evil. In this attitude one finds therefore a strongly marked tendency towards a purely monistic orientation of life and a rejection of the natural world.

To the second view there corresponds a theory of human nature which is much more balanced in that it takes equal account of the human and the divine. The all-permeating spirit here is one of love, a love for a world which is indirectly a creation of God and as such good, as well as a love for God Himself. Psychologically one finds here a firm faith that has arisen naturally without conversion, sufficient trust to accept the natural parts of life without suspicion or bitterness and yet enough humility to recognize their ultimate imperfections and the need for a higher supplement, the divine revelation.

To the third type, finally, there corresponds a theory of human nature that is over-confident. Here we find a full acceptance of all purely human powers and faculties and a sturdy optimism that this world, as it is, is a whole that needs no further supplement or help from beyond. If it were not for the fact that so many men who subscribed to this view have in all sincerity protested their adhesion to the Christian belief in the transcendent end of human life, one would be inclined not to take this last attitude as a Christian attitude at all. At any rate we must note here a strong tendency towards a bifurcation of life in that this last view makes for an encouragement of Christian beliefs together with a toleration of a purely pagan conduct: this results from the conception of the spiritual and the natural-material world as two mutually independent and self-sufficient spheres of life. According to the first and second views these two spheres of life hang together; whereas according to the third view they are completely separated from one another.

The relationship which one holds to exist between natural and divine law will also automatically determine the validity one can attribute to the dictates of reason and revelation respectively. On the first view a great probability of contradiction between the dictates of reason and revelation is assumed, but truth will be ascribed to revelation alone and the results of rational inquiry will be disparaged as satanic illusions likely to contradict revealed truth. The third view, having postulated an absolute independence between the two spheres of reason and revelation, will gladly tolerate the co-existence of two contradictory truths. It is only according to the second view that a complete harmony between reason and revelation, and hence between natural and divine law, is presupposed. Each, authoritative in its own order, can never contradict the other, since both kinds of law are an emanation of the one *lex aeterna*.

Translated into politics, these considerations strongly influenced throughout the Middle Ages the degree of sovereignty or autonomous legislative and administrative power that people believed should be granted to Church and State (or to secular and ecclesiastical tribunals) respectively. According to the first view any autonomously exercised power of the State could be nothing but the temptation of the Devil to lure men along the path of

eternal damnation. The State, both in origin and in its functioning, was evil and could be turned to good account only by a complete submission to the Church, to the holy depository of revealed
truth. According to the second view both State and Church were
to exercise an autonomous power in the secular and ecclesiastical
sphere respectively. The problem of encroachment or of a conflict of laws hardly arose when it was postulated that reason and
revelation could not contradict one another. The sphere of the
State was limited only by its own limitations, i.e. by the fact that
human reason could not be a guide towards supernature. But
within that sphere there could be no question of a submission
to an extraneous institution. And lastly, according to the third
view, there was to be no limitation whatever upon the power of
the State. Since all ecclesiastical laws, except those of a purely
spiritual nature, affected man's natural life they had to be subject to
the approval of that authority which was the expression *par excellence* of man's natural life, of his reason. For all practical purposes
the sovereignty of the State was unlimited by any Christian
considerations. The State could do whatever it thought fit
to do.

It will be easily recognized that all these problems raised by a
Christian political philosophy are the expression of the fundamental dualism between flesh and spirit, nature and supernature,
man and God, which is at the very basis of all Christian thought.
The three basic types which we have just described are all attempts
to come to terms with that dualism; but from a purely philosophical point of view it appears to be impossible to judge as to
which attempt is the most successful one. The first lays itself open
to the charge of '*vilificatio naturae*' and hence to an implied dero-
gation from God's goodness and glory. The third view, by doing
the very opposite, pushes God far beyond the stage on which
the scenes of human life are laid. Both views—and this fact might
commend the second solution—are in the last analysis a refusal
to face up to the requirements of a dualistic conception of human
life: they do not take full account of the importance of the doctrine that man is embedded in nature and yet can transcend it.
They tend towards monism, for they always belittle one of the
two poles of the Christian world-picture. The second solution,

however, is based partly on the faith natural to a happy temperament and partly on the spirit of compromise and mediation. In so far as it is the former, it must remain a purely personal solution, acceptable to all those who combine the intellectual acumen with the sweet *naïveté* of faith of a St. Thomas Aquinas; but in so far as it is a compromise, it shades off, imperceptibly to start with, but irresistibly under the duress and pressure of real life and political struggle, into the first or the third type. The tragedy and failure of this attitude in Richard Hooker will be the subject of the present essay.

2

The historical facts for which these theories were meant to account, either critically or apologetically, are too well known to need anything but the briefest reference. Through the fortuitous combination of the determined policy of the bishops of Rome and the general conditions prevailing in Western society, the Church had become a monarchical institution with the Pope at its head. It was partly owing to the urge of a Christian conscience and conviction, and partly owing to the simple fact that so many existing tribunals were ecclesiastical institutions, that men lived not only according to customary and statutory but also according to ecclesiastical law. In cases of dispute concerning the latter, only the Church as the Spouse of Christ, the 'continuation of the word incarnate' and the depository of revealed truth could be considered a valid court of appeal. At the head of this Church there stood the bishop of Rome, generally recognized as Pope by the pressure of his own policy as well as by the fact that in all disputes as to canon law people finally turned to the bishop whom they held to be the successor of St. Peter himself.[1] Thus there had grown up from below as well as from above a centralized ecclesiastical judicial system. Owing to the nature of the case, the Church was

[1] Cp. A. L. Smith, *Church and State in the Middle Ages*, Oxford, 1913, Lecture I; H.X. Arquillière, *L'Augustinisme Politique*, Paris, 1934, *passim;* E. Bernheim, *Mittelalterliche Zeitanschauungen, in ihrem Einfluss auf Politik und Geschichte*, Teil. I, Tübingen, 1918, *passim.*

not only the ruler of rulers but also a tribunal in the first instance —an institution directing and ordering social life in co-operation with those secular institutions which served a similar purpose. And it was the social and political framework of feudalism that had furnished the practical experiences which made such a co-operation possible. The demand for a double loyalty as implied by the first and second type of theory could best be satisfied by a feudalistic conception of allegiances. Feudalism furnished the legal conceptions and social conditions for the kind of system that underlay the first and second type of Christian political philosophy. Here the king could hold his kingdom as a papal fief[1] and the ecclesiastical courts could be considered as franchises on an equal footing with the courts baron or the courts leet. Only when the monarchy began to challenge the notion of a feudal hierarchy successfully, and managed to assert its claim to a direct lordship over all manner of subjects of whatever feudal status within a certain defined territory, the idea of an overlordship of the Papacy became untenable and the independent jurisdiction of the canon law became impossible. As the monarchy drew its tight judicial net over a certain territory, the state which was thus founded could, by its very nature and origin, be but a secular state and Christian only in the sense of the third type of political philosophy. It offered no scope for a dual administration of social affairs. As we shall see, Hooker virtually admitted this by borrowing from Marsilius.

But those were not the only facts a sixteenth-century political philosophy had to take into account. Side by side with and partly encouraged by these political developments, there had also taken place certain religious developments. The conflict that is constantly created by the dual character of human consciousness, by the friction between the emotive and the intellectual

---

[1] Cp. such expressions as '... we will do liege homage to the Lord Pope ...' Petit-Dutaillis, *Feudal Monarchy in France and England*, London, 1936, p. 330; and 'Rex ... homo fit papae ...' in G. Bonwetsch, *Geschichte des Mittelalters*, Leipzig, 1931, p. 55. See also Z. N. Brooke, *Pope Gregory's Demand for Fealty from William the Conqueror*, E.H.R., Vol. XXVI, 1911. O. v. Gierke, *Political Theories of the Middle Ages*, Cambridge, 1938, p. 14, and St. Thomas, *Quaestiones Quodlibetales*, 12, Qu. 13, art. 19, ad 2nd: 'Reges sunt vassalli ecclesiae.'

factors, has also been fully reflected in man's attitude towards religion. It is to a very large extent this conflict which dominates the history of religion. Where the intellect prevails, men accept a religion that is an orderly and systematized institution and lay special stress on knowledge rather than on religious intensity. All personal inspiration and fanatical enthusiasm are looked upon with suspicion and all claims to new revelation and sudden regeneration are rejected. Where emotion prevails, knowledge is rejected as a subtle device to separate man from God. The contact with the divine is here of a purely personal nature and based on a continuous inspiration of the elect. The conflict between the two attitudes is the fundamental conflict between theology and mysticism—or between objectivism and subjectivism. It seems that the human mind cannot choose the one or the other but is condemned to seeking a continual adjustment between these two poles. Philosophy in fact has not been able to pronounce in favour of either attitude; it has merely been able to show that there is no final reasonable choice to be made. And thus religious history has shown that we are dealing here with a fundamental clash between two opposite standpoints. The one commends itself because of its emotional intensity and the unshakeable certainty of conviction and hence of satisfaction that springs from it; the other commends itself because it encourages people to discuss rationally what they consider to be true and because it does not draw a sharp line between those who feel themselves to be elect and those who are considered to be rejected. But since the respective advantages lie in entirely different fields, one cannot even expect men to weigh the merits of each attitude against those of the other and to decide after the test: each man, for reasons unknown, inclines to the one or the other side; and once he has taken his stand there is no possible argument that will persuade him of the correctness of the opposite.

It is no cause for surprise then, when we find that from the earliest times there were deeply religious men who challenged institutionalized Christianity, the Church, its laws and traditions, and tried to supplant it by a direct and personal contact with God. Politically such challenges meant a protest against the idea that the Church of Rome was the sole depository of revealed truth.

Such movements were sporadic in the thirteenth century; later they became more widespread. And by the middle of the sixteenth century almost one-half of Western Christendom gave them their full support. All these protests had one thing in common; they denied that the ecclesiastical institution, known as the Church of Rome, had a monopoly of revealed truth and that all other churches could partake of this truth only to the degree to which they were dependent upon and attached to the hierarchy whose apex was in Rome. God, they claimed, could choose any man or any congregation as the direct recipient of the Holy Spirit. Such movements destroyed the orderliness and stability which had been the expression of the old idea that God had revealed Himself once and had left one institution as the guardian of that revelation on earth. Instead there arose innumerable Churches, each claiming that it had been directly inspired by God and that it had therefore both the right and the duty to declare the content of divine law.

To understand rightly the peculiarity of the sixteenth-century situation and the special problem which it posed to Christian political philosophy, we must recall the ferment caused by the dissolution of feudalism. This had gathered momentum during the preceding two centuries, and had fostered an inclination towards the emotional and subjective religious attitude. At the same time the breakdown of scholastic philosophy through the criticism of the Nominalist school had caused widespread disillusionment and had forced men once more to see religion as a personal and moral, rather than as a cognitive, problem.[1] Both trends united in laying stress on the emotional factors in religious experience and tended to cast aspersion on reason and its competence: they encouraged a preference for the first type of political philosophy.

Coupled with this situation was the fact that the Papacy, by the beginning of the sixteenth century, had virtually ceased to function

---

[1] For Petrarch see E. Gilson, *The Unity of Philosophical Experience*, London, 1938, p. 104 ff.; and for Cusanus, E. Cassirer, *Individuum und Kosmos in der Philosophie der Renaissance*, Leipzig, 1927; it is significant that that movement seized that aspect of St. Augustine which had been almost completely neglected so far: the *Confessions*.

in the sense in which it had functioned during the Middle Ages proper. By the nature of its very vocation it had become engrossed in the politics and diplomatic affairs of this world and had not been able to preserve the original attitude that power and wealth were only means towards an end. Internal corruption and greed had sapped the vitality of the ecclesiastical hierarchy; and abuses in the administration and the resulting weakness of the Church had undermined its prestige and had lent the most plausible support possible to the counter-challenge that was being made in the name of personal religion. And gradually the growing monarchies of Europe took away from the Church of Rome one power after another. All these movements were closely intertwined and acted as mutual encouragements to one another: but the final result in the sixteenth century was that the political philosopher had no longer to deal with the problem of a secular State and a Church in a feudal society—but with secular states and a large number of independent religious congregations each of which claimed to be a depository of revealed truth and showed a decided preference for the first type of political philosophy. Their challenge was opposed by that of the secular state which in turn could but adhere to the third type of political philosophy. The two powers that were thus left in the field subscribed to the first and third type of philosophy respectively. Neither would give way to the other; and the social framework of feudalism that had in an earlier age afforded scope for compromises had been destroyed or was in a state of advanced dissolution. This fact was finally responsible for the bitterness of the ensuing struggle between the two contestants. But what was to become of the second type of philosophy and of the theory of human nature it was based upon?

3

Richard Hooker made it his task to put forward in the sixteenth century once more the second type of Christian political philosophy. Although he did not remain alone, he was one of the first to do so. Almost at the same time Bellarmine, and a little later Suarez, took up the same tradition. But Hooker occupies a special position among these thinkers. For he was not only concerned with the theory of law but also with the practice of an extremely vigorous and enterprising political organization: the Tudor State. And unlike Bellarmine he was too close to the political reality of that institution to be able to afford to condemn it. As a result, his arguments were understood to have a closer practical relevance and thus his influence was assimilated and developed—not altogether in his spirit—in the course of continual political arguments.

His ideas did not survive in their original purity and with their original meaning, but were transformed and became part of the living tradition of English political thought. The other writers had their doctrine preserved in its purity, and their influence was confined almost entirely to the evolution of the theory of international law. But it is just the fact that Hooker's thought became absorbed that has made it so difficult so far to form an exact and clear picture of the real nature of that thought: he has too often been considered the father of Anglicanism and has thus usually been interpreted as the conscious originator of an idea which, though it developed largely on the basis that he had furnished, neither had been envisaged nor would have been approved by him. Hooker did not want to put forward any new ideas at all; nor did he ever think of defending a system which was new. Hooker was an apologist for the Tudor constitution; but he defended it only because he believed it to be something very ancient. To understand what Hooker really meant we must not allow ourselves to be misled by the outcome of his teaching: e.g. Locke, or Anglicanism. We must call up 'a mist over the face of time', forget what has happened since Hooker's days and what he himself could never have known, and look deeper into the past than most historians of Hooker's thoughts have done so far.[1]

What can be known about Hooker's life is sufficiently well known through his biographer Walton and Professor Sisson's

[1] A. P. d'Entrèves, *Riccardo Hooker*, Torino, 1939, is the only attempt at a truly historical approach to Hooker's thought.

recent corrections of that biography.[1] He was an Elizabethan Englishman of a type so very different from the current popular conception of the sturdy sea-dog, the worldly humanist and the bawdy and brilliantly witty poet. If it is true that the characteristic note of the Elizabethan age was precipitancy and that Elizabethans tended to act first and to theorize afterwards, Hooker was not a very typical Elizabethan. His temper and disposition have indeed been admirably summed up in the epithet by which he is so well known: the judicious Hooker. He was a very learned scholar; and from the tone of his writings we can easily gather the sweetness of his temperament and the loving spirit with which he approached the world in general and his fellow-men in particular. Kindness and a readiness to reconcile opposites were the dominant notes of his mind. He had a sharply developed power of criticism. But there is not the slightest sign of bitterness or arrogance in his criticism; only an assertion of disagreement. Hatred of any kind was in fact alien to his nature. He was serious and very single-minded in his devotion to the task which he had set himself and pursued it without ever being tempted by worldly preferment or by the more attractive pursuit of public preaching in a great London institution. But, at the same time, he had a sufficiently great sense of humour not to become sour or self-righteous in his devotion to God and to his work.[2] His serious single-mindedness never tempted him into a moral puritanism. His approach to all problems was essentially intellectual and his persuasive force lay in his own sincere conviction of the importance of intellectual argument.

Together with all this there went an appreciation of an understanding of the goodness of the past and of all existing conditions. This was largely conditioned by his piety which could not have allowed him to appear bitter or resentful of divine providence; turning away from all evil because he could not hate, he tended to see more harmony and pleasantness than there probably was.

It must be left to the psychologist to decide whether Hooker's

---

[1] C. J. Sisson, *The judicious Marriage of Mr. Hooker and the Birth of the Laws o. Ecclesiastical Polity*, Cambridge, 1940.

[2] I believe in fact that there was a certain similarity in character between Hooker and St. Thomas Aquinas.

temperamental disposition was the cause or the effect of his philosophy. But since the two were obviously interdependent, the historian may be permitted to choose as his starting-point the less complex and develop from there the more intricate intellectual edifice. With the predisposition described above, Hooker approached the great political problem of his age. Brought up and educated in a medieval environment he could not but be concerned with the problems it posited; and being of such a disposition he could not but choose the second type of political philosophy as his fundamental position: the temper with which he had been endowed was in fact capable of doing full justice to each of the opposite poles of the dualistic Christian world-picture. He thus understood how the first and the third types of political philosophy tended to upset the balance which only the second type of philosophy kept so admirably.

The real problem which thus confronted Hooker and many others was how to maintain a political system in which secular and ecclesiastical powers co-operated in the sense of the second type of political philosophy. Or, in other words: it was necessary to refute the exorbitant claims of all those people who believed in a newly discovered source of revealed law and who arrogated to themselves the right to a final decision in all matters affecting the conduct of life. This was a double task: because there was first the claim of the newly established churches to be better repositories of revealed truth than the Church of Rome and secondly the growing conviction that divine law could simply override and dispense with natural law. To make such a refutation by pointing at the all-embracing power of the secular state did not require much ingenuity in the sixteenth century: kings and their statesmen saw to that. But to make such a refutation and at the same time put the secular state into its proper place was a matter of considerable difficulty—for the old Church of the Middle Ages was no longer a politically effective institution, and everywhere the Monarchy had been stepping into the place vacated under pressure by the Church. The bishop of Rome, as the head of the Papal State, was still an important factor in European affairs; but he had no longer sufficient strength to be the centre of a united Christendom. And so there gained ground the idea—which was firmly planted in the minds of so many Englishmen even after the Council of Trent—that the Pope was one among many secular rulers, but that the Church over which he presided as bishop of Rome could no more be granted any political rights in England than could the Monarchy of France.

Some people, especially at the beginning of the sixteenth century, had simply blinded themselves to these political realities. To them the Papacy needed but an internal reform; but they were not even prepared to go as far in their proposals for a reform as the originators of the conciliar movement in the previous century had gone. But others, gifted with a keener political insight, understood that very little was to be expected from the Papacy and that the ecclesiastical organization had to be regulated in a new way if it was to continue to fulfil its proper function. These considerations governed the attitude of Stephen Gardiner: a profoundly religious man in the Catholic sense, he supported the Monarchy because it was the one effective political force in which the ecclesiastical organization might find protection. His Caesaro-Papism was grounded on the realization that the Pope in the early sixteenth century was incapable of upholding the Catholic or medieval tradition of faith and the necessary institutions. He thought therefore that 'the king was the only bulwark against the oncoming storm'.[1] Gardiner wanted the *ecclesia anglicana* to continue to be the Church in England; not the Church of England. He saw no ground for local developments in belief and ritual. He simply wanted the common tradition to be maintained, and Janelle suggests that Gardiner did not worry very much about the problem of the unity of Christendom because to him the Catholic medieval tradition was so clear that it needed neither definition nor a special institution to preserve it.[2] The actual

---

[1] P. Janelle, *Obedience in Church and State, Three Tracts by S. Gardiner*, ed. with an introduction, Cambridge, 1930, p. xv. But it is wrong to conclude from the evidence of one of Gardiner's occasional tracts that he believed in obedience to the King for its own sake as Janelle suggests; op. cit. p. lxvii. Gardiner's misfortunes under Henry's successor and his attitude towards some of Henry's pretensions are sufficient proof of his loftier motives. Cp. Ch. H. McIlwain, *Constitutionalism Ancient and Modern*, Ithaca, N.Y., 1940, p. 105.

[2] Op cit., p. lxi.

idea behind Gardiner's conception can be understood quite clearly from the reply which he drafted on behalf of Convocation to the Commons' petition to the King in 1532. He urged the necessity of maintaining 'the conception of an organic and self-controlled ecclesiastical system' which was to act together with that of the secular authority. He considered it essential to maintain the co-operation of the two independent powers. The authority of Convocation was grounded upon Scripture and on the determination of the holy Church and could therefore not be made dependent on the King's assent.[1] Gardiner sought royal protection for the Church; but he could not give up the ancient idea of co-operation of two independent and—each in its own sphere—autonomous institutions. He simply believed that through the papalization of the Monarchy that system would be more effectively safeguarded than by an adherence to the tottering Papacy.

We can discern here a clear and unequivocal attitude towards the problem of sixteenth-century politics, although Gardiner's vision did not reach far enough to enable him to formulate it in any other way than a very simple and unsophisticated theory of obedience to the Monarchy. His attitude however is like Hooker's a refusal to see in the English Reformation much more than a political re-orientation of the *ecclesia anglicana*; and an implicit denial of anybody's right to found a new Church or to seek revealed truth by any method other than the hitherto known one. Another explicit statement of the same attitude can be found in Bishop Jewel, who wrote very soon after the accession of Queen Elizabeth when Englishmen began to hope once more for some political stability. He explained that only to ignorant men it looked as if the *ecclesia anglicana* had left the Church of Christ and embarked on a course of its own. But, he wrote, 'we have put ourselves apart not as heretics are wont, from the Church of Christ, but as all good men ought to do, from the infection of naughty persons and hypocrites.'[2] Anglicans are not like Anabaptists, but strictly orthodox[3] and he expressly wished to establish the continuity of tradition between the English reformers

---

[1] See M. Powicke, *The Reformation in England*, in E. Eyre, *European Civilization*, Vol. IV, London, 1936, p. 391 f.

[2] *Apology*, IV. ix. 12.   [3] Ibid., III. ii. 1.

and the medieval critics of the Papacy. Neither the one nor the other had ever departed from the Catholic faith; they had merely complained about the bishop of Rome.[1] He naturally repudiated the Pope[2]; but apart from that he could find no fault with the institution of the ecclesiastical hierarchy[3], and insisted that all ministers had to be appointed in the orderly manner by the Church: nobody was to be allowed to style himself a Priest and to interpret Scripture 'as he lists'.[4]

Whitgift took up his pen in defence of the same ideas at a time when the attack had become very much more pointed and virulent. But there was not the slightest doubt for him that it was his opponents who were thinking of innovation.[5] The Church of England, to Whitgift, is the old and ancient Church. 'I would rather die', he writes, 'than be the author of schisms, a disturber of the common peace and quietness of the church and state.'[6] Like Jewel he explained that the *ecclesia anglicana* is still the same medieval Church. The abuses have been reformed; but it is an error to believe that the whole Church has been transformed[7] and that therefore people have a right to continue the transformation. He too defends the existence of the ecclesiastical hierarchy by pointing out how it is a necessary guarantee of order and peace in the Church. And his main argument for not tolerating the Pope as the apex of this hierarchy is that no man can have enough ability and insight to rule the whole world at once. An archbishop can rule over a province; but nobody can rule over all provinces.[8]

Such was the general background of ideas developed in sixteenth-century England. They fulfilled the twofold purpose of

[1] *Apology*, IV. xvi. 1.

[2] Ibid., II. vii. 5.

[3] Ibid., II. iii. 1.

[4] See L. Pullan, *Religion since the Reformation*, Oxford, 1924, p. 47.

[5] Whitgift's theoretical position was, however, weak, for he was a real Calvinist in religion and merely defended the Church and its relation to the Tudor State because he was the sort of man who would have defended any *status quo*.

[6] *Works*, Parker Society, Vol. III, p. 321.

[7] Ibid., Vol. II, p. 439.

[8] Ibid., Vol. II, pp. 417, 245.

defending the Tudor Monarchy as a Christian and not a purely
secular state; and of denying the more thoroughgoing Protestants, who came to be known as Puritans, the right to dominate
the community in the name of a divine, revealed law of which
they were the self-styled keepers. But these ideas were never
developed in a satisfactory manner. Their propounders were themselves more often than not tinged with a certain amount of Puritan theology and thus had very little ground to stand on except
their vested interest in the established order and the all too
human inclination towards conservatism. But ultimately the
question went deeper: it affected the theory of human nature and
the general problem of divine, natural and human law. So when
Hooker was drawn almost accidentally into the controversy
and when it was brought home to him that there was a fundamental question of philosophy and theology involved[1] he could
no longer remain satisfied with the numerous answers offered; he
withdrew into the country in order to meditate in quietness upon
the great problem of his age.

The problem involved in fact the ultimate and fundamental
problem of man's place in the Universe and the kind of conduct
that was appropriate to it. Hooker's work, written towards the
end of the sixteenth century, is a statement of a case against the
most powerful and far-reaching psychological and philosophical
developments of the period of the Renaissance and the Reformation. These developments led in the end to a human consciousness and outlook that made the second type of Christian political
philosophy impossible.

4

The dialectic of historical processes is exceedingly complex:
hardly ever do movements or periods follow chronologically
upon one another. They rather seem to exist side by side at all
times; and the twin force of economic appropriateness and gradual
intellectual clarification renders now the one, now the other, more

[1] For an account of Hooker's first clash with Travers see J. Strype, *The Life
and Acts of John Whitgift*, Oxford, 1822, Vol. I, pp. 340-346, p. 40 ff.

intense and thus allows the historian to identify it as the dominant trait during a given period of time. We must therefore search for the antecedents of Renaissance and Reformation in the very beginnings of Western Civilization itself.

The inroads that were made by self-seeking and adventurous men on the feudal organization of society were the earliest manifestations of the human spirit of self-confidence and enterprise and of the belief in man's power to control his destiny, to subject it to his will and to gain whatever fruits he set his mind upon. The direct result of this movement was the growth and development of urban life. The early merchant had lived on the fringe of feudal society; and although in a comparatively short time the towns themselves were fitted into the existing social framework they nevertheless continued to bear witness to the spirit by which they had been founded[1]. The capitalistic nature of their enterprise, together with the easy opportunity they afforded for social intercourse and education, stimulated the growth of a dynamic and ever-changing civilization, which made them an alien element in a purely feudal and rural society. But they acted naturally like a leaven and it was not long before they started to challenge the political and religious order that had been developed before they had reached their maturity. It was in and through town life that the lay-spirit asserted itself.

From a purely practical point of view the lay-spirit was a challenge to the early medieval conception of the threefold division of society into peasants, soldiers and priests. Theoretically it meant even more: it was the foundation of the belief that laymen, educated and enterprising as they were, had no need of an institution that should mediate between them and God.[2] The successful and

[1] For the history of that spirit and a description of the socio-economic setting in which it flourished see H. Pirenne, *Medieval Cities*, Princeton, 1925; Weber's famous theory which sees in the development of Calvinism the incentive to the development of this spirit is narrow, for it takes too unified a view of medieval economics as being dominated by 'traditionalism'. Weber was not wrong in stressing the connexion between Calvinism and Capitalism; but those elements in Calvinism which favoured the development of the Capitalist spirit were already the results of age-old tendencies.

[2] Cp. G. de Lagarde, *La Naissance de l'Esprit Laïque au déclin du Moyen Age*, Paris, 1934-1946.

self-confident merchant felt little need for an institution for such a mediation. For the powers of his own intellect and the shrewdness of his enterprises were perfectly self-sufficient. Coupled with this belief in the self-sufficiency of the layman there was the natural resentment of canon law interference, of irksome restrictions on laymen dictated by the temper of ecclesiastical law and of the immunities of clerks. It was in the fifteenth and sixteenth centuries that the attitudes that had thus been developed reached their full maturity and formed together with a number of other influences the basic traits of Renaissance and Reformation.

There is a common tendency in much Renaissance and Reformation thought and outlook: namely the belief in the self-sufficiency of the human being. In typical Renaissance thought we meet this belief as the confidence in man's natural and rational capacities to reach whatever goal he may appoint himself. The resurgence of Epicureanism in Valla and Politian, the pride in one's intellectual effort in Pontano and Alberti and the affirmation of human dignity and autonomy in Pico and Ficino are all manifestations of the same current.[1]

And in Reformation thought—or rather in Protestant piety and religious feeling—it appears in a very subtle form as the complete submergence of the human in the divine. Both Luther and

[1] See Ph. Monnier, *Le Quattrocento*, Paris, 1901, Vol. I, p. 48 ff.; W. F. Schirmer, *Antike, Renaissance und Puritanismus*, München, 1933, p. 89; E. Cassirer, op. cit. pp. 88-103, p. 68; P. O. Kristeller, *The Philosophy of Marsilio Ficino*, New York, 1943, pp. 119-120. Burckhardt's famous description of the Renaissance as the emergence of the complete individual is narrow. It is more generally correct to say that the Renaissance meant not so much a shift in ultimate values as the growing conviction that man can attain to his values through his own individual efforts. This will cover both Burckhardt's point and a good many cases besides. Gilson's dictum that the Renaissance is the Middle Ages without God, is, I think, false; in the light of the evidence accumulated by F. Olgiati, *L'anima dell'Umanesimo e del Rinascimento*, Milano, 1924, we must conclude that the orientation of Renaissance thought was no less transcendent than that of medieval thought. The difference between medieval and Renaissance thought does not lie in the goals sought but in the methods employed. We characterize as medieval the belief that man, on the secular side, must be a member of a larger social unit, and on the spiritual side stands in need of sacraments; and it is the general mark of the lay-spirit that man is self-sufficient and can reach his appointed goal without the help of these institutions.

Calvin started with a thorough revival of the doctrine of the complete depravity of man and deduced from it that only grace, and nothing but grace, can ever regenerate man and lead him to everlasting peace and happiness. One could hardly imagine a more pessimistic theory of human nature; and yet, just because it was such an extreme theory it automatically bore in itself the affirmation of its very opposite: salvation through faith alone. To Luther faith was the only means of regeneration. But whereas to St. Augustine there never could be any final assurance as to whether God had bestowed grace on the man who had faith, to Luther faith itself was already regeneration. Faith by itself secured the certainty of regeneration. The burden of proof was thus thrown on man, and not on God. Certainty of election and of salvation can be found by every individual man if he will only have faith. Here the Lutheran, and the Protestant in general, becomes as independent, self-reliant and self-sufficient as any Renaissance man. 'He is a priest before God, taken charge of by no priest, and a King over the world.'[1] The same sentiment was developed even more explicitly in Puritanism proper. 'The life of faith', one Puritan wrote, 'does not only bring us on to justification, but in time brings us to the assurance of it.'[2] Hence the indestructible optimism of Puritanism. The historian witnesses here in fact a curious psychological spectacle: there is man, dejected and depressed beyond words and hope by the consciousness of his depravity; and yet at the same time he is assured that a pure act of faith in God, something which he himself and only he himself is capable of accomplishing, can put a sudden end to his state of despair and give him an absolute certainty of salvation. 'Puritanism was indeed without any feeling for the twilight zones of the mind, it could do nothing with nuances or with half-grasped, fragmentary insights and oracular intuitions . . . it was all or nothing, white or black, God or the Devil.'[3]

In this sense then, the Reformation was not so much the counterpart of the Renaissance but rather an attempt—thoroughly

---

[1] A. V. Harnack, *History of Dogma*, Oxford, 1899, Vol. VII, pp. 209 ff.
[2] Quoted by Perry Miller, *The New England Mind*, New York, 1939, p. 50.
[3] Ibid., p. 45.

successful—to express Renaissance consciousness in terms of theology.[1] And it can easily be seen that that tendency towards self-sufficiency undermined the very basis of the second type of Christian philosophy. For there it is assumed that man's natural life with its natural faculties is only one part of his whole life— and that in order to complete it, a supplement is needed that will draw its strength and efficacy from a non-human source. Protestantism, and more specifically Puritanism, had no use for such a conception and finally came to be a denial of the view that life in this world was incomplete, could never reach perfection and could find its ultimate goal only in the next world. It asserted instead that men can have certain knowledge of their election and thus can reach a state of perfection in this world: the godly are, in a certain sense, already cleared of sin. In the seventeenth century, moreover, official Presbyterianism invented the Covenant of Grace in order to give an expression to such a consciousness: it was the perfect social order for the elect. The more radical Puritans, following the same bent, became millennarians and perfectionists: they believed that they were charged with bringing about the immediate heaven on earth,[2] or the inauguration of the state of Nature.[3] They certainly showed no patience with a constitution that gave political expression to the idea that natural man needs a non-human supplement to guide him along the path that leads to the future salvation of the soul. Hence their inveterate opposition to clericalism and sacramentalism, the two chief supplements of the human part of man's existence, and to any form of church-state relationship that was designed for the maintenance of these supplements in general and to Episcopacy in particular. But the chiliastic hopes of Puritanism were no more modern or new than the self-reliant individualism of Renaissance man.

[1] K. Burdach has traced this development of thought in the opposite direction. He sees in the Renaissance an expression of the theologico-mystical idea of regeneration and the reformation of human nature, which was the driving force of the thirteenth-century religious revival. Cp. *Der Dichter des Ackermann aus Böhmen und seine Zeit*, Berlin, 1926-1932, p. 95, 142; *Reformation, Renaissance und Humanismus*, Berlin, 1926, pp. 44 ff, 95 ff., 100 ff.

[2] Fifth Monarchy men.

[3] Diggers.

The voice that thundered against Episcopacy in Elizabethan England was prompted by the very same thoughts that had prompted the medieval townsmen to resent the jurisdiction of ecclesiastical tribunals. It was for the spiritual satisfaction and for the economic advantages to be derived from the abolition of Episcopacy that the Puritans found so many adherents and active supporters among laymen.[1] Laymen hoped that the advance of Puritanism would bring in its train the complete secularization of the state. They hoped to acquire a monopoly of government and conduct it entirely in the spirit of the pursuit of worldly and material ends. They joined forces with Puritan theologians in an attack on the medieval church-state, because they wanted the state to become completely secular and because they wanted to 'empty religion of its social content'.[2] It was an ill-omened alliance as the seventeenth century was to show; but during the sixteenth century this combination proved a powerful force against the tradition of a church-state partnership. Laymen also imagined that a state whose subjects were divided among themselves in matters of religion would be compelled to adopt—in order to maintain itself—a purely neutral attitude towards religion and hence become a secular institution.[3] But the Elizabethan lay-supporters of Puritanism, like Knollys, Walsingham and Leicester would most probably have been horrified had they been able to anticipate the development of seventeenth-century Presbyterianism in England: for, far from satisfying their wishes to assist the evolution of a secular state, it almost succeeded in turning England into a complete theocracy.

But there were other minds in sixteenth-century England in whom a different trait of Puritanism remained dominant. In them, Puritanism had nothing whatever to do with secularism; but was on the contrary a recrudescence of certain medieval tendencies against which many medieval philosophers and theologians had

---

[1] See C. H. Garrett, *The Marian Exiles*, Cambridge, 1938, p. 7; A. F. Scott-Pearson, *Thomas Cartwright and Elizabethan Puritanism*, Cambridge, 1925, pp. 266, 345, 411–2; R. G. Usher, *The Reconstruction of the English Church*, London, 1910, Vol. I, pp. 270–1.

[2] The phrase is Professor Tawney's.

[3] See G. Ruggiero, *The History of European Liberalism*, London, 1927, p. 396.

protested. Protestantism was in fact a revival of Augustinian theology at the expense of the Thomistic synthesis. It denied free will
and the doctrine of salvation through faith and merit; it disparaged
all purely human powers and together with the freedom of the
will it rejected the soul's rational faculties on which the former
was based. It cast aspersions on one side of the dualistic Christian
world-picture and extolled the other. It revived the consciousness
of human wickedness and of the impotence of all human effort
and, in an attempt to give God His due, fostered a hatred for His
creatures. Together with this we find the acceptance of a doctrine
which, though it had been developed philosophically only during
the later Middle Ages, was well in accord with certain mystical
traits of earlier times: the doctrine of the primacy of will over
reason. According to that doctrine, religion was not something
to which the intellect could yield assent; but something that altogether transcended the intellect, and the strength of which lay in
the directness of its emotional appeal.[1] Everybody, whether
learned or unlearned, could therefore set himself up as an authority
on religious matters and make himself a mouthpiece of divine law.[2]
All that was required was an emotional preparedness or a moral
conviction. This stressed the importance of the will as opposed
to the intellect.

How firmly this second trait of Puritanism was intertwined
with the one described above is shown by the fact that it was
just this strong recrudescence of medieval ideas that proved the
most powerful incentive to worldly activity. By stressing the
voluntary rather than the intellectual element in religion, it became imperative that everybody who wanted to count himself
among the elect should prove by worldly success both to himself

[1] For Occam's influence on Luther see H. Hermelink, *Die theologische
Fakultät in Tübingen vor der Reformation*, Tübingen, 1906.

[2] Wolsey's attitude was typically medieval and in keeping with the scholastic tradition. When Latimer was accused of heresy he was summoned before
Wolsey. The latter, when he discovered that Latimer was not a 'light-headed
fellow that never studied' but well read and learned, was without further
questioning convinced that he could not be 'infected with this new fantastical
doctrine of Luther'; in K. Garvin ed. *The Great Tudors*, London, 1935, p. 209.
It did not occur to Wolsey that religion may be a matter independent of the
intellect.

and to his fellow-men that he in fact *was* one of the elect. A complete renunciation of the world and the impulse to dominate it may both spring from the same source.[1]

Hand in hand with this conviction that faith is a matter of the purity of the heart rather than a matter for the understanding, there went the suspicion of worldly knowledge and intellectual achievement. In so far as Puritanism was a revival of strong ascetic tendencies it was a direct reaction against the dominant Renaissance outlook. It suspected the practice of worldly arts and discouraged the pursuit of worldly pleasures. All these things were considered evil in that they distracted the human soul from an immediate contact with God. In short: the exclusive orientation towards the divine left neither time nor opportunity for the contemplation of the world or the appreciation of man.

In the political field such tendencies could not but lead to the demand for theocracy—for the complete subjection of all secular institutions to the judgement of divine law and more particularly to the judgement of those men or bodies that claimed to be the depositories of divine truth, the congregations or the newly founded churches. All human law, at best derived from a natural law that was only the dictate of a corrupt reason and at worst imposed by the folly and wickedness of ambitious tyrants, was considered pernicious and hence invalid. The only lawful rule for the conduct of life was the word of God—revealed in the Scriptures and understood and interpreted correctly by the elect. As a criticism of the militant and virile Renaissance Monarchy this doctrine was the dynamite of sixteenth-century political theory.

These two trends of Puritanism were firmly intertwined; between them they threatened to destroy the basic assumptions of the second type of Christian philosophy: the first trend by encouraging the third type, and the second trend by encouraging the first type. They upset the balance of the dualistic world-picture either in the one or in the other direction. But it must be observed that, though the two traits are logically contradictory, they supported each other dialectically. And neither the one nor the other was specifically modern in any sense of the word. Both were

[1] Hence the Calvinistic impetus to Capitalism was not a modern trait—but due to the fact that Calvinism itself bore many medieval traits.

firmly rooted in the medieval tradition. Renaissance and Reformation were therefore accentuations of medieval tendencies. And they became the seed-bed of the modern world, not because they were modern in themselves but because they over-stated certain aspects of the Middle Ages to such an extent that the pendulum finally, through its own increased momentum, swung to the opposite extreme. The development of modern ideas was therefore aided most not by the rejection but by the accentuation of medieval ideas; and Renaissance and Reformation must be looked upon as periods of transition and preparation.

A particularly cogent illustration of this theory is offered by the growth of empirical philosophy. No more precise characterization of that philosophy can be found than the remark of Hobbes that the terms 'secular' and 'spiritual' had been invented in order to make men see double. This, if anything, was a complete rejection of the medieval world-view that had been shared by everybody, namely that 'the visible is controlled by the invisible, the tangible by mysterious forces and constant divine interventions, the expedient by a law which moves the whole of nature and is the breath of God':[1] in short that the secular and the spiritual *together* formed the whole of Reality. Nobody in the medieval world would ever have dreamt of making the experience of one part of it a test of the existence of the whole. But people had become accustomed, through the influence of a Protestant outlook, to regard the spiritual and the secular as two antithetical modes of existence, and had made the decision in favour of the greater Reality of the spiritual mode of existence. The idea of a one-sided world had become so familiar that now people saw nothing unusual in the notion that the world was still one-sided but that the side that counted was the secular one. To over-stress the spiritual was typically medieval; but once the stress was carried beyond a certain point the pendulum was encouraged to swing to the opposite extreme. An empirical philosophy could not have gained ground if Protestantism had not prepared the human mind for the shock by overstretching medieval notions.

Hooker wanted people to abandon the one-sided world-picture and the consequences to which it would lead. He himself seized

[1] M. Powicke, *Stephen Langton*, Oxford, 1928, p. 19.

explicitly on many of its more specific manifestations; the wider and general issue which we have described he never mentioned. Partly because he assumed it to be understood—and many thinkers are more remarkable to the historian for what they do not consider worth mentioning than for what they explain in great detail; and partly because he himself was not fully aware of it. For it is only the historian who can, in retrospect, understand a thinker in his own historical context more clearly than he could understand himself. Hooker was in fact more alive to the purely medieval aspects of Puritanism and less aware of it as a seed-bed of modern ideas. He saw in it an accentuation of certain medieval tendencies—and therefore confined himself to opposing it by a medieval counter-argument. The startling fact, however, is that a number of sixteenth-century developments in both economic conditions and thought provided a soil in which these medieval tendencies could produce entirely new shoots. That was not, and perhaps could not have been, understood by him; it became the direct cause of his failure.

CHAPTER TWO

HOOKER AND ST. THOMAS

PURITANISM in the late sixteenth century meant many things. The name was applied to ministers who refused to wear what they called Popish vestments; to political pamphleteers who objected to Episcopacy; and it was not long before men who refused to drink and make merry on Sundays were teasingly referred to as Puritans. At first the name was used in a derogatory sense. But soon all sorts of people, often for very different reasons, accepted it with pride.[1] But for the present purpose our main concern is to find out what Hooker believed Puritanism to be; for it was against what *he* thought Puritanism meant that his attack was directed. It is quite conceivable that he erred as to some of the things he thought Puritanism meant; but from the historian's point of view that is of little consequence for Hooker's thought itself. We must first attempt to find out what kind of question Hooker asked, i.e. what kind of situation he thought confronted him. It is then quite a different task to ask whether Hooker had actually asked the right kind of question and whether he had understood correctly the real situation that confronted him.

Hooker believed that fundamentally the propagators and supporters of Puritanism were prompted by other than philosophical or theological considerations. The 'unquiet wit of mind'[2] was the

---

[1] Most historians have proceeded empirically and have investigated as Puritanism all those manifestations which were called Puritanical. See M. M. Knappen, *Tudor Puritanism*, Chicago, 1939, p. 339. I have so far employed a different method. I have defined a certain type as puritanical and have then proceeded to trace its manifestations.

[2] IV. viii. 4.

psychological condition for the whole Puritan attack and the arguments that supported it. To Hooker radical reformers are restless spirits; they hate slow methods of change and by their blind fanaticism makes everything worse in the end.[1] Their violent objection to the present constitution is the typical 'conceit of the vulgar sort . . . whensoever they see anything which they mislike and are angry at . . . [they] think that every such thing is scandalous'.[2] But he realized that to understand the psychological condition of Puritanism is not to refute it; and thus we find interspersed with his own arguments a full analysis of the Puritan standpoint.

To begin with, he pointed out, the Puritans are rash and thoughtless: for they take as a *prima facie* criterion of right and wrong simply what Rome dislikes or likes respectively.[3] They go so far as to say that even in matters indifferent we ought to do the opposite of what Rome does.[4] But they do not stop at this, and are intent on a firmer foundation for their beliefs: they proclaim them to be a direct command of God as it is revealed in the Scriptures. But, true to his original assumption that Puritanism was due to a psychological disorder, Hooker does not give them any credit for this statement. He says it is the greatest evil if men begin to think that it is the 'will of God to have those things done which they fancy; their opinions are as thorns in their sides, never suffering them to take rest till they have brought their speculation into practice'.[5] They make, to put it quite bluntly, the Bible a peg for their own opinions and one could accuse them therefore of blasphemy: they say indeed that God has laid down rules which He has not laid down[6] and if they are not more careful they will all believe in the end that the Spirit of God testifies the things which really the spirit of error suggests.[7] Hooker knew that the Scriptures are far too general and vague to be interpreted literally. If a person is ingenious enough he will find support for any sort of argument in them; 'a marvel it were if a man of so great capacity . . . could espy in the whole Scripture of God nothing

[1] VII. i. I.
[2] IV. xii. 2.
[3] IV. ix. 2.
[4] IV. x. 3; IV. iii. I, 2, 3; IV. iv. 3.
[5] In, VIII. 12.
[6] III. xi. 21.
[7] III. viii. 15.

which might breed at the least a probable opinion of likelihood that divine authority itself was the same way somewhat inclinable'.[1] They plead the law of God, and misconstrue it, and call these results of their imagination God's command.[2] In the end they get so biased that they can no longer think straight and can not read even the Scriptures properly. Every sentence there is to them nothing but a confirmation of their own 'conceits'.[3] And how completely arbitrary their interpretation of the Scriptures actually was, is revealed by the fact that they can never agree among themselves.[4]

It is important to note that Hooker, since he believed the Puritans to be philosophically wrong, was bent on finding an unphilosophical reason for their opinions; because in his view the methods of philosophy would sooner or later have led them away from error. From this insight the analysis proceeds to a deeper observation: the Puritan appeal to Scripture was not an appeal for men to use their reason to decipher the word of God, but a direct affirmation of the fact that man had to be 'inspired' in order to know anything at all.[5] The process whereby Puritans interpreted the Bible was called 'inspiration'; and the laws for human conduct thus arrived at were not laws derived by men but laws grounded on the word of God.[6] To find rules for conduct is therefore, according to Puritanism, a matter of pure inspiration and not of reason. A man who is not intelligent enough 'to utter five words in sensible manner, blushes not in any doubt concerning matter of Scripture to think his own bare yea as good as the nay of all the wise, grave and learned judgements that are in the whole world.'[7] They do not even attempt to show 'some commission whereby they are authorized to sit as judges and we required to take their judgement for good in this case'.[8] They 'simply oppose their *methinketh* unto the orders of the Church of England'[9]. Hooker of course admitted that there had been people who were called directly by God to preach the word; 'but then He does ratify

[1] In, II. 7.
[2] III. v. I; VII. xiv. 9; In, VIII. 5.
[3] In, III. 9.
[4] In, IV. 6.
[5] III. viii. II.

[6] III. vii. 4; In, VIII. 7.
[7] II. vii. 6.
[8] IV. iv. 2.
[9] Loc. cit.

31

their calling by manifest signs and tokens Himself from heaven':[1] Even the Apostles did not change the heathen laws by a mere *methinketh* but gave proof through miracles of their divine inspiration.[2]

All this amounts in Hooker's eyes to an open attack on man's rational faculties. In some simple cases, Hooker admitted, it is of course plain what is right and what is wrong, but in others only a trained intellect can decide, and individual discretion is no guide in complicated matters. The Puritan theory of the utter depravity of human nature, however, had naturally led to the disparagement of human reason, and the above described kind of inspiration was left as the only guide to conduct to fall back upon. The light of nature, reason, is made hateful with men, Hooker observed. It is considered an 'unlucky comet'. People 'think they cannot admire God as they ought to if in things divine they should attribute any force to man's reason'.[3] And after having summed up the various Puritan objections to the use of reason, such as St. Paul's warning against philosophy or the contrast between the clumsiness of reason and the easy clarity of the word of God, he concludes that the Puritans hate reason 'as if the way to be ripe in faith were to be raw in wit and judgement; as if reason were an enemy to religion, childish simplicity the mother of ghostly and divine wisdom'.[4]

This deprives the Puritan platform of all rational foundations, and the most Hooker can say for them is that *some* things which they maintain do *seem* to have been 'out of Scripture *not absurdly* gathered' as far as *some* men can *probably conjecture*.[5] But if people want others to follow them, Hooker thinks, and if they want to turn the whole world upside down by condemning and criticizing other things, they must make sure that their first 'foundations and grounds be more than slender probabilities'.[6] It is certainly wrong that the 'bare authority of their word should persuade in a cause so weighty'.[7] Only if they could prove the voice

---

[1] VII. xiv. 11; Cp. v. x. 1.

[2] IV. xiv. 2.

[3] III. viii. 4.

[4] III. viii. 4; Cp. also In. III. 14.

[5] II. vii. 9.

[9] II. i. 3; Cp. In. v. 6.

[7] IV. x. 2.

of their conscience to be right could they expect others to follow it and claim the right to defy the whole world.[1] To the Puritan, however, the voice of conscience, as expressed in his mind, was 'certain' *par excellence*, and thus incapable of further proof. The mere fact that it was 'conscience' was its criterion of certainty. To admit that it was only probable was to admit that anything else than faith, e.g. reason, might be its source.

Such an approach, Hooker recognized, created necessarily a division of human beings into two classes—a division for which there could be no rational foundation whatever. Those who considered themselves godly because they were sufficiently forward to claim that they were inspired set themselves apart from other men and believed that they might apply their own standards to their thoughts and actions.[2] These godly men form the real congregation and are the source of all divine law on earth—but in reality, Hooker argued, the authority which they claimed to exercise had been arrogated and could not be justified rationally. To form a church by the segregation of the self-styled elect was a fantastic plan to Hooker. Even heretics, let alone those that are not 'elect', are members of the universal Church of Christ.[3] The whole doctrine of the elect was to him nothing but pride and arrogance. But it was not enough for Puritans to introduce that arbitrary division into society; true to their fundamental tenet, they did not believe that human or natural law, promulgated or discovered by reason, could have any validity whatever. Hence they concluded that a Christian man's liberty was lost if any law were imposed besides the Gospel of Jesus Christ.[4] And, since the congregation of the godly and the elect had a monopoly of inspiration for the correct interpretation of the Gospel, that congregation became the highest and practically only valid authority to make any law. In the end, all power in society would be exercised by those that styled themselves the godly; 'for confusion unto the wise and the great, the poor and the simple, some Knipperdolling with his retinue must take the work of the Lord in hand'.[5] All

[1] In. v. 3, 6.
[2] In. III. II.
[3] VIII. iv. 6.
[4] III. ix. 3.
[5] VIII. vi. 14.

other authority, and especially that of purely secular institutions, will be set aside until the magistrate has been reduced to the position of a mere handmaid to that new form of Church. And if the Puritans were really consistent they would not tolerate any human agents in church government at all because they say that 'from the greatest thing unto the least about the church, all must needs be immediately from God'.[1]

Divine law then becomes the only rule for the conduct of society and of life—for every other kind of law is at best merely due to reason and hence can have no valid authority. Thus the Puritans would even discard the knowledge of the civil law and would have everything judged by elders according to divine law. Hooker in fact related the story that in a 'famous kingdom' a reformer once proposed that in order for the kingdom to flourish, it was necessary to abolish all lawyers 'whose courts being not pulled down, the new church consistories were not likely to flourish'.[2] The Puritans wanted to divide the whole kingdom of England into a number of independent parishes. The Queen herself would just simply be a member of one of these parishes or churches and as such would be subject to what it declared to be the divine law.[3] Unity of authority, the only guarantee of peace in society, would disappear. And Hooker did not for one moment believe the Puritans when they said that they had no designs on the Queen's authority and powers. They say that, Hooker thought, in order to avoid undue criticism and suppression while they are in a minority.[4] The best proof of their ultimate plans is that the Puritans are not really prepared to accept the decision of an authority—at least not unconditionally, but only if it happens to agree with the voice of their conscience.[5] They are bent on the establishment of a political order where all authority is vested in the divine law, where the congregations of the godly are the proper judges of that divine law, and where any other form of law is abolished or at least completely subordinated to divine law. This order they believe will finally inaugurate the golden age[6] and put an end to all the evils that beset mankind.

[1] VIII. vi. 5.
[2] VII. i. 1.
[3] VIII. viii.
[4] VIII. ii. 15.
[5] In. VI. 1, 2, 3.
[6] VII. i. 4.

The Puritans themselves, though they might have admitted the one or the other point, would have rejected, and in fact did reject, so summary an interpretation of their ideas. But Hooker's analysis although fuller and more penetrating added little to the points which Whitgift and Bancroft had made earlier. The Puritans had been characterized as wild and irresponsible sectarians before. It was alleged that they let every boy rage at pleasure and that they advocated that every man 'should have his fancy and live as he lists'. They had been called stumbling-blocks to the weak and a rejoicing to the wicked; and behind their ideas it had been assumed there was little but the restlessness of their spirits, their arrogance, covetousness and self-love.[1] Their Bibliolatry had never really been taken seriously and it had been said long before Hooker that they were merely using the Bible as a peg for their fancies, that they were building a theology around their arrogance and that they were 'murdering Scripture to serve their own purpose'.[2]

As to politics, their opinions were considered due to factiousness and the desire to rebel. They were held not only to attack royal prerogative but to call in question any form of civil government. They wanted the magistrate to become a mere instrument in the hands of their elders and believed their absolute order of ecclesiastical government to be sufficient for the ordering of society.[3] They wanted the basest and simplest, rather than the wisest and most experienced, to govern and they considered the rule of the many better than the rule of one because they wanted to make the state 'popular'.[4] The result of all this could only be confusion, dissoluteness in behaviour, factions and enmity.[5] For the supreme authority which hitherto had been vested either in King or in

---

[1] R. Bancroft, *A Sermon preached at Paul's Cross*, in G. Hicks, *Bibliotheca Scriptorum Ecclesiae Anglicanae*, London, 1709, Vol. I, pp. 252, 257, 285; Whitgift, *Works*, Parker Society, Vol. I, p. 131, Vol. III, p. 321, 429.

[2] Whitgift, op cit. Vol. I, pp. 59–60, Vol. III, pp. 468–9; op. cit. p. 254.

[3] Bancroft, op. cit. p. 286, p. 303; Whitgift, op. cit. Vol. III, pp. 189 ff., p. 426, p. 486.

[4] Whitgift, op. cit., Vol I, p. 302, Vol. II, pp. 240–1; Vol. III, pp. 196, 274, 275.

[5] Whitgift, op. cit., Vol. III. p. 208

Pope was now to be vested in Presbyters.[1] The authority of the latter was to supplant that of the King, and the result would be that the whole kingdom would be broken up into a large number of congregations.[2]

Bearing these possible consequences in mind, Bancroft referred to the doctrine of the *Vindiciae contra Tyrannos* as identical with that of the Puritans. He had recognized very shrewdly that all these ideas tended towards some form of political pluralism—to a form of government where sovereignty was not vested in a unitary state but was split and resided in a large number of ecclesiastical congregations.[3] And thus he warned his listeners of the intolerable state of affairs that would be created for them if they should ever have a Puritan system of government forced upon them. If the present unitary form of government were overthrown, anarchy would result. The unfortunate events in France during the second half of the sixteenth century were the best demonstration of the disaster to which Puritanism could lead a country: it was irresponsible to lend support to Puritanism on the assumption that England was not France and that such things could never happen on this side of the channel.[4] Hooker himself was very much aware of the strength of this argument and pointed to the disasters wrought by such arbitrary, radical and violent a reformation as the Puritans advocated, in France, Westphalia, Flanders and Scotland.[5]

In vain did the Puritans protest their loyalty to the Queen and their truly religious zeal.[6] Their opponents, partly for propaganda purposes, refused to draw any distinction between them and their continental counterparts. Whatever they said or did was not judged on its own merits but interpreted in terms of

[1] Bancroft, op. cit., p. 292.

[2] Whitgift, op. cit., Vol III, p. 184.

[3] Bancroft, op. cit., p. 297.

[4] Ibid., p. 298.

[5] IV. xiv. 6.

[6] See A. F. Scott-Pearson, *Thomas Cartwright and Elizabethan Puritanism*, Cambridge, 1925, p. 88 and pp. 219 ff. for Cartwright's arguments against the separatist Harrison.

what the Huguenots and Anabaptists on the Continent had done.[1]

Hooker's analysis of Puritanism was deeper and, not being designed for political propaganda, less malicious. But fundamentally he was in agreement with the other opponents of Puritanism. He saw much more clearly than anybody else had done so far the general attitude and philosophy that was behind the Puritan platform and in terms of which its various points appeared as the expression of one consistent spirit. According to this analysis, stated in the most general terms, the foundations of Puritanism lay in hatred; in hatred of the natural world, hatred of its social institutions and hatred of human nature. Puritans insisted on the complete depravity of man and refused to place any confidence whatever in his rational and in his natural faculties. And, yet, automatically, this desire of self-abasement generated, as it was being indulged in, its very opposite: an arrogant pride. The Puritan who felt that he was one of the elect could indeed ride rough-shod over all cautious objections and doubts, for he knew with certainty what the divine truth was.[2] The religious objectivism which expressed itself as the complete annihilation of human nature before God was really indistinguishable from a complete religious subjectivism: this dialectic enabled men to pass their personal prejudices and irrational convictions as divine commandments.[3]

---

[1] Hooker, VIII. vi. 14; Whitgift, op. cit., Vol. I, p. 106, Vol. II, pp. 100, 243, 402; Vol. III, pp. 295, 321, 485; Bancroft, op. cit., p. 263. Apart from Guy de Bré's famous book on continental Anabaptism, there were the minor works of R. Some, *A Godly Treatise*, 1580, and of G. Gifford, *A Short Treatise*, 1590, which drew the same analogy.

[2] This Puritan dialectic is clearly portrayed in their sermons and diaries. A preacher would get his audience writhing with agony at the consciousness of their depravity and then immediately hold out to them the hope of full and gratuitous redemption through an act of faith. For examples see W. Haller, *The Rise of Puritanism*, New York, 1938.

[3] The facts related and analysed by William James in his *Varieties of Religious Experience* seem to be instances of this dialectic emotionalism. To other types of religious experiences his conclusions do not apply. It was only through Puritanism that religious experience became what James thought it was.

The discriminatory power of natural reason lost all significance. Nature and the kingdom of grace were considered according to Luther's maxim *mundus inimicus Dei*, two antagonistic forces. And once grace had triumphed, it abolished and supplanted every natural inclination and faculty: *gratia tollit naturam*—that was the final quintessence of Puritanism.[1]

This outlook naturally foreshadowed one of the most rigid systems of moralism human experience has ever known. The Puritan would condemn any pursuit of pleasure that was not orientated towards the super-natural.[2] And for all those activities that were obviously only concerned with the maintenance of temporal life, he sought an indirect divine sanction by holding that in order to be lawful they had to be commanded by holy Scripture. He asserted in fact, as Hooker put it, that whatsoever is not done by the word of God, is sin.[3] From this basis the Puritans derived the right of their corporate societies to defy the authority of the secular state. This was not so much a theoretical derivation as a natural consequence. If divine law was to supplant all other law, it was only natural that those institutions or bodies that were in possession of divine truth should overrule those that were not. The growth of the conventicle movement in the eighties of the sixteenth century was to Hooker therefore more than a disorderly act of disobedience to an Act of Parliament: it was an attack on natural law and the authority of the secular state that followed from it.[4]

---

[1] In fairness to the Puritans we must remind ourselves also of the other side of the picture. To many Puritans it seemed that the Church was simply used as a bulwark to protect privilege against reform. There was much social chaos and moral corruption in such places as Cheshire and Kidderminster as described by Baxter. Puritanism in this sense—and it was a sense which wholly escaped Hooker—was an attempt to revitalize Christian morality and to adapt it to the needs of a population which was being driven from its old feudal status into an increasingly commercial society. Cp. W. Haller, *The Rise of Puritanism*, New York, 1938, pp. 116-7.

[2] For the meaning of Puritan moralism cp. J. W. Allen, *English Political Thought*, 1603-1660, London, 1938, p. 282.

[3] II. iv. 1, 3.

[4] Hooker's *Laws of Ecclesiastical Polity* was published as an authoritative defence of the Conventicle Act, 1593, C. J. Sisson, op. cit., p. 13; Bancroft had

Hooker's opposition was roused, in the last analysis, by the Puritan attack on natural law and the disparagement of reason. He saw that Puritanism was both an appeal to and a justification of the irrational elements in human nature. And when he set to work to state his counter-argument, he was probably aware of the fact that the human mind was standing at one of the cross-roads of its history. Hence the weighty words with which he opened the Preface to the *Laws of Ecclesiastical Polity*: 'Though for no other cause, yet for this; that posterity may know we have not loosely through silence permitted things to pass away as in a dream . . .'[1]

2

Human life consists of continuous intercourse between human beings. Discussion, exchange of views, a clash of opinions, frictions, agreements or disagreements; those are the basic relationships between man and man. The human mind has naturally developed certain methods to cope with these relationships. But what is the character and nature of these methods? Are they primarily rational or irrational? If the methods are of a rational nature then there is some hope that by prolonged discussion men might find grounds for agreement that are intrinsically compelling, i.e. from which they cannot possibly withhold their assent. But if these methods are primarily of an irrational nature, there can ultimately be no solution but a head-on collision. At best it might end in an agreement to differ; and at worst it will end in the decomposition of the world into energy-rays. For in this case there can be no discussion that will end in a compelling agreement; all that is possible is a statement of the respective positions and a recourse

unearthed all the relevant facts in connexion with the Classis movement and had presented them in his *Dangerous Positions*, ed. by R. G. Usher, Camden Society, 3rd series, Vol. VIII. But he was only concerned there with the purely political aspect. For a more impartial representation of the relevant facts see Ch. Burrage, *Early English Dissenters*, Cambridge, 1912, and W. A. Shaw, *Elizabethan Presbyterianism*, E.H.R., III.

[1] One can almost discern a note of disillusionment in these words. He is writing as if he thought that he had not much chance to persuade his opponents.

to a non-philosophical method of finding a working solution. Hooker was firmly convinced that human nature was profoundly rational, and that if this were only rightly understood there would be no need for terrible apprehensions. This conviction was most probably the consequence of his temperamental disposition and of the interpretation of Christian faith and dogma to which the former obliged him to adhere. His own nature being what it was, he could but see that Christianity taught that man must find a proper balance between the two poles of the Christian dualistic world-picture.

In Puritanism, however, Hooker recognized a straight denial of the rationality of human nature. If men were to accept the Puritan teaching on this matter, they would frivolously throw away the gift of reason and resort to a method of human intercourse that could but lead to collisions and a never-ending strife from which there was no appeal but to violence and fanaticism. For, if men believed that human nature was irrational, they would certainly act as if it were and thus furnish the very proof for their assumption. Hooker therefore realized that he had to exhort man to avail himself of his rational faculties and not to abandon them lightly and give himself over to an incorrect view of human nature.

Even Christ used to argue, Hooker wrote, and continued that 'there is as yet no way known how to dispute or to determine of things disputed without the use of natural reason'.[1] But the Puritans would not accept this view. And what made them so especially dangerous was their very refusal to argue about it rationally: 'let any man of contrary opinion open his mouth to persuade them, they close up their ears, his reasons they weigh not, all is answered with a rehearsal of the words of John: We are of God, he that knows God hears us'.[2] The Puritans, by excluding reason, allowed authority only to faith and thus to an irrational factor. Hooker as a Christian neither would nor could deny the authority of faith; but he saw that if human society was to be saved from chaos, faith had to be synthesized with reason. He had to show that as far as man's natural life was concerned irrationality neither need nor ought to have any authority over it. Although, he said, the spirit leads us to truth and goodness, its

[1] III. viii. 17.　　　　　　　　[2] In. III. 14.

workings in us are so privy and secret, that we stand on a plainer ground when we use reason as the criterion as to whether our inspiration is from God or not.[1]

3

Hooker was not the first philosopher to attempt to refute the Puritan case. If we grant the general assumption that Lollardy was an early manifestation of Puritanism[2] we find that Pecock was a direct forerunner of Hooker. Pecock's philosophy had to cope with exactly the same kind of Bibliolatry and the consequent denial of reason and natural law that Hooker had to deal with. It is moreover not improbable that Hooker was acquainted with some of Pecock's works. After the latter's condemnation, his books had been burnt; but some odd copies survived. And it is known to-day that during Hooker's lifetime a copy of the *Repressor* was in the possession of the antiquarian John Stowe,[3] and that Whitgift owned a copy of *The Book of Faith*.[4] Whether Hooker had access to the former work we do not know; but there is every reason to suppose that Whitgift, who knew of the nature of Hooker's work, drew his attention to Pecock's *Book of Faith*. At any rate if Hooker was acquainted with the work of Pecock, we must conclude that it served him as a warning not to make the situation worse by following in Pecock's footsteps.[5]

[1] III. viii. 15.

[2] Cp. J. Gairdner, *Lollardy and the Reformation in England*, London, 1908.

[3] Ch. Babington, introduction to *The Repressor of over much blaming the Clergy*, London, 1860, p. lxv. It found its way into the Cambridge University Library during the last quarter of the sixteenth century.

[4] J. L. Morrison, introductory essay to *The Book of Faith*, Glasgow, 1909, p. 13.

[5] There is little ground for the assertion that Pecock's views on natural reason and its function were identical with those of Hooker. See V. H. H. Green, *Bishop Reginald Pecock*, Cambridge, 1945, p. 230-1, and Ch. Babington, op. cit., p. xxvi, also Hallam, *Middle Ages*, London, 1853, Vol 3, p. 388. It is certainly true that with Pecock reason outstripped faith and that Hooker too was carried in the end towards an ever-increasing rationalism. But there was method in the evolution of Hooker's thought; whereas Pecock's thought is based on confusion.

Pecock was first of all prompted by much less laudable motives than Hooker. He was incurably vain; and it is difficult for a modern reader of his works not to believe that he used the Lollard Bibliolatry merely as an opportunity for showing that the Bible was not at all perfect and that his own expositions were at any rate clearer.[1]

As against the Lollard belief that faith in the literal text of the Scriptures is the only guide towards salvation, Pecock asserts the priority of reason. The rules of conduct have to be known; and, since knowledge is a rational faculty, faith can only be considered a poor substitute for reason. There is nothing positive in faith itself; and whenever possible it must be supplanted by the more certain knowledge that is derived from reason. If Scripture and reason, for instance, should be found to contradict each other, it is the former that must be adjusted to the latter.[2] Scripture must never interfere with reason, for the former's appeal is mainly emotional and of an admonitory character.[3]

The moral law which is known through reason is more important than the moral law which we know by faith alone[4] and the tables of Moses are not a sufficient guide for life[5], and therefore it is necessary to list all the essential virtues by 'doom of reason'.[6] The four tables which Pecock himself drew up with the help of reason comprise all of God's laws.[7] One can really only believe if there is some kind of evidence; hence all faith must be subject to the judgement of reason,[8] and a

---

[1] He keeps on stating that his tables and expositions are clearer and better than everybody else's. *The Donet*, Early English Text Society, ed. E. V. Hitchcock, London, 1929, pp. 142 f., 119 ff., 117 ff., 81 f.; quoted as D; *The Rule of Christian Religion*, Early English Text Society, ed. W. C. Green, London, 1927, pp. 11, 365 ff.; quoted as Ru.

[2] *The Repressor of over much blaming the Clergy*, ed. Ch. Babington, London, 1860, I. 5; quoted as Re.

[3] Re, I, 13.

[4] Re, I, 15.

[5] D, pp. 20, 140, 142.

[6] D, p. 22.

[7] D, p. 161.

[8] *The Book of Faith*, ed. J. L. Morrison, Glasgow, 1909, pp. 129, 131, quoted as BF.

truth must be accepted on faith only until there is better evidence for it.[1]

All this shows clearly that to Pecock the distinction between reason and faith did not lie in the difference of the subject-matter of which they imparted knowledge, i.e. in the difference between natural and divine law respectively; but simply in the fact that the one was trustworthy and the other was not. The subject-matter, the law that was to guide man towards salvation, could really be known by either method: with certainty by reason, without certainty by faith. There are several attempts in Pecock to give a justification for the asserted primacy of reason over faith. He says for instance that whatever 'the doom of kindly and well disposed reason allows and approves is a governance of God's law',[2] indicating thereby that he considers reason the gift of God and hence naturally infallible. Christ, he also argues, would have been mean, had He taught a faith that could not stand the test of reason.[3] The dictates of reason are the law of nature; but the law of nature is the law of God—hence reason leads ultimately to the law of God.[4] He indicated thereby that reason to him was not a pagan instrument but a faculty which led to divine truth.

Pecock therefore warned laymen against all unlearned expounders of the Bible.[5] Only reason was fit to judge the Bible. This power to explain the Bible is a purely intellectual power and does not depend in any way on a man's character, as the Lollards, who were prepared to listen to the commands of the 'godly', believed.[6] Even the Bible must be interpreted by reason.[7] He showed special insight when he explained that certain kinds of faith were really caused by strange 'humours' such as Melancholy. The results of such faith could only be called superstitious and it is

[1] BF, p. 136.

[2] Re, IV, 5.

[3] BF, p. 132.

[4] *The Folewer to the Donet*, ed E. V. Hitchcock, Early English Text Society, London, 1924, p. 164; quoted as F.

[5] Re, I, 16.

[6] Re, I, 17.

[7] F, p. 10.

necessary therefore to subject such faith, derived from 'inspiration', to the test of reason.[1]

Against the main Lollard thesis, that reason was unreliable, he set the argument that wherever reason may be weak, it can find aid in the formal syllogism.[2] He could certainly not admit that reason was to be excluded altogether: if man does not follow reason, he said, his way of serving God is not better than that of the beasts.[3] Reason was in fact the greatest authority that God ever made,[4] and it is just through the exercise of reason and of freewill that men differed from the beasts.[5] Will always had to conform to the judgement of reason.[6]

To Pecock reason and faith were only two different modes of knowledge of one and the same kind of truth. He thought that he could confound the Lollard insistence on the exclusiveness of faith by proving that faith, contrary to the Lollard assumption, was an unreliable, but reason an infallible, mode of knowledge. Faith, he actually wrote, is a kind of knowledge derived from a person whom we can trust. But knowledge derived from 'natural wit' must needs be more reliable.[7] And in any case, faith cannot be autonomous because in order to have it, we must have some form of reason for it.[8] All this shows clearly either that Pecock was never able to form a clear conception in his mind of the two distinct realms of nature and supernature with the two modes of knowledge appropriate to them; or that he was simply carried away by his own ardour against the Lollards so that he simplified the whole problem to the extent of asserting merely the opposite of what they believed, i.e. the primacy of reason over faith as against the primacy of faith over reason.

But the problem was not as simple as all that. To do what

---

[1] Ru, p. 459; Hooker accepted the Church as a historical reality, i.e. as the continuation of the Incarnation. Hence he could derive both Bible and faith from the authority of the Church. Pecock being only interested in the vindication of reason as such, attempted to base Bible and faith on the latter.

[2] Re, I, 14; there is no ground for believing, as is often done, that to Pecock or to any medieval thinker, reason and the syllogism were identical.

[3] Ru, p. 228.

[4] F, pp. 9–10.

[5] D, pp. 12 ff.

[6] F, p. 180.

[7] BF, I, 1.

[8] BF, I, 2.

Pecock had done was to open the door to the denial of the existence of supernature altogether, for he implicitly denied that faith could impart knowledge of a number of things of which reason could not impart knowledge. He must have unconsciously felt the danger of his virulent rationalism, for again and again one finds passages in his works which contradict his general argument.[1] If one takes his vanity into account there is a strong presumption in favour of the conclusion that he simply lacked the intellectual stature that was required to deal with such a problem. There was always the danger of a pagan rationalism behind the assertion that reason was superior to faith; and it could therefore hardly commend itself to a Christian like Hooker to follow Pecock in his attempt to refute Lollardy by reversing the terms of their statements. It is certainly true to say that Pecock failed to reach a real synthesis of faith and reason.[2] But just this fact shows how very unlike Hooker he was; for Hooker, though the intellectual circumstances of the sixteenth century lured him along a different path, had understood that the problem could not be solved by a mere conversion of the Puritan thesis into its opposite.

4

Hooker was intellectually infinitely superior to Pecock. He really understood the problem involved, and therefore did not let himself be tempted into an easy-going rationalism which might have led—as it did in fact with so many seventeenth-century thinkers—to some form of natural religion. He had probed the problem, and his analysis of the Puritan standpoint had probably suggested the only fitting answer. It is usually only necessary to ask the right kind of question in order to find out what the right

[1] In Ru, p. 461, he writes that in matters supernatural we must be satisfied with a literal interpretation of the Bible and in F, p. 10, he says that the literal sense of the Bible had to be found by reason. Sometimes he takes faith to be a supplement of reason, as in D, p. 108, and asserts that there are truths which are above reason, Ru, p. 84. These statements contradict the larger part of his chief argument.

[2] V. H. H. Green, *Bishop R. Pecock*, Cambridge, 1945, p. 129.

kind of answer would be. Hooker must in fact have recognized in Puritanism the traditional tenets of medieval Augustinian philosophy. For an answer to it he naturally went to St. Thomas Aquinas. Hooker did not expressly explain that that was what he did. But if one compares the general character of medieval Augustinian philosophy with the character of Puritanism as seen by Hooker; and Hooker's answer with the fundamental principles of Thomistic philosophy, then one will clearly recognize what was at the root of the *Laws of Ecclesiastical Polity*. There was of course no real philosophy behind the Puritan arguments at all. They sprang from a deep inner conviction and an attitude of mind, and there does not exist a philosophical summary of them in the sixteenth century apart from the one which Hooker had prepared himself. Their views were actually a denial of philosophy and of a philosophical mode of argument. If Hooker marshalled a philosophical argument against Puritanism, he did it in order to satisfy his own craving for philosophical clarity, and because in order to argue at all one had to assume that one's opponents' case was based on thoughts that could be expressed in philosophical terms. Strictly speaking, however, all that can be said about the assumed correspondence between Puritanism and Augustinian philosophy is that the two had been prompted by a similar approach to religion.

It had been the tendency of medieval Augustinianism to deny the separate and independent existence of philosophy and to make the latter completely subordinate to theology. Thus the Augustinian philosophers had tended to deny that there was a sphere of life with which reason could deal competently and autonomously. This fundamental idea was closely connected with their general view of God. Without His special and continuous aid neither man nor the world could continue to operate or even to exist. Man, in order to know and to act, stands all the time in need of a special divine illumination and grace; and the world can only exist and operate through *rationes seminales*, that are contained in each object in which is thus pre-formed every successive shape which it can ever assume. In all this we find a complete dependence on Platonic Idealism: there is an ideal world which through the special goodness of God directly operates upon this world which could not continue to exist without this special mediation. 'Because the form has not in itself the power to create form . . . he[1] prefers to find it pre-formed in the *ratio seminalis*; it is because the intellect has not in itself the power to construct the intelligible that he will have it draw from God the elements of the immutable and necessary; it is because the will has not in itself the principle of the four cardinal virtues, that he will have these powers impressed upon it by their divine archetypes.'[2]

In short: Augustinian philosophy denied the efficacy of second causes and made both man and nature completely dependent on divine grace by not allowing them any kind of either causal or rational efficacy. This was the philosophical theory which had stood behind the view that human nature was depraved and could only be regenerated through a special act of divine grace, that faith therefore had to supplant reason and that divine law was to be substituted for natural law, and which Hooker apparently assumed to stand also behind Puritanism. Both Puritanism and Augustinianism sprang from the same source, namely, from the fear that one might subtract from God's power and glory if one attributed any kind of efficacy to the world He had created. *Attribuere quod est Dei creaturae periculosum est.*[3]

St. Thomas had turned against these theories of Augustinianism because he found them to be too Platonic. The Platonic theory of Ideas he took to be incorrect because he had accepted Aristotle's criticism of Plato. There were two opposed theories of the operations of natural things and of knowledge. On the one hand Plato drew the natural consequence of the scepticism of his predecessors, who had denied that sense-knowledge is reliable or that bodies could be known, as they were in a state of constant

[1] St. Bonaventure.

[2] E. Gilson, *The Philosophy of St. Bonaventure*, London, 1938, p. 429; for a general description of Augustinian philosophy see also P. Mandonnet, *Siger de Brabant et l'Averroisme Latin au XIII siècle*, Louvain, 1908, and E. Longpré, *S. Augustin et la pensée française*, Paris, 1932; for the Augustinian psychology and metaphysics of illumination see Cl. Bäumker, *Witelo*, Münster, 1908, pp. 372-7; 460 ff; 469.

[3] There is no attempt in Hooker to deal with Nominalism. We therefore presume that he did not consider Puritanism to be the result of any Nominalist influence.

becoming. He therefore transported the reality, intelligibility and ideas of things into a super-real world. In this world there lay, according to him, all efficacy and all truth. On the other hand there stood Aristotle who rejected the scepticism that was latent in Plato. To him there is a certain stability in the world which can therefore be known by man through the senses. And hence things have efficacy in the state in which we know them, i.e. in this world. Knowledge need not be explained through a world of exterior intelligibles but through an active intellect which produces the intelligible.[1] Thomism was due to the purely philosophical decision that Aristotle was right and Plato was wrong. Behind the philosophers whom he criticized, behind Ibn Gebirol, Avicenna and St. Augustin, St. Thomas saw Plato. Plato to him was the common father of all those *qui rebus naturalibus proprias subtrahunt actiones.*[2]

Hooker rejected Augustinian philosophy for different reasons. He was less concerned with the purely philosophical problem of the theory of Ideas than St. Thomas. But he was confronted by an immensely urgent and practical question: how to maintain the belief in the autonomy and efficacy of natural reason in those spheres of life where the irrational authority of faith can only do more harm than good. Moreover he had little sympathy with the fact of conversion or with the fear that by attributing some efficacy to man and nature one might not be attributing enough to God. He had never been one of the great doubters to whom Christianity was primarily a matter of conscience and who could therefore not bring themselves to an automatic and spontaneous acceptance of Christian faith. Hooker belonged to those men to whom faith is something natural—not something which their conscience can either reject or accept.

[1] See E. Cassirer, *Individuum und Kosmos in der Philosophie der Renaissance,* Leipzig, 1927, pp. 17 ff. The scepticism which caused Plato to place all real efficacy into the super-sensible world corresponds to the despair of human nature which compelled the Augustinian philosophers to attribute efficacy to God alone.

[2] See E. Gilson, *Pourquoi Saint Thomas a critiqué Saint Augustin,* Archives d'Histoire Doctrinale et Littéraire du Moyen Age, 1926-7.

5

Hooker therefore went back to that medieval thinker who—though for different reasons—had built up a case against Augustinianism.[1] He began his great work with a summary of Thomistic philosophy which takes up the better part of the first book. Most of the arguments are telescoped to such an extent that to a reader unacquainted with the main principles of Thomism they may fail to carry conviction. But Hooker's philosophically inclined sixteenth-century reader must have quickly grasped what he was trying to do. The summary was made in Hooker's own language, not encumbered with any philosophical pedantry or technical jargon, and bears witness to the extent to which the grandiose system of Thomistic philosophy had been assimilated by Hooker. He could write about these matters with ease and grace, probably forgetting half the time that he was propounding philosophy, thinking that he was merely briefly expounding what everybody knew or ought to know. What to him, at any rate, had become so familiar as to be obvious rather than a matter for controversy.

At times, for the sake of greater clarity and brevity, he even changed the Thomistic terminology though he was always intent on preserving its meaning. He does this for instance when he is describing the powers with which the soul is striving for perfection.[2] In other places, as for instance when he is discussing the various types of human law[3] where he is obviously just paraphrasing the famous passage from the *Summa Theologica*,[4] he adopted the sixteenth-century terminology for these matters.[5]

Hooker used the Thomistic method to perfection. His real

[1] Hooker's connexion with St. Thomas has been noted by many historians.

[2] I. xi. 4.

[3] I. x. 10.

[4] I, II. 95, 2 ad Resp.

[5] *Ius civile* was divided into *mixtum* and *merum* according as to whether it contained any natural law or not. Hotman, *Inst.* I, ch. 2; Bachoven, *Inst.* I, 2, § 1. Hooker used the English equivalents 'mixed' and 'merely' for the same distinction.

endeavour was to reconcile as many conflicting opinions as possible and to establish a synthesis rather than to press one doctrine to its ultimate conclusions. Hence the catholicity of his quotations and his persistent refusal to quote St. Thomas where, in his view, a doctrine followed from reason as much as from the authority of the 'greatest of the school divines'. It is of course possible (though it means precisely nothing) to interpret any statement of Christian philosophy that is couched in sufficiently general terms, as Hooker's statements in fact are, in terms of Thomistic philosophy. Especially since both Hooker and St. Thomas took Aristotle as their point of departure. But the mere fact that Hooker should have been so staunch an Aristotelian puts him, as a Christian thinker, into the same class as St. Thomas—for Thomism is a Christian Aristotelianism *par excellence*. To St. Thomas, as to Hooker, Aristotle was practically synonymous with reason. Furthermore the general hierarchical order of Hooker's system corresponds so closely to that of St. Thomas that we must speak of very much more than mere interpretation when we say that Hooker was a Thomist. And finally, the crucial test can be made at all those points where Hooker is completely consistent in his Thomism not only against the Platonic-Augustinian school but also in regard to the Nominalist critics of St. Thomas. With St. Thomas he maintains an Aristotelian empiricism against Plato.[1] And against St. Augustine the specific doctrine that man can have no knowledge of God but through a process of abstraction from initial sense-experience.[2] He expressly states that angels are immaterial[3] and thereby sides with St. Thomas in the latter's famous dispute with St. Bonaventure on this matter. In the much debated doctrine about the relationship between soul and body, Hooker again shows himself an uncompromising Thomist by adding—in order not to leave the slightest doubt—as a footnote the statement, which was in itself not strictly relevant to the argument, that the soul is the form of man and that it needs a body.[4] He thus declared himself against the Augustinian school which maintained that the soul was a substance and that the union of

---

[1] I. vi. 1.   [2] I. iv. 1.

[2] I. ii. 2.   [4] I. iii. 4.

body and soul was a union of two substances and not a union of matter and form.

He also pronounces unhesitatingly in favour of the Thomistic conception of God as Reason against the doctrine always latent in Augustinianism and openly set forth by Occam and his disciples that God is primarily Will.[1] This last point is of special importance because much of the Lutheran and Calvinist teaching on predestination and the elect had been derived from and grounded in Occam's philosophy. It is significant that Hooker should assert the Thomist conception of a universe governed by reason, which thus could partly at least be understood by man's rational faculties and before which he did not appear completely helpless and lost, as against the idea of Occam that the universe was subject to blind and unpredictable will, and that man, incapable of fathoming the divine arbitrary decisions, remained helpless and unprotected at the mercy of God. After these crucial tests the positive evidence of a complete correspondence between Hooker's teaching and that of St. Thomas becomes even more significant.[2] We shall deal with the implications of Hooker's Thomism later; for the time being we shall only examine what arguments Hooker drew from St. Thomas in order to establish his position against Puritanism and to show what place was due to reason in the conduct of human life. The following paragraphs are a summary of Hooker's and St. Thomas's arguments.

Everything works for an end.[3] No certain end can be obtained unless there is a regularity in action fit to obtain it. Such a canon we term a law. Such a canon is given to all creatures by a superior, i.e. by God. God's being is the source of this *lex aeterna*, which in turn is the source of all other law.[4] God's will is always prompted by his reason: and it is actually this reason which is the *lex aeterna* and which God has set down for Himself to follow.[5]

[1] I. ii. 5.

[2] For a systematic exposition of that correspondence see Appendix A.

[3] In this and the following notes, the first reference is to Book I of Hooker's *Laws of Ecclesiastical Polity*. The other references are to the respective works of St. Thomas—ii. 1; S.Th. I, II, 3; S.c.G. IV, 1.

[4] ii. 2; S.c.G. III, 115; S.Th. I, II, 91, 1, and 93, 3.

[5] ii. 5; S.Th. I, II, 93, 1.

This *lex aeterna* is the plan of divine wisdom according to which everything is guided to its proper end.[1] This law is the source of all other law; i.e. of the law of natural agents, of celestial law, of the law of nature or reason, of divine law and of human law.[2] In all these laws the *lex aeterna* manifests itself.[3]

Natural agents observe the law set down for them because they cannot do otherwise; voluntary agents, i.e. men, observe it by giving their free consent.[4] It follows that nothing can work according to the laws set down for it except with the efficacy of God. It is He who bestows efficacy on all things and on all men.[5] God works in fact through Nature, using her as an instrument.[6] Man, like all other creatures, aspires to the greatest degree of conformity with God he is capable of. He does this by seeking knowledge and truth and the exercise of virtue.[7] The exercise of virtue, i.e. the pursuit of goodness, lies essentially in an obedience to the divinely ordained order; every disturbance of this divine order is sin.[8] But there are two different ways of finding out what is good: Man can either attain to a knowledge of the cause of a thing's goodness or simply discover the signs of goodness, such as, that all men account a certain thing as good: for the voice of all men is the sentence of God.[9] If all men hold a thing to be good, they must have learnt it from Nature—and Nature is but God's instrument. By it we learn from Him.[10] For God has endowed every man with reason and has thus enabled him to discover for himself the order which he ought to follow.[11] Hence

[1] ii. 6; S.Th. I, II, 93, 1.

[2] iii. 1; S.Th. I, II, 91, 1 and 93, 3.

[3] iii. 1; S.Th. I, II, 93, 4 and 5 and 6.

[4] iii. 2; S.Th. I, II, 91, 2; S.Th. I, II, 93, 4 ad Resp.

[5] iii. 4; S.c.G. III, 66.

[6] iii. 4; S.c.G., III, 70; S.Th. I, 22.

[7] v. 3; S.Th. I, II, 71, 2 ad Resp.

[8] vii. 7; S.Th. II, II, 142, 1 ad Resp.

[9] See Appendix B.

[10] viii. 2; this is an application of a Thomist epistemological principle: 'dupliciter aliquid cognosci potest: uno modo in seipso; alio modo in suo effectu in quo aliqua similitudo eius invenitur.' S.Th. I, II, 93, 2 ad Resp.

[11] viii. 3; S.Th. I, 84, 5 ad Resp.: 'Signatum est super nos lumen vultus tui, Domine', Ps. iv, 6–7.

man can learn the will of God by using his reason: it can guide him in so far as it is the light of His countenance.[1] To consult reason is therefore to consult God, and all laws thus made only appear to be made by men. They are however really made by God and only discovered by men.[2] This argument is based on the assumption that second causes have an efficacy of their own. All created causality is in fact an analogue of creative causality, for to be a cause is to participate finitely in the infinite fecundity of the creative act.[3] And the same applies, *mutatis mutandis*, to reason. God in His goodness has thus associated man with His own divine government.[4] And St. Thomas quotes 1 Corinth., iii. 9: 'Dei sumus adjutores'.[5]

A law is a rule which directs men to good conduct. For all voluntary agents this rule is the sentence of reason. A law then is that which reason defines to be good and which therefore must be done. It compels obedience because it is the command of reason.[6] The main principles of reason are apparent in themselves[7] and natural law consists of those dictates of reason which are thus imposed upon the will; such as 'parents are to be honoured' or 'small difficulties are to be endured for the sake of greater good'.[8]

The gist of this argument is that reason, because it is the imprint of the divine countenance on man, can and ought to be relied on. It is the proper guide to the discovery of that law according to which man must regulate the conduct of his natural life if he wishes to avoid sin, i.e. if he wishes to conform to the divinely ordained order of the Universe. By following reason man is ultimately following God and exercising his rational autonomy only apparently. He is really only co-operating with God, for nothing can

[1] viii. 3; S.Th. I, II, 19, 4 ad Resp.
[2] viii. 3.
[3] S.c.G. III, 70; I follow Gilson's exposition of Thomism.
[4] S.c.G. III, 113.
[5] S.c.G. III, 21.
[6] viii. 4, 8; S.Th. I, II, 90, 1 ad Resp.
[7] viii. 5.
[8] viii. 5, 6; S.Th. I, II, 91, 2, and ad 2nd; 94, 2.

be done or can happen except by virtue of God's efficacy, or without the perpetual aid and concurrence of the supreme cause of all things.[1]

There are always cases where rules of conduct have to be defined more specifically than is done by natural law. It is necessary therefore to deduce with the help of reason special rules from natural law, so that it may be easy to see in every circumstance what is the right thing to do.[2] Such special rules are called human laws. These laws are nothing but the rational application to concrete and sometimes varying conditions of the general principles of natural law. It follows therefore that a provision of human law that is at variance with natural law is not a law at all, but a corruption of law.[3] These human laws differ of course according to time and circumstances for which they are made. They are not less good than natural law although, through the variety of human circumstances for which they are made they have no universal validity.[4] One must further distinguish between two kinds of human law. Some human laws forbid or enjoin what is *malum vel bonum in se*; others enjoin or forbid what are *in se indifferentia*. The former kind is known as 'mixed human law' and the latter kind as 'merely human law'.[5] In any case, however, human law is completely dependent on natural law, and it is only reason which allows us to deduce the former from the latter.[6]

With this theory Hooker had succeeded in establishing the claims of reason in the natural order of life. Or one might invert this and say that he had succeeded in defining one part or aspect of human existence as purely natural and thus subject to the dictates of reason. It does not matter that these ideas were not original. Hooker showed a most penetrating understanding when he discovered that they were relevant to the question under

[1] viii. 11; S.c.G. III, 66, 67.

[2] x. 5; S.Th. I, II, 91, 3 ad Resp.

[3] x. 10; S.Th. I, II, 95, 2.

[4] x. 9; S.Th. I, II, 95, 2 ad 3rd.

[5] x. 10; S.Th. I, II, 95, 2 ad Resp.

[6] St. Thomas describes the method by which mixed human law is derived as *conclusio* and that by which merely human law is derived as *determinatio*, ibid., and In Eth. 5, 10, Lectio 12c.

discussion, i.e. when he recognized the very Augustinian traits against which St. Thomas had developed his theory, in sixteenth-century Puritanism.

But the argument does not end here. After having defined the order of nature and the human faculties that control it and operate in it, Hooker, still agreeing with St. Thomas, proceeded to add to it the order of supernature. Most ends, he continued, are desired as means to further ends. But in order to avoid a *regressum ad infinitum*, there must be a final end that is desired for nothing but itself.[1] What is desired as a means is desired with a strength proportionate to the end it is desired for. What is desired as an end in itself is desired, however, with an infinite strength; for only that which is an infinite good can be desired with infinite strength: and this infinite good can be nothing but God.[2] Neither wealth nor any good of the corporeal order[3] nor felicity or any other good of the spiritual order can be the final end of man.[4] The last end of an intelligent creature can only be the vision of God.[5] It is thus that Christian philosophy points towards supernature, beyond the confines of nature. And in order that man, though weakened through the Fall, may nevertheless recognize the rules necessary to guide him in accordance with the supernatural requirements through life, God has *revealed* a law to man. This revealed law cannot be found by reason, for it concerns the supernatural and not the natural aspect of human life. The divine law is therefore primarily known to man through faith. And just as we have seen that supernature rounds off the world of nature by setting man a final end which he can desire for itself and with infinite strength, so divine law rounds off the system of rules for conduct. In this way faith, by which divine law is known, supplements reason, by which natural law is known. The two realms of nature and supernature co-exist in perfect harmony, because in the last analysis they both flow from God's *lex aeterna*. Hence there can

[1] xi. 1; S.Th. I, II, 1, 4 ad Resp.

[2] xi. 2; S.c.G. IV, 54; S.Th. I, I, 2, 8 ad Resp.

[3] xi. 2; S.c.G. III, 32; S.Th I, II, 2, 5 ad Resp.

[4] xi. 2; S.Th. I, II, 2, 7 ad Resp.

[5] xi. 2, 3; S.c.G. III, 25.

be no real contradiction between reason and faith. For everlasting felicity, Hooker concludes, we need both nature and Scripture.[1] They are jointly, and not severally, a complete guide.[2] He has now reached the final point in the argument where he might have said with St. Thomas: '*Gratia non tollit naturam sed perficit.*' He could now put his finger on exactly that point where the Puritan argument according to him failed: it did not achieve a distinction between nature and supernature and the respective human faculties. The Puritan's exclusive appeal to the Bible was just such a negation of reason and of natural law as was not permissible according to Hooker's view of the order of creation. He had shown to his own satisfaction that the whole Puritan case was based on an incorrect picture of the world. The Puritan confusion of the two orders of nature and supernature had, according to his analysis, no basis in facts. Puritanism, therefore, was an error of judgement.

But it is just at this point that the historian can understand and appreciate the unsolvable conflict that underlay the whole argument. To the Puritan as to the Augustinian type of religious thinker the view that a religious question could be an error of judgement was completely meaningless. Religion to him was not a matter of knowledge, i.e. an epistemological problem; but a matter for his conscience, i.e. a moral problem. The primary question was not: what are the facts? but: what shall I do? What was all-important was the decision of man's conscience whether it should accept divine grace or not; whereas to Hooker the acceptance of divine grace was not a matter for doubt. The problem for him was to find the place of divine grace in the general scheme of things. The Puritan, when confronted with the question of his conscience, must have considered Hooker's analysis probably wrong and certainly irrelevant. Once he had gone through the struggle of deciding that he must accept God, he could hardly be expected to make this decision with any reservations by allowing a proper place and scope for just those purely natural factors, such as reason, which had been most instrumental in preventing him from making a decision.

---

[1] I.e., faith. [2] xiv. 5.

We find then towards the end of the sixteenth century an exact repetition of a medieval situation. Where St. Thomas had defended the efficacy of second causes and the independence of philosophy against the Augustinians, Hooker defended the autonomy of reason against the Puritans. The point at issue was the same. It was the conflict in religious thought between the epistemological and the ethical approach. The arguments involved were very largely identical. The revival of Augustinian thought through a radical Protestantism had brought about through Richard Hooker a revival of Thomism. There was hardly a single new argument—in the philosophical sense—on either side. But originality is hardly ever a measure of any consequence. What counts is the acumen with which a situation has been analysed. And on that account Hooker deserves full credit. That as a philosopher and theologian he did not see the unsolvable conflict, cannot be held against him. That insight is due to psychological understanding.

It helps us to understand, however, why one particular point in Hooker's argument, which sounded so conclusive from his own standpoint, failed to carry conviction with the Puritans. Hooker could in fact easily show that even the most ardent Puritan and opponent of the use of reason acknowledged in the end the judgement of the wise. For if one ever quoted such a judgement against them they either deprecated its wisdom or quoted another one to refute it. This means that in reality the Puritans did not practise what they were preaching, and showed due respect for reason.[1] But they were using reason just in order to show how useless reason was.[2] By this argument, if one granted Hooker's fundamental approach to the problem of religion, Puritanism stood convicted of self-contradiction. Hooker had reduced it *ad absurdum*, for the whole Puritan argument was, through the mere fact that it was being put forward at all, a constant refutation of itself. In this way philosophy can always deal with any argument that is directed against philosophy; philosophy cannot as a mode of knowledge be successfully attacked on a philosophical basis. This is obvious. But at the same time, a defence of philosophy

[1] II. vii. 8, 10.　　　　[2] III. viii. 4.

57

on none but philosophical grounds cannot, for the same reason, be convincing. And this is as obvious. It is unlikely that the opposing parties understood that at the time, but the fact that their endless controversies never produced any results might have made them suspect it. To-day with the help of psychological analysis we can see the problem in its proper light, although we have to admit that we are, with that insight, no nearer to a solution than our sixteenth-century forefathers were.

To sum up Hooker's philosophical achievement, we cannot do better than to quote Gilson's description of the meaning of the thirteenth-century Thomist position: 'In such a doctrine it is easy to see that far from derogating from the glory of God in insisting on the perfection and efficacy of creatures, we only exalt it in exalting them. For the Christian philosophers of the classical period it was always a mistake to belittle nature under the pretext of exalting God. *Vilificare naturam* is a philosophical error in itself, for a nature cannot be conceived unless we attribute to it the means of acquiring its own power of perfection. But it also does wrong to God, for God is the pure actuality of being, and since it is by creating that He communicated being to creatures, it must needs be that in communicating the likeness of His being He communicated also a likeness of his causality. . . . A universe without genuine causality would be a universe unworthy of God . . . all injustice towards the causality of creatures becomes an injustice towards the goodness of God.'[1] Hooker would indeed have wholeheartedly subscribed to St. Thomas's statement that the existence and efficacy of second causes and, by implication, of human reason, is evidence not of a lack of power in God, but of the immensity of His goodness.[2] 'Detrahere actiones proprias rebus est divinae bonitatis derogare.' This was what Hooker meant when he said that an 'earnest desire to draw all things under the determination of bare and naked Scripture, has caused here much pains to be taken in abating the estimation and credit of man'.[3] And he warned his readers that St. Augustine when he had exhorted people not to listen to men but to God, had not meant

[1] E. Gilson, *The Spirit of Medieval Philosophy*, London, 1936, pp. 144-5.
[2] S.c.G. III, 70.
[3] II. vii. I.

that they should not listen to him, St. Augustine, either. He had merely meant that they should not listen to men that contradicted God.[1] To Hooker as to St. Thomas, the attempt to deprecate man and his nature was tantamount to a denial of God's goodness. And this attitude is at the basis of every kind of Christian humanism.

6

St. Thomas had been accused in the thirteenth century by St. Bonaventure and his disciples of yielding to naturalism. No matter how sound the Thomistic reasoning was, to insert the efficacy of nature and of human reason between God and natural effects was considered extremely dangerous: 'Attribuere quod est Dei creaturae periculosum est.'[2] How well justified this warning was is well proven by the final position which Hooker was driven to assume. For when he came to the last part of his work, to the defence of the Tudor Constitution, he discovered that his theory of the nature and use of reason could be interpreted in a very generous fashion. There was indeed nothing in it that would prevent him from looking upon the dictates of reason as the direct commands of God, and thus from excluding, at least, for all practical purposes, God from the government of society. The role of divine law—and of an independent Church based on a mystery that was beyond the reach of secular organs of government—was thus minimized and reason became almost omnipotent. And all this was developed by a slight shift of emphasis from Hooker's purely Thomist premises. His ideas on this matter are best studied in his account of the origin of episcopacy.

The Puritan objection to episcopacy was based on the idea that in the primitive Church all pastors had had equal authority and that therefore episcopacy was a human innovation and a violation of the divine command. Hooker defined episcopacy by giving an account of its origin in which he showed in the most striking fashion that the dictates of reason are really equivalent to divine

[1] II. vii. 6.

[2] E. Gilson, *The Philosophy of St. Bonaventure*, London, 1938, p. 476.

59

commandments. To start with, he admitted that originally all churches had been governed by a number of bishops, also known as presbyters, who had all enjoyed an equal amount of authority.[1] Very soon, however, people had discovered that there were conflicts and disagreements among them and that it would stand them in good stead to be under the control of one superior. Therefore one of the presbyters was appointed to rule over the others.[2]

Hooker thus attributed the evolution of episcopacy to a purely *natural* process; it was the need for a supreme authority which made men realize that they ought to have a bishop whose authority was to be superior to that of the other pastors. And similarly he said that, since bishops used to fall out among one another, metropolitans were appointed at the Council of Nicea to redress the situation and to rule over the bishops.[3] Again he explained the origin of archbishops by a purely rational reflexion: it was experience which taught that they were needed, human reason therefore dictated that they ought to be established.

The final meaning of this theory is clearly revealed by Hooker's own comments. He says that bishops were in fact set up either by the whole Church or by the Apostles themselves; and, since the latter had been guided by the Holy Ghost, episcopacy must be considered divinely ordained. He did, however, not say what the status of episcopacy would be if bishops had first been set up by the whole Church. The actual derivation of episcopacy, whether by direct divine order or by the indirect divine sanction of human reason, was not held by Hooker to be a problem of any great significance, because the one was as good as the other. All he knew was that there was a need for a ruling authority; and that that need could be met either directly by divine command or indirectly by human reason. In either case episcopacy must be considered to have been divinely ordained. Seeing that he attributed equal efficacy to divine orders and to human reason, we must infer that he attributed implicitly supernatural powers to human reason— since we cannot take him to mean that there was no realm of supernature. He knew that human reason was able to deal with such needs and, as it was God's gift to man, its dictates could be

[1] VII. v. 1.
[2] VII. xi. 5.
[3] VII. viii. 10.

considered equivalent to the voice of God. In another place
Hooker said that the ruling authority of bishops was derived from
Christ through the Apostles. This fact is never doubted by him.[1]
And yet he thought that that authority was clearly based on the
will of the Church as a whole and that one could therefore
imagine it to have been repealed if circumstances should have warranted it.[2] It looks almost as if Hooker believed in a dual basis
of episcopal authority. But this idea is not the result of any lack
of precision in Hooker. It is due to his firm conviction that the
divine and the human basis of episcopal authority, namely
Christ's command and the will of the Church, really amount to
one and the same thing. There is therefore no need to distinguish
between the two only apparently different opinions. As human
reason comes from God, its dictates are as competent and effi-
cacious—because as divine—as the will of Christ itself or as the
orders of the Apostles inspired by the Holy Ghost. It is therefore
possible for Hooker to mention the two bases of episcopal authority in one breath and use the one as much as the other as an
argument in support of his thesis that episcopacy is a necessary and
integral part of a divinely ordained church government.

In this sense Hooker can say that there are bishops who are
superior to other bishops for causes which 'the wisdom both of
God and man' has approved.[3] He is writing as if the two were
really one.[4] Hooker then, evolved in the end a conception of a

---

[1] VII. v. 8; VII. iv. 3; cp. also V. lxxviii. 12.

[2] VII. v. 8.

[3] VII. viii. 5; cp. the following quotation: 'Inequality of pastors is an ordin-
ance both divine and profitable.' VII. xiii. 5.

[4] All this is a social contract theory: but a theory that is conceived in the
Aristotelian, not in the Hobbesian sense. In the former, authority over others
arises naturally because it is necessary if men want to live together in society.
A formal contract is superfluous. In the latter a formal contract is necessary
because man's wish to live in society is not prompted by nature, and hence an
artificial agreement to do so and to establish the necessary institutions is required. In the former theory there is no conscious choice on the part of man.
And since God has created human nature the Aristotelian contract is as much
God's work as it is man's. If interpreted in an Aristotelian sense, Hooker's ideas
about the equivalence of the two sources of episcopal authority will not strike
us as absurd. They are odd if one attempts to interpret Hooker in terms of
Hobbes's theory.

truly omnipotent reason. The fine and important distinction which he had derived from St. Thomas between reason and faith as two supplementary methods of finding natural and divine law respectively, was wiped out. Reason now was held to extend beyond the sphere of the natural order; it was really equivalent to faith in that its commands extended over the same sphere of the supernatural order and were considered equivalent with divine commands and with revelation: '. . . of His[1] approbation the evidence is sufficient if either Himself have by revelation in His word warranted it, or we by some discourse of reason find it good of itself.'[2] Hooker had thus at last established the complete autonomy of human reason over the whole of life.

He was certainly not altogether clear as to the exact consequences of his theory. When he discovered its practical application he hesitated—as we shall see in the following chapter. But there can be little doubt that he was just beginning to commit exactly that error into which St. Bonaventure had said all Thomistic philosophy would fall: naturalism. Nevertheless Hooker, as the medieval man he was, must not be mistaken for a modern rationalist. If pressed for a final opinion on this point, he would not have said that that which reason can discover exists or is valid; but that reason can discover everything that exists and is valid. Reason is neither the measure of the universe nor its law; but God in His infinite goodness bestowed so much reason on man as to make him practically independent, even of God Himself. This is where the philosopher has to leave the matter; but the historian's interest is not exhausted, and he must follow the fate of Hooker's attempt to revive Thomism in very unfavourable circumstances and finally trace in them the reasons for his ultimate failure. The inclination towards naturalism or rationalism was a logical consequence of Thomism; but it was a mere accident that Hooker's thought encountered in another direction a storm which it did not weather.

[1] God's.
[2] VII. xi. 10.

7

It had been Hooker's original idea to define clearly two spheres of life in which reason and faith reigned supreme respectively. In the order of nature he had vindicated the control of man's rational faculties and had subjected all irrational impulses to their judgement. He was fully aware of the existence of the irrational factors that enter into man's natural life and that often threatened to dominate it, the appetites. But here as elsewhere he had faithfully followed St. Thomas who had subordinated the will, and therefore the appetites, to reason. The two springs of human action are knowledge and will. The will always wills the good—but the good is of course what rational knowledge apprehends as such.[1] Sensual and rational appetite differ like the two degrees of knowledge that correspond to them. The former makes us desire a good apprehended by the senses and the latter makes us desire a good apprehended by reason.[2] The will must be inclined towards that which reason proposes as good. But since reason never proposes the highest good but always a relative or partial good the proposal is also only partial. Hence the will is free to follow reason, or not, to the extent to which the good proposed is only partial.[3] And as long as reason does not show that an end it proposes is necessarily good, the will can take it or reject it. The will is only obliged to will it when reason sees the necessary connexion between the particular good proposed and the highest good. 'If reason have taught it rightly to be good, yet not so apparently that the mind receives it with utter impossibility of being otherwise, still there is place left for the will to take or leave'.[4] The will, in short, is free. But the necessity of its being controlled by reason is clearly established.

In the last instance, therefore, the irrational can reign supreme

[1] I. vii. 2; S.Th. I, II, 8–19 *passim*.
[2] I. vii. 3; S.Th. I, 80, 2 ad Resp; *De Veritate*, XXII, 4 ad Resp. and ad 1st.
[3] I. vii. 6; S.Th. I, II, 13, 5 ad 1st.
[4] I. vii. 6; S.Th. I, 82, 2.

only through faith, i.e. in the order of supernature. Everything that is connected with nature is amenable to reason. This is a most important point—for it shows what Hooker thought reason competent to solve. Reason to him was not only a mechanical process that could also be performed by a calculating-machine. The meaning of reason was to him the same it had been to the Middle Ages and to Antiquity: it implied an intuitive as well as a discursive element. For, if reason is competent to deal with all the problems arising out of natural life, it must be able to do more than to infer conclusions from premises: it must be, in a sense, able to invent the premises themselves. To say that reason dictated the proposition 'do good and avoid evil', only makes sense on the implicit understanding that reason is an intuitive power. Or, in other words, that intuitively known truth was not an irrationally known truth but possessed all the characteristics of rationally discovered propositions, such as that they are universally true among rational beings. Disagreement in regard to them does not spring from certain emotional or other unphilosophical sources, but has its roots in a philosophical error which can be eliminated through discussion. In short, according to this conception, the powers of reason were enormously wide and varied. Hence the great desirability of maintaining its services for the regulation of human intercourse.

What Hooker had opposed most determinedly in Puritanism was the willingness to hand over to irrational forces the control of those spheres of life which he knew could be controlled by reason. Puritanism, in other words, was an attempt to give wider scope to the irrational forces in the human mind. To the Puritan such irrationality, being the antithesis of human reason, was likely to be of a divine nature. But we have seen above that Hooker was in no way prepared to grant that assumption and repeatedly branded it as conceit, as desire to disturb an existing order, or as greed; in short as all those irrational appetites known as such to medieval and ancient philosophy. But Hooker's counter-argument could only be successful if the fundamental assumption that reason had intuitive as well as discursive powers was accepted. It so happened, however, that just this assumption was undermined by the development of seventeenth-century philosophy and that Hooker's argument therefore lost its force among the very generation for which it had been designed.

It was one of the basic elements in the revolution of philosophical thought brought about by Bacon and Descartes that all knowledge has an a-rational[1] basis. The one explained how knowledge was to be derived from sense-experience by a rational process called induction; and the other showed how all knowledge proceeded from self-evident principles with the help of a rational process known as deduction. Both were at one in that they asserted that all knowledge is based in the last analysis on something other than reason, and that the term reason could in justice be applied only to the inductive and deductive process. In a sense then, one could see in that revolution already a critique of reason—though it did not go so far nor was it as pointed as the one which was put forward one hundred and fifty years later. The practical effect of such ideas is obvious: by reason people gradually came to understand a human faculty which was capable of effecting induction and deduction respectively; but which could not be credited with any intuitive powers. Only the processes of induction and deduction deserved the name of rational activity. The material upon which this activity is performed is discovered by non-rational methods. As a result the meaning of the term reason became much narrower during the seventeenth century. It lost its connotation of sensibility and good conduct and retained only that of good logic.[2] How much narrower the meaning of the term reason precisely did become during the two centuries following Hooker's argument can best be shown by a comparison of the teaching of Hume and that of Hooker on a certain point in moral philosophy.

Hooker argued that heretics obstinately followed 'their own ambitions or otherwise corrupted affections; instead of framing their wills to maintain that which reason taught, they bent their wits to find how reason might seem to teach that which their wills were set to maintain.'[3] Hume would have understood the

---

[1] Not necessarily irrational.

[2] Cp. M. Roberts, *The Modern Mind*, London, 1937, pp. 121 ff.

[3] III. viii. 8.

problem—for it was one with which he also was intimately concerned. But he would have been surprised at what he could have but called Hooker's *naïveté*. To Hume, reason was altogether powerless to be anything but the slave of man's passions and to do anything but justify what his affections inclined him to. He thought of reason, in fact, in the narrow sense, as a mechanical process devoid in itself of any power to judge wisely or to understand intuitively. He could therefore only have wondered at Hooker's idea that reason ought to control the affections and that it was a very reprehensible weakness for a man to allow his affections to control his reason. In Hume's eyes this would not have been weakness but human nature; and to believe that man could do anything else was to refuse to see the facts.

To Hooker, on the other hand, who used the term reason in the wider sense, nothing was more natural than that man should make use of his rational powers to control his affections. To refuse to do so was an unforgivable error and a refusal to use those faculties with which God had endowed man.[1] This refusal was a sin; for it was of the essence of sin to refuse to conform to the divinely ordained order of the Universe.[2]

[1] With Hume we stand at the beginning of *Romanticism*. It was only natural that men should one day refuse to let reason in the narrow sense stifle their best impulses and emotions and smother their vitality. Hume's criticism destroyed the Age of Reason. But if Hooker had prevailed we would never have got to Hume. For the latter's criticism applied only to reason in the narrow sense. Once reason had been emptied of its intuitive content it was essential to further development for Hume to show how hollow it was. And thus the storm of the Romantic revolution broke loose.

[2] That the medieval philosophers were no more naïve in that respect than Hume, and had no illusions as to the possible strength of affections over reason, is shown by the following argument of St. Thomas: a person in whom concupiscence dominates considers good whatever he desires, even if his judgement contradicts the universal judgement of reason; and, in order to neutralize this sophistry of the passions, man must safeguard himself by moral habits through which it will become almost conatural to him to judge soundly of his end. S.Th. I, II, 58, 4–5 ad Resp.; cp. E. Gilson, *The Philosophy of St. Thomas Aquinas*, 1929, p. 321. St. Thomas was shrewd enough to recognize the usefulness of habits. But looking at reason from a different point of view from that of Hume he was not tempted to conclude that habits rather than reason determined what was good.

We find then that Puritanism, quite incidentally, worked in favour of the acceptance of modern philosophy; and in turn its triumph in seventeenth-century England must have been assisted very considerably by the fact that Hooker's great counter-argument had lost its force. For to claim for reason what Hooker had claimed was only sensible if reason was understood in the wider sense; it could not sound very convincing when people understood it in the narrower sense. For then it was only all too obvious that man would need an additional source of knowledge to enable him to cope with the problems of this his natural life. Some people found these additional sources in empirical observation of self-evident principles, and others, with a more religious bent of mind, sought them in divine inspiration.[1]

Hooker's failure was due to the fact that he saw in Puritanism only what it essentially was: the revival or accentuation of a medieval idea. He did not recognize that it bore in itself unwillingly and unwittingly the seeds of the modern world. Puritanism in itself was medieval; but by loosening up the medieval synthesis it helped modern conceptions to establish themselves. And these modern conceptions in turn prepared and assisted the triumph of Puritanism in the seventeenth century. Hooker's argument was unsuccessful because it did not cope with this dialectical process but was directed exclusively against the Puritan revival of the medieval anti-Thomist trend.

[1] After the middle of the eighteenth century they sought them in emotional vitality.

CHAPTER THREE

HOOKER AND MARSILIUS OF PADUA

THROUGH his general philosophy, Hooker had committed himself to certain political principles. Details might be adjusted; but there can be little doubt that he understood when the plan for his work was conceived that it also implied a political system. The two principles that do in fact emerge from it are the following: faith, being a method of finding supernatural truth, must be guarded by an institution which does not derive its *ratio essendi* from any merely rational arrangements for the better government of human society. The Church, as the guardian of revealed law, must, in order to fulfil its function always be the Apostolical Church, the continuation and extension on this earth of the Word Incarnate. As such it must be independent of those institutions that have been set up by human reason to ensure the smooth regulation of purely human affairs. And, furthermore, the Church must stand to the organs of secular government in the same relationship in which faith stands to reason. It must be a supplement to secular government and take over the leadership and control of human conduct at exactly those points where natural reason becomes impotent, i.e. wherever problems of conscience are concerned, and where men are to conform to the divine law because natural law, i.e. human reason, has become silent. Church and State therefore are to co-operate in the government of society, the one representing faith and the other reason; both together ensuring that men are guided not only towards life, but towards a good life—'good' being understood of course in the Christian, not in the Aristotelian, sense. But each making an independent contribution towards the discovery and maintenance of the whole body of law according to which a Christian man must live.

By implication Hooker's mind was set automatically against any form of Erastianism: for Erastianism would destroy the independence of the Church. And also against the idea that a new Church has been or ought to be, founded by the Reformation movement. For that would destroy the continuity of the Church. When Hooker began to ponder over these problems of the Tudor Constitution, he kept these ideas firmly in his mind. Two roads were actually open to him. He could either appear as the critic of that constitution and explain that in such and such points it did not satisfy what he considered to be the requirements of a Christian constitution; or make himself the apologist of that constitution by availing himself of the fact that so many of its features had purposely been left undefined, and by interpreting it in such a way that it satisfied what he considered to be the requirements of a Christian constitution.[1] Apologist or critic: but, Hooker's nature being what it was, there was never a real choice for him. He had to become its apologist. It appears, to begin with, that to disapprove of existing conditions would have smacked to Hooker of impiety towards God. For Hooker was profoundly Christian in his interpretation of human history as the work of divine providence.[2] Psychologically he was too well adjusted to existing conditions to be capable of the bitterness that is always a necessary ingredient in an enthusiastic and wholehearted criticism. 'A thing very scandalous and offensive it must needs be thought', he writes, 'if either kings or laws should dispose of the affairs of God, without any respect had to that which of old has been reverently thought of throughout the world, and wherein there is no law of God which forces us to swerve from the way wherein so many and so holy ages have gone.'[3]

---

[1] For an example of the lack of definition in the Tudor Constitution see F. W. Maitland, *Defender of the Faith and so forth*, E.H.R. Vol. XV. 1900, p. 120.

[1] Hooker noticed for instance that the Christian 'diocese' grew out of the Roman 'province'. He concludes that God arranged the Roman constitution in such a way that it would be capable of furnishing a basis for a Christian order of society. VII. viii. 7. To the modern historian, this fact is a proof of the human character of the Christian diocese. To Hooker this fact was proof that even the Roman Empire was divinely ordained.

[3] VIII. ii. 17.

So he began by saying that there were good reasons to observe the ecclesiastical laws of England and none to impugn them.[1] This shows already that Hooker's conservatism was not of the naïve kind that can find no other justification for the acceptance of the *status quo* than the fact that it *is* the *status quo*. Hooker saw in the existing conditions the result of a long historical development, and recognized that that development could only have taken place in the way it did because rational human beings had approved of it and had supported it. A criticism of the present would imply a criticism of the past and thus a neglect of the role played by human reason in past ages. 'What have we', he said, 'to induce men into the willing obedience and observation of laws, but the weight of so many men's judgement as have with deliberate advice assented thereunto; the weight of that long experience which the world has had thereof with consent and good liking?'[2] To Hooker, the appeal to historical precedent and to history in general is always an appeal to human reason.[3] For it is just this reason which one must presume to have been as operative in the past as it is now. And the same is true for his appeal to authority: it is not an appeal to the irrational or the inscrutable, but an appeal to reason—exercised by someone else. But since that reason is, in all human beings, an exercise of the same divine gift and an interior reflexion of the highest, divine reason, such an appeal is extremely rational. That he should make it bears witness to the fact that he really did believe in what he had taught about the nature of reason. In such an appeal to authority we find an expression of his own humility and consciousness that his own reason might not be as good as that of others. 'The things which so long experience of all ages has confirmed and made profitable, let not us presume to condemn as follies and toys because we sometimes know not the cause and reason of them.'[4]

Hooker's conservatism was, however, also strengthened by a very deep insight into the nature of politics—an insight which Burke is usually said to have been the first to have had. Hooker understood that once a revolution is started and the old well-established order done away with, there was no stopping and no

---

[1] In, vii. 1.　　　　　　　　　　[3] Cp. Appendix B.
[2] IV. xiv. 1.　　　　　　　　　　[4] IV. i. 3.

return to security. For then every man could rightly claim authority in place of the old abolished institutions. Nobody could trust anybody not to covet that authority, and the only salvation, i.e. the only chance for arresting the continuous insecurity and turmoil, would lie in the establishment of the rule of one man who would be strong enough, by violent measures if necessary, to suppress all other turbulent spirits. And one would then have to be so grateful for such an opportunity to occur at all that one could not even be very particular as to whether the kind of government thus established was the right and proper kind. It was in this sense that Hooker, in the Preface, told his readers the lamentable experiences of the Genevans with their revolution or reformation. The Genevans had had to accept Calvin, though his demands were severe and his proposed rule would amount to tyranny, for the sake of mere peace. Had they not accepted his rule, they would not have been able to put a stop to the turmoil at all; but Calvin would return only if he were given some guarantees that he would not merely be a 'tenant at will' under the multitude.[1] If tradition and stability are once swept away there is considerable difficulty if one wishes to return to a new stability. Unlike Burke, he did not vituperate Calvin and the Genevans but accepted the *fait accompli*; pointing out however what dangers for England there lurked behind such a revolutionary settlement. Hence 'as for the orders which are established, since equity and reason, the law of nature, God and man, do all favour that which is in being, till orderly judgement of decision be given against it; it is but justice to exact of you (the Puritans) and perverseness in you it should be to deny, thereunto your willing obedience'.[2]

Both Hooker's nature and his insight forced him to become the apologist of the Tudor Constitution. He did not merely describe it and then claim—as conservatives usually are wont to do— that that constitution was the best of all possible constitutions. He had his own principles to which, he was convinced, every good constitution ought to conform. It all depended then on whether he would be able to give an interpretation of the Tudor Constitution in terms of his own principles. There were two

---

[1] In ii. 4.   [2] In vi. 5.

circumstances that must have made him confident as to a successful interpretation: there was firstly the fact that Elizabeth and her advisers had, wherever possible, left points of constitutional law undefined. This policy stood all parties in good stead—as Elizabeth could always for want of a precise definition fish in muddy waters, and other groups would not be needlessly offended by the promulgation of a constitutional doctrine which they disliked. Secondly there was Hooker's own disposition to be reasonable, not to argue about trifles and not to force a hard-and-fast theory on a political organism. In short, things were made easier for him because he was not a doctrinaire. But how difficult things really were, is shown by the fact that he failed in spite of these propitious circumstances.

2

For the general conception of this interpretation, Hooker availed himself of ideas that had been put forward at various times, and for the practical realization of which Bancroft was working while Hooker was writing the *Laws of Ecclesiastical Polity*. The basic conception was the idea of the actual identity of Church and Commonwealth in sixteenth-century England. The first to formulate it expressly had been Gardiner.[1] Whitgift had accepted the most valuable suggestion and turned it into good account during his controversy with Cartwright: he denied that there was any distinction between Church and Commonwealth as far as England was concerned.[2] The idea was particularly useful in so far as it could be made to explain so plausibly the concept of Royal Supremacy. If there were only one society instead of two, what was more natural than that there should be one head only both in matters civil and in matters ecclesiastical? And, closely connected with this idea, there was another which showed that the 'Anglicans' had a subtle understanding of the nature of historical development. They admitted in fact that one could not

[1] *Oration of true obedience*, in *Obedience in Church and State*, ed. P. Janelle, Cambridge, 1930, p. 93.
[2] *Works*, Vol. III, p. 160.

always take for granted the identity of Church and Commonwealth and the justifiability of royal supremacy over the former. There are times and societies in which such an identification would be entirely unwarranted. In Turkey and in ancient Rome, for example, where neither the magistrate nor every citizen was a Christian, such an identification would be absurd. But in sixteenth-century England, they argued, conditions have altered. Every citizen is also a Christian and the highest magistrate is a Christian too. Hence one could not possibly deny the identity of Church and Commonwealth. Cartwright, Whitgift wrote, 'separates the Commonwealth of England as far from the Church of England as he can do the Commonwealth of Turcia from the Church of Christ in Turcia'.[1] By refusing to see the historical development that had actually taken place, the Puritans betrayed a lack of understanding of the nature of social life and development in general. Their world-picture was completely static, and they could not conceive that it was just this fact of continuous historical development which made it imperative for men to change and to adapt forms of government and institutions if they wanted them to continue to serve the same ends. If institutions are not adapted, they would only become impediments instead of means towards the organization of society according to Christian principles.

The Puritans, however, would simply not admit that *now* that the magistrate is a Christian, the situation is different from what it was when the magistrate was a heathen. They stubbornly denied the fact, which is so plainly written in history, that the magistrates can become Christianized and need therefore no longer be regarded with the suspicion with which the heathen magistrates of Rome had been regarded. To pagan magistrates, control over the Church had been rightly denied for the very same principle for which it ought to be granted to a Christian magistrate.[2] Now that the magistrate himself had become a Christian there was simply no point in having the same kind of Church government as in the times when the magistrate was a Nero.[3]

[1] *Works*, Vol. III, p. 297.
[2] Whitgift, *Works*, Vol. III, p. 180.
[3] Ibid., p. 218.

On the basis of such a conception of the identity of Church and Commonwealth, Gardiner and Whitgift had erected a somewhat sketchy but plausible theory of government. The King, naturally enough, was, as the head of that society, the highest authority in both its aspects, i.e. both in Church and in Commonwealth. But, just as he was presumed to act in civil affairs through his council and with the advice and consent of Parliament, so he was presumed to act in ecclesiastical affairs through the bishops with the advice and consent of Convocation. There were believed to exist two administrative systems under the King: the one controlled society in so far as it was a Commonwealth; and the other controlled the same society in so far as it was a Church. Both systems acted under the King and in mutual co-operation to guide Englishmen, both in their social intercourse and in their private lives along the paths prescribed by natural morality and Christian duty. Gardiner had expressed himself to that effect in the famous reply which he had drafted on behalf of Convocation in 1532 to a petition by the Commons to curtail the independent powers of the clergy.[1] He had urged there the necessity of maintaining a self-controlled and organic ecclesiastical system acting together with that of the secular authority. Whitgift had put forward a very similar idea: 'The Archbishop does exercise his jurisdiction under the prince and by the prince's authority. For the prince having the supreme government of the realm, in all causes and over all persons, as he does exercise the one by the Lord Chancellor, so does he the other by the Archbishop.'[2]

In this sense, then, the independence and autonomy of the Church was thought to be preserved without prejudice to the idea of the Royal Supremacy. All these ideas were couched in very general terms, and at the time when Whitgift was writing his replies to Cartwright he was probably a bit doubtful himself as to how they would actually square with the practice of the Tudor Government. Richard Bancroft was probably the first man in whose mind these ideas began to take a more concrete shape and who proposed to put them into practice. Usher says that it was indeed Bancroft who first suggested to Whitgift that

[1] Cp. Chapter I, above, p. 17.
[2] *Works*, Vol. II, p. 246.

the High Commission could be 'made into a permanent court of ecclesiastical law, controlled by the Church and used mainly for supplying that coercive power which the bishops lacked'.[1] And he adds that by 1592 this development of the High Commission was complete. This trend in the Church became of course even more pronounced after Elizabeth's death. James quite consciously pursued a policy in which he exercised his ecclesiastical supremacy through Convocation alone. Parliament became more and more excluded and naturally grew to resent that it should not be allowed to meddle with ecclesiastical affairs. But here James did not show himself a tyrant; only a thorough disciple of the conceptions of government put forward by Gardiner, Whitgift, Bancroft—and Hooker. Usher is indeed of the opinion that the real reconstruction of the English Church took place with the canons of 1604. Here the bishops took the initiative, and the King, as Supreme Head of the Church, acted through Convocation. What Elizabeth had often ambiguously hinted at and what Hooker, Bancroft and Whitgift had envisaged, now began to take shape. It was this aspect of Stuart policy which became one of the chief causes of the bitter conflict between King and Parliament. This is well known; but it is important to observe how deeply royal supremacy was rooted in medieval conceptions, and how parliamentary opposition to it was the embodiment of that lay-spirit to whom the idea of a dual system of government and a dual conception of society was repugnant. It was absurd to suspect Charles or Laud of Roman Catholicism; but it was perfectly correct to see in them the defenders of the very same philosophy that had produced, under different political conditions, the medieval Respublica Christiana.[2]

When Hooker began his work he drew on these ideas; and when he had finished he had helped to shape and to define them. His fundamental approach was that of Aristotle. In the beginning of the eighth book he treated Aristotle in fact in exactly the same

[1] R. G. Usher, *The Reconstruction of the English Church*, London, 1910, Vol. I, p. 107.

[2] Cp. J. N. Figgis, *Respublica Christiana*, in *Churches in the Modern State*, Appendix I; London, 1913.

way in which St. Thomas had treated him.[1] The end of society is not to enable men to live, but to enable them to live well. But to live well men need the guidance of religion. Therefore the State, the institution entrusted with the government of society, cannot be concerned with secular matters only. If it is, it does not fulfil its proper function. The secular State and the ecclesiastical hierarchy must therefore co-operate as one institution in the government of society. And such a society is, if it does fulfil its purpose of enabling men to live well, *eo ipso* a Church. Or, in other words, if the members of a Commonwealth embrace the true religion, the Commonwealth is automatically a true Church.[2] And to formulate this doctrine of the identity of Church and State in scholastic terminology Hooker says that there is one substance: Society; and that that substance has two accidents: Commonwealth and Church.[3] 'Such societies as do embrace the true religion' are churches.[4] Thus he can call a church any society of men 'united unto some public form of regiment and . . . distinguished from other societies by the exercise of Christian religion'.[5]

All societies can therefore be classified under three headings: (1) Infidel societies, where Church and Society are two distinct bodies; (2) Catholic societies, where Church and Society are one body but where sovereignty is divided between Pope and Emperor or King; (3) Anglican society, where Church and Society are one body and sovereignty is not divided.[6] Hooker does not say so but it appears clearly from this scheme that the Puritan insistence on treating Church and Commonwealth as two distinct bodies is completely illogical: for it infers from the special conditions of a present-day society the consequences that legitimately follow only from the conditions existing in a heathen society.

Since every society should have only one head, it follows that a Christian society should also have only one head. The fact that this society has two accidents, Church and Commonwealth, can make no difference. That the king is the supreme head of this

---

[1] VIII. i. 1; *De Regimine Principum*, I, 14.   [4] VIII. i. 2.

[2] VIII. vi. 6.   [5] VIII. i. 2.

[3] VIII. i. 5.   [6] VIII. i. 7.

society means in fact that (a) all foreign powers are excluded from exercising any authority; (b) no one part of the society has a power to exercise any authority; (c) God is superior, i.e. the king has to maintain divine law, not to make it; and (d) Law itself is superior to the king, i.e. the dictates of reason, natural law, must be followed.[1] The highest authority then, in English society is, as Hooker put it, 'Parliament with Convocation annexed thereunto'.[2] That is to say: the king as the supreme head of society has under him two different systems: the civil system, his council and his Parliament, and the ecclesiastical system, the clerical hierarchy and Convocation. These two institutions correspond to the two accidents of society, Commonwealth and Church. Between the two systems there is a complete separation of powers: '. . . our laws do neither suffer a spiritual court to entertain those causes which by law are civil; nor yet, if the matter be indeed spiritual, a mere civil court to give judgement of it.'[3] This separation is theoretically achieved through the definition of the natural and the supernatural order—and is philosophically justified by it. The two administrative systems have to co-operate because they supplement one another as faith supplements reason.

The general conception underlying this scheme of government was that the State as the secular organ of government of society derived its authority from the will of the people and the consent of the governed.[4] But the Church, i.e. the ecclesiastical hierarchy, as the spiritual organ of government of society, derived its authority from the Apostles. Hooker always extolled the unearthly derivation of that authority of the priesthood and more particularly of episcopacy in the most exalted language.[5] The continuity of the English Church with the early Apostolic Church was one of the corner-stones of his argument.[6] It would have been indeed impossible for him to admit that the institution which guarded and administered divine law which could, by definition,

[1] VIII. ii. 3.
[2] VIII. vi. 11.
[3] VIII. viii. 9.
[4] I. x. 8; VIII. vi. 8.
[5] See Chapter II for the exact meaning of his theory.
[6] V. lxxvii. 1, 2, 3,; VII. i. 4.

not be discovered by reason, owed its authority to any purely human makeshift or expediency. The ecclesiastical power which had been vested in the Queen by the Act of Supremacy was therefore to be understood in a special sense: it was to be exercised according to the laws of the Church. The Queen herself had no right to use the ecclesiastical hierarchy for any purposes but its own.[1] And it follows that Hooker must have looked upon the whole system as if it limited the power of the Queen in the Church by divine law, just as it limited her power in the State by natural law.

3

Having put forward these ideas as to the nature of the Tudor Constitution, Hooker could maintain that that constitution fulfilled all the Christian requirements and that there was little reason to find fault with it and certainly none for upsetting it. He could proudly say: ' . . . we offer the laws whereby we live unto the general trial and judgement of the whole world.'[2] The key-point in the whole argument is, as we have pointed out, that the continuity of the Church has never been broken and that Englishmen had lived for many centuries according to similar arrangements. To doubt the wisdom and convenience of these arrangements is presumptuous: and, in any case, the burden of proof that these arrangements are *not* good is on the Puritans.[3] The Puritans saw in the English Church a half-hearted attempt at a revolutionary reformation: to take this view and to urge that that revolution be carried on to a successful and radical conclusion was, to Hooker, an absurdity.

The way in which Hooker conceived the continuity of the Church did not allow him to look upon those acts, usually referred to as the Reformation, as a revolution. He no more looked upon the English Reformation as a revolution than medieval observers

[1] VIII. ii. 17.
[2] I. i. 3.
[3] I. xiv. 5; I. i. 3; VII. i. 4; VII. vii. 2; IV. iv. 2.

had looked upon the Councils of Nicea or of the Lateran as revolutions. He admitted of course that there had been carried out in the reign of Henry VIII some necessary and beneficial reforms. But these reforms had not been the beginning of a new Church. To him the Christian world was still divided into two parts, East and West; and the so-called Reformation had made no difference to that division by introducing a third division.[1]

Only the Puritans 'seem to imagine that we have erected of late a frame of some new religion'.[2] There was no doubt to Hooker that the constitution of the Church had never undergone a real revolutionary change.[3] There was therefore no need, he thought, of justifying or producing the authority on the ground of which the Reformation had been carried out.

The error which Hooker here committed was, in a way, for a sixteenth-century Englishman, an excusable error. Only to very few people had the Reformation appeared as a real revolution. To most observers it had merely meant a speeding-up of a process which had been going on for centuries: the submission of all institutions, courts and bodies in England to the Monarchy. The way in which the Reformation had actually taken place, the method by which Roman Catholic Cathedral Chapters had become Anglican Cathedral Chapters, etc., had been so gradual, and the practical difference this had made to the average Englishman so slight, that he could well be excused for not being able to observe the one important fact:[4] that Henry VIII had effectively blocked the channel through which grace had flowed—according to the medieval idea—into the English Church. In this sense, Henry's actions were different in quality, not only in quantity, from those of his predecessors who had curbed papal influence here and there. But once an Englishman had adjusted himself to the insight that the Pope was no longer a politically effective head

[1] Cp. F. Le van Baumer, *The Concept of Christendom in Renaissance England*, *Journal of the History of Ideas*, Vol. VI, 1945, p. 145, for the corresponding views of Bilson and Laud.

[2] IV. ix. I.

[3] VII. vii. 2; IV. ix. I.

[4] Cp. F. M. Powicke, *The Reformation in England*, Oxford, 1941, p. 2.

of the Church, there was little in the Reformation that looked like a real revolution.[1]

In addition to these points, there were certain features in Elizabeth's own policy which were most certainly designed to foster the illusion on which Hooker had been able to build his theory. Elizabeth again and again encouraged her bishops to act on their own initiative and sometimes even on their own authority, in order to give the impression that the Church was indeed the autonomous and independent institution it had always been.[2] Convocation itself was given a certain amount of legislative independence[3] and it was finally due to Elizabeth's own policy that Bancroft could carry out his plans in regard to the High Commission and pursue a course that led to the canons of 1604 and finally culminated in the Jacobean High Church. Elizabeth's policy, Janus-like, faced in two directions. Sometimes she showed her teeth and left her subjects with the very clear idea that the Tudor Monarchy was a secular State in which a secular institution was sovereign. Here, as we shall see presently, she might have pointed towards Marsilius of Padua. And sometimes she did everything she could to create the impression that very little had been changed since the Middle Ages and that all those that criticized were to be treated like unruly opponents of an age-old institution rather than as critics of a very recent innovation.

Here she furnished herself the basic assumptions of Hooker's argument: for had he been compelled from the very beginning to admit either that the Church was not continuous with the old Church or that it was no longer independent, he could not have reasoned the way he did. In the first case he would have had to explain on what grounds and by what divine authority the continuity had been broken and a revolution been accomplished. This he could have done only by conceding Puritan Bibliolatry and

[1] Sir Thomas More was one of the very few Englishmen who had no doubts as to the real revolutionary nature of the Reformation.

[2] Cp. M. M. Knappen, *Tudor Puritanism*, Chicago, 1939, p. 270; for an important example such as Parker's injunctions, see Strype, *The Life and Acts of M. Parker*, Oxford, 1821.

[3] Cp. Article *Convocation* in *A Dictionary of English Church History*, ed. S. L. Ollard, 1912; N. Sykes, *Church and State in England in the XVIIIth cent.*, Cambridge, 1934, pp. 298 ff.

thus their Augustinianism with its disparagement of human nature and reason. And the best proof of the fact that he wanted to defend reason rather than merely apologize for the Tudor State is that he did not concede their Bibliolatry and merely argue in favour of a different interpretation of the Scriptures— which would have been easy enough for a man of his learning. In the second case he would have had to explain how the English Church was, if it was under the control of a secular State, a Christian Church at all. This he could not have done, because an Erastian Church was to him no more a Church than it was to the Puritans. For in that he agreed with his opponents: just as St. Thomas had agreed with St. Bonaventure, that natural reason cannot go the whole way.

Hooker, in short, had understood the equivocal policy of Elizabeth very well and tried to make use of it for his own purposes. But without the Thomistic conception of reason and faith, of nature and supernature, Hooker would not have been able to conceive his interpretation of the Elizabethan Constitution. And what is particularly important is that Hooker was one of the first thinkers, since St. Thomas, who had grasped the significance of Thomist thought on this matter clearly enough to apply it to practice.[1] Hooker's solution was of course different from that of St. Thomas. To begin with, the latter's ideas on this matter had never been expressed coherently in any one place, so that in fact there is some doubt among scholars what it exactly was that he taught on the relationship between Church and State.[2] The most exact pronouncement that St. Thomas ever made on this question was that the Church should stand to the State as the soul to the body.[3] This simile, however, had been used before St. Thomas in many diverse senses.[4] In order to understand its specific

[1] See Chapter IV for a full explanation of this statement.
[2] The most important relevant passages in St. Thomas are: S.Th. II, II, 147, 3; S.Th. II, ii, 60, 6 ad 3rd; comm. 2nd Bk. sentences, last passage; De Regimine Principum, Ch. XIV.
[3] S.Th. II, ii, 60, 6 ad 3rd.
[4] See J. Hergenröther, Katholische Kirche und christlicher Staat in ihrer geschichtlichen Entwicklung und in Beziehung auf die Fragen der Gegenwart, 1872, and W. Müller, Der Staat in seiner Beziehung zur sittlichen Ordnung bei Thomas von Aquin, Münster, 1916, pp. 46 ff.

meaning, it is therefore necessary to interpret it in the light of St. Thomas's philosophy: it then looks as if he meant to attribute to the Church a general supervisory function while he reserved to the State, in its own sphere, i.e. in regard to the natural-human problems of life, an independent competence. This fundamental conception of the two distinct orders of nature and supernature, each requiring different laws found by different faculties and yet supplementary to one another, was clearly understood by Hooker.

There is no doubt, however, that St. Thomas accepted the supremacy of the Pope and considered it a deadly sin to deny it. In Hooker's times the political situation had, however, changed fundamentally. The Papacy had become politically weak, whereas the Tudor State was in the days of its fullest maturity.[1] Unless he wanted to become a Utopian he had to come to terms with these realities; and he found that he could do so best by using the ideas that had been worked out before him and by adapting them to and justifying them by his own philosophical standpoint. What is important is that he did not copy St. Thomas unintelligently and slavishly, but that he understood him so clearly that he could use the former's theory of the two orders of nature and supernature and their relationship in order to build a new theory on it that would satisfy the conditions of sixteenth-century England.

4

The Puritans were probably very little perturbed by the fact that Hooker had not followed St. Thomas slavishly and had been truer to his spirit than to his letter. But that he had so obviously

[1] Hooker's logic might have compelled him to accept the Papacy. For he justified the existence of a bishop by pointing at the quarrels among presbyters and the necessity for one superior to rule them. Similarly he justified the existence of an archbishop who had to compose the quarrels among bishops. So logical rigour would have compelled him ultimately to admit that a Pope was needed to rule archbishops. But historical circumstances forced him to forgo logic. For had he upheld the Papacy, he would have put the Church at the mercy of an Italian potentate.

abandoned the form of Church government practised in the primitive Church and enjoined—as they thought—by the Bible, that they could never forgive. The Puritans, and this was a necessary consequence of their Bibliolatry and their denial of natural law, considered the Church an association which had been founded by a divine charter, the Scriptures; and the existence, scope and function of which was exactly defined by that charter. Any independent move or development of the Church was considered to be *ultra vires*. The Church was not a living group-personality but a chartered company, limited and defined in every respect by the terms of a charter. It was therefore immaterial to the Puritans what sort of an interpretation Hooker might give to the Tudor Constitution: as he could not deny, and indeed only made it plain beyond doubt, that the Church under this constitution differed from the primitive Church, his whole argument was, as far as they were concerned, beside the point. This Hooker knew, and he endeavoured therefore to explain that the Church was not like a chartered company: but had a group personality that was capable of development in every direction, of adapting itself to all circumstances and yet remaining always the same person.

When seen in its proper light, this aspect of the controversy was a first round in the great argument between Romanists and Germanists in Jurisprudence as to whether societies were real persons or not. Hooker, as we shall show presently, believed that societies were real persons; but unlike the nineteenth-century jurists whose ideas to that effect were determined very largely by romantic conceptions of a super-individual group-mind, Hooker derived his theory entirely, *via* St. Thomas, from the principles of Aristotelian philosophy. One can therefore not find in him the strong irrational element that dominates all modern group-personality theories, which therefore discredit a purely individual will and judgement and tend to sacrifice the latter to such irrational factors as the group-mind or the general will.

Hooker started by explaining that the Church, although directing man towards a supernatural end both by compelling him to keep the divine commandments and by allowing him to partake of divine grace through the sacraments, was still a society; and as such a natural organism, with natural functions and with natural needs. Hence the Church is partly bound by natural law and partly bound by supernatural law.[1] As far as natural law is concerned, Church government can be carried on according to the same precepts according to which any other form of government is carried on; i.e. through the rational discovery of means that will be best conducive towards a certain end. And as circumstances changed, the form of Church government had to change. If it did not change, the Church might ultimately become an obsolete institution defeating the very purposes for which it had been created.[2] It is therefore necessary for men to find out by reason what laws ought to be framed for the good of the Church.[3]

For the distinction between the natural and the supernatural aspect of the Church as a society, Hooker availed himself of the distinction between matters of faith and matters of government which had actually been introduced by the Puritans themselves as the distinction between discipline and doctrine'.[4] In this distinction Hooker went further than the Puritans had meant to go; for he added immediately that matters of discipline were to be left to the rational discretion of the Church, while only in matters of doctrine the Church was bound by the revealed divine law.[5] This inference, though based on what had originally been a typical Puritan notion, was not accepted by the Puritans who maintained that Hooker 'mis-distinguished' between doctrine and discipline.[6] But Hooker was unperturbed and thought himself justified by the fact that even Christ had distinguished between 'accessory' and 'necessary' things.[7] Whatever the theological rights or wrongs in this distinction were, it enabled Hooker to see in the Church, which was already the supernatural aspect of society, another society or organism with corresponding natural functions.

[1] I. xv. 2.

[2] III. ii. 1.

[3] III. ix. 1.

[4] III. iii. 2, 3; this distinction became in fact one of the corner-stones of constitutional doctrine, since it was held that the Royal Supremacy was not to be *in sacris* but only in matters of government.

[5] III. ii. 2.

[6] loc. cit.

[7] III. iii. 4.

This organism had of course a natural life, just as every other social organism; and it was just through that natural life that it was firmly anchored in this world and could thus fulfil its function as a bridge between this world and the next or as a practical means of divine grace or of contact with this world. To the Puritan, the Church was a society without natural functions; its sacramental powers were practically non-existent and thus it failed to establish the bridge between nature and supernature. It was a society of the elect, i.e. of those men that were already in a state of grace and who did not need to seek any assistance for attaining that state through the Church. In short, to the Puritans the Church did not represent a supplement to natural society—but an alternative to it. Or, as Hooker himself put it, the Church and the Commonwealth were corporations severed perpetually in substance.[1]

Having recognized in the Church a natural society, he proceeded to apply to it the Aristotelian principle that everything natural has the natural power to provide for its own preservation. 'All things natural have in them naturally more or less the power of providing for their own safety.'[2] And since the making of laws is necessary for the preservation of the Church, the Church must be presumed to have by *nature* powers to make laws for its own government. In this respect, of course, the Church does not differ from other societies: for all societies are naturally endowed with full powers to guide themselves.[3] And as that power, in a society, is the power to make laws, law-making power resides naturally in every natural society.[4] The power to make laws may be exercised either by the assent of every individual or by a delegate or representative on behalf of his constituency or by one's forefathers: what the latter assented to has become custom and posterity has to accept it. For later generations live in the same society as their forefathers, and that society is an 'immortal corporation'. 'The act of a public society of men done 500 years sithence stands as theirs who presently are of the same societies, because corporations are immortal; we were then alive in our

[1] VIII. i. 2.

[2] VII. xiv. 3, he does not acknowledge his debt to Aristotle.

[3] VIII. ii. 5.

[4] VIII. vi. 3.

predecessors, and they in their successors do live still.'[1] In this way Hooker described the fact which he had only too clearly seen, namely, that sixteenth-century Englishmen were living according to a law that had been made centuries ago. In all this there is no allusion to a group-mind or an irrational super-individual personality; merely the application of a principle of Aristotle's philosophy of nature. So Hooker could finally conclude that 'nature itself does abundantly authorize the Church to make laws and orders for her children . . .'[2]

The Church then is a corporation; and since all corporations are perpetual they are alive in the sense that they abrogate old laws and make new ones in order to cope with the ever-changing conditions of the political and social situation,[3] by exercising the natural power that is naturally inherent in all social organisms, i.e. the power to make laws. It was largely for this reason that Hooker was so careful to draw a distinction between 'assemblies' and 'societies'. To the Puritans, he said, a Church is a mere assembly for the performance of a public action. When the action is ended, the assembly dissolves itself and is no longer in being. Whereas the Church, which is a society, continues both before and after the actual assembly of its members.[4] Hooker thus expressed quite clearly the theory that the Church in so far as it was a natural society was a corporate personality which could at all times freely make provision, according to rational principles, for the best way of governing itself. With this conception of the Church as a corporate personality which was not the slave of its foundation charter, Hooker could meet the Puritan objection that the English Church was different from the primitive Church. He could justify the difference by pointing to the Church as a living personality that developed. His theory was a natural-law theory of group personality. The juristic concepts he used were those of natural law; and to the final realization of the nature of corporateness he was driven by the extreme Puritan claim that anything the Church did over and above the commands of the Scriptures was *ultra vires*.

[1] I. x. 8.
[2] VIII. vi. 1.
[3] VII. xiv. 3.
[4] III. i. 14.

The Puritans protested that they had no intention of destroying the corporate character of the English Church. They began in fact by appealing to that very corporation, asking it to reform itself according to the precepts of the true word of God. They wanted this corporation to remain in existence, although they would not endow it with the same natural rights and powers with which Hooker had endowed it. But neither Travers nor Cartwright nor any other Puritan was ever given credit for these protestations. It was always taken for granted by Hooker that there was no real difference between continental Anabaptism and English Puritanism.[1] He refused to believe that separatism and the establishment of conventicles was not the final aim of Puritanism. It is curious to watch how that opinion of Hooker and of his friends produced its own verification.

To begin with, the Puritans had appealed to the Church itself to reform itself. The appeal had been rejected by a narrow majority apparently on the ground that most clergymen did not see any reason why the Church should conform in all minute details to the prescriptions of the Bible as interpreted by certain theologians. Now if the Puritans had shared Hooker's conviction that the Church should legislate for itself, they would not have gone further. But the fact that now they appealed to Parliament to reform the Church proved beyond doubt that they would not grant the Church the natural right to make laws for its own government; but considered these laws to be contained in the Scriptures, and were prepared to have the Church coerced into accepting them. The appeal to Parliament then was in itself a rejection of the idea that the Church was a corporate personality in natural law. From the Puritan point of view this was a perfectly intelligible rejection, since they denied the validity of natural law altogether. But no sooner had Parliament, for reasons which need not concern us here, refused the appeal, than the Puritans resorted to self-help. They set up conventicles; they used the meetings known as 'prophesyings' for their own purposes and began thus to drift into separatism. And at that moment the difference between continental Anabaptism and English Puritanism became practically negligible. Puritanism became an attack on the life of the

[1] See Chapter II, p. 36-7.

existing Church, since it professedly aimed at a reconstruction of ecclesiastical life and government from independent units upwards. We can therefore observe a curious historical process. Whitgift, Hooker and Bancroft, as the foremost exponents of the idea of the corporate continuity of the English Church, held that Presbyterianism, in England at any rate, had certain Anabaptist implications. Their opposition to Puritanism was partly determined by this belief. But it was only due to this opposition that Puritanism ultimately did develop fully what they had thought it implied: separatism.[1]

Their initial opinion had been based, however, on more than a prejudice. They knew that the situation in England was such that a Presbyterian reconstruction of the Church would not really be possible without a thorough revolution. In Geneva the political situation had been altogether different. There the traditional Church had been no longer in existence and its corporate character had been destroyed in any case by the departure of the bishop and his clergy.[2] Thus when Calvin had come to Geneva in 1536, there had only been a half-ordered government in existence; there had been no ecclesiastical laws at all and people were simply doing whatever their pastors persuaded them to do.[3] In a certain sense there had been a *carte blanche* in Geneva. But in England the situation was entirely different. There was an orderly government of both Church and Commonwealth in existence and one could not possibly proceed, as one had done in Geneva, as if England too were a *carte blanche* on which one merely had to write down the law enjoined by the Scriptures. When the Puritans nevertheless did not desist from the attempt, people became suspicious: they began to understand that through its Bibliolatry Puritanism was committed to a course that would finally lead to separation. The Puritans would willingly try all the existing constitutional channels for bringing about change. But since they

---

[1] For the logic of the situation which forced Puritanism into separatism see M. M. Knappen, *Tudor Puritanism*, Chicago, 1939, pp. 212–14; 152, 157; A. F. Scott-Pearson, *Thomas Cartwright and Elizabethan Puritanism*, Cambridge, 1925, p. 311.

[2] In. ii. 4.

[3] In. ii. 1.

owed their allegiance solely to the word of God they would, if unsuccessful, simply brush them aside and set up new churches. It was with this suspicion in mind that Whitgift embarked upon his inquisitorial policy for which he was so sharply criticized by Burghley; that Bancroft published his *Dangerous Positions*; that Hooker wrote the *Laws of Ecclesiastical Polity*; and that Parliament in 1593 passed the Conventicle Act.

5

In this way Hooker had made his point secure against the Puritan opposition. But in order to make his plea carry conviction, he had to give a somewhat fuller account of Tudor constitutional theory and practice. And it was just here that Hooker realized that he was confronted by difficulties which it was well-nigh impossible to overcome. It would have been easy enough to account in terms of Aristotle's philosophy for the practice of the Tudor State; but to do so in terms of the Christian version of Aristotle was a more complicated matter.

The point was that the Tudor State was a thoroughly secular state, organized and administered for purely secular ends. And that most Elizabethan Englishmen were aware of this fact is nicely illustrated by Harvey's pointed remark that 'we are not living in Plato's Republic, nor in the Utopia of Sir Thomas More, but in the *Res Publica* of Sir Thomas Smith.'[1] There can hardly be imagined a more open statement of the theory of the purely secular state than the work of Sir Thomas Smith, which went even so far as to deny natural law. The Elizabethan State was in fact administrated as if the end of human life were the attainment of peace, security and happiness in this world. Every other aim was made subservient to this idea; and the institution whose task it was to guide men according to the requirements of a further, a supernatural end, fared accordingly. It became in all but name a state-department. The practice of the Elizabethan State in regard

[1] G. Harvey, *Marginalia*, ed. by G. C. Moore-Smith, Stratford-upon-Avon, 1913, p. 197.

to the Church was Erastian; not necessarily in the sense in which Erastus had understood it—but in the sense in which we have come to use this term to-day. There is no need to mention any but the most striking examples.

Though it was asserted again and again that the Queen's Supremacy did not mean that she held priestly office; that it did not apply *in sacris* and that it did not make the Church a state-department, we must not forget that these descriptions of the Queen's Supremacy were put forward officially in order to appease over-critical minds. An examination of the practice of the system, however, revealed sooner or later, that the Queen's Supremacy implied a good deal more than was admitted. There could be no doubt as to the fact that the Queen was the supreme judge in all matters ecclesiastical. She appointed bishops and her sanction was necessary for the formulation of doctrine. All ecclesiastical jurisdiction was derived from her,[1] and even when she confined herself to what was known as enforcing Christian discipline, i.e. when she merely saw to it that the clergy did their duty without professing to define what that duty was, she still, by implication, reserved to herself the right to know when the clergy did not do their duty. And since nobody, by any stretch of the imagination, could claim that the Queen was in possession of revealed truth and therefore a proper judge of divine law, one could only conclude that her ecclesiastical policy was guided by the same principles which guided her civil and foreign policy: by considerations of reason of State or by what she herself preferred to call the 'mysteries of kingship', meaning thereby the maxims of statecraft, and not any mystical powers.

The Reformation of Henry VIII had been completely revolutionary in spite of the appearances to the contrary noted above.

---

[1] The legal controversy that was raging round the canon law soon revealed that the Church was not an autonomous institution making its own law. The lawyers contended that the ecclesiastical courts were under the common law or at least drew all their authority from statute law. In reply the clergy could but argue that they were exercising the Queen's prerogative as defined by the Act of Supremacy, and could therefore not be brought under the jurisdiction of the common law. Neither argument spoke in favour of the Church's autonomy. Cp. R. G. Usher, *The Rise and Fall of the High Commission*, Oxford, 1913, pp. 157, 167, 226, etc.

The real nature of the secularization of the English Church is revealed by an examination of this fact. To begin with, the effective and legal conception of the complete sovereignty of King in Parliament dates back to the Reformation, and the process whereby the former was evolved cannot be distinguished from the latter.[1] After the Reformation there was really nothing Parliament could not do; and a constitution in which this principle was valid was obviously a secular constitution—at least, secular in so far as Parliament was a secular body.

Thus no decision of a general council was valid without the assent of King in Parliament. England had indeed become an '*imperium*'[2] and in that it resembled the Roman Empire, rather than the Holy Roman Empire.[3] The Act in Restraint of Appeals carried indeed the doctrine of *Praemunire* to a point where the difference between the medieval and the sixteenth-century state of affairs was no longer one of degree but became one of kind. And similarly the submission of the Clergy[4] completely altered the status of the ecclesiastical hierarchy in England: it was cut off from Rome and could no longer partake of the divine grace that had originally been bestowed upon the Church of Rome. The most obviously revolutionary innovation, however, was the new status of the Canon Law. In the Middle Ages the King's courts had endeavoured to curtail the jurisdiction of the ecclesiastical courts and had stolen one matter after another from them. But the ecclesiastical courts themselves, where their jurisdiction was recognized, had always continued to administer the canon law of the universal church. After the Reformation, the canon law

---

[1] Cp. the discussion in Ch. H. McIlwain, *The High Court of Parliament*, New Haven, 1910, p. 103, Note B; it appears that McIlwain does not distinguish sufficiently carefully between the theory of Parliament's legislative capacity, which was indeed only fully developed by Bentham, and the actual instances where Parliament made law, which can be found as far back as the reign of King Edward II.

[2] 1533, 24 Henry VIII, c. 12.

[3] For a discussion of the meaning of the maxim 'Rex in regno suo est imperator' see G. de Lagarde, *La Naissance de l'esprit laïque*, Paris, 1934–1946, Vol. I, p. 164.

[4] 1534 Henry VIII, c. 19.

administered in the ecclesiastical courts of England had become the King's canon law—a term which is an odd contradiction in terms: for the law is either the King's, and then it is secular, or it is canon law and spiritual and then there is no real sense in which it is the King's law.[1]

This then, was Tudor practice. By what theory could such a practice justify itself to the eyes of a Christian observer? Elizabeth and her statesmen took good care to explain very thoroughly in what sense they thought Tudor England to be a Christian State. They assumed that religious faith proper had nothing whatever to do with outward behaviour or with matters political. Problems of conscience were purely private and personal problems: they were not to affect any citizen's conduct in regard to either State or Church. And conversely, Elizabeth presumed to have the right to exact civil obedience from her subjects whether they could reconcile it with their consciences or not. As long as subjects obeyed, 'no windows were to be let into their souls'. They were at liberty to believe whatever they pleased. Conformity, in short, was made a matter of obedience to the law; not a matter of conscience. As a matter of obedience to the law—to which after all the whole realm had assented by Act of Parliament—the State was perfectly justified in coercing its citizens into conformity.

The fact that a distinction between conformity through obedience to the law and conformity through conscience was made, clearly showed how matters stood: it was apparently held that religion as something purely spiritual could have no influence on, or any significant relation with, the world of politics and human behaviour. Or, in other words, a strict separation between the two worlds of religious and of secular life, between nature and supernature was pre-supposed. And when the Elizabethan State began to persecute and to suppress non-conformity by force, it always

---

[1] For the question of Canon Law see F. W. Maitland, *Roman Canon Law in the Church of England*, London, 1898, pp. 81 ff. See especially p. 90: Before the Reformation the State limited the sphere of action of the ecclesiastical courts; after the Reformation the State dictated the decisions to the ecclesiastical courts. William I for instance had accepted ecclesiastical law as long as *he* was allowed to carry it out. This was very different from Henry VIII's attitude. Cp. Z. N. Brooke, *The English Church and the Papacy*, Cambridge, 1931, p. 163; also p. 145.

insisted that its victims had been convicted of treason, not of any religious offence;[1] as if a man could be expected to hold one view in religion and a diametrically opposed one in politics.

Nevertheless, the fact that the Tudor State in the late sixteenth century acted on this principle, proves that behind its practice there stood the same theory of religion as had stood behind the doctrine of Marsilius of Padua; namely the Latin Averroists' theory of the two truths. It was indeed implied, though practically never formally pronounced, by the school of Latin Averroists which had flourished towards the end of the thirteenth century, that nature and supernature were two realms so completely separated from one another, that a proposition that was true in the one, could be false in the other, and vice versa[2]. Siger of Brabant and

[1] Persecution of Catholics started only when the latter began to assert the political consequences of their religious convictions. And then the State was interested in these consequences *only*. The Catholics were all tried on charges of treason. The same is true for the Puritans. Penry was tried and condemned under 23 Eliz. c. 2. which was an Act against 'seditious words and rumours uttered against the Queen'. See J. Strype, *The Life and Acts of John Whitgift*, Oxford, 1822, Vol. II, p. 175–6. It was stated officially that the State's objection to dissenters and nonconformists was not based on any positive religious conviction but on the fact that they refused to obey the law. The same point was made by Burghley in his *The Execution of Justice in England*; in the *Proclamation against Jesuits*, 1 April, 1582; and in the Statute 27 Elizabeth, c.2. For Walsingham's similar attitude see Conyers-Reed, *Mr. Secretary Walsingham*, Oxford, 1925, Vol II, p. 294: also pp. 339, 265. Burghley went to a great deal of trouble to prove that Campion was executed for treason and to conceal the fact that the issue was really a religious one. Cp. A. G. Smith, *William Cecil*, London, 1934, p. 200. Cp. *Proclamation of June 11, 1573*, by the Queen. *Puritan Manifestoes*, C.H.S. LXXII, London, 1907, p. 153; and Elizabeth's letter to the Emperor Ferdinand, Nov. 3, 1563, in C. G. Bayne, *Oxford Historical and Literary Studies*, Oxford, 1913. The Elizabethan establishment 'meant that the common bond of her people would in future be not their religion but their nationality' W. Haller, *The Rise of Puritanism*, New York, 1938, p. 7.

[2] To St. Thomas, who believed in a complete hierarchy of being, there could only be one truth. Siger of Brabant, however, denied implicitly the fundamental premise that there is a hierarchy of all being. He looked upon nature and supernature as two separate, parallel fields of existence, and consequently there was nothing absurd to him in the notion of two truths. Siger wrote as if it were possible to consider nature without any reference to supernature and thus adhere to the dictates of reason though they obviously contradicted those of faith which were true in the realm of supernature. When he

his followers had been forced into that position by the logic of the situation. On one side they had to recognize the truths of Aristotle; on the other side they were, as Christians, committed to revealed truth. They thought the only way out of this dilemma was to assume that the two truths could well contradict each other since they applied to completely different realms.[1] The Thomistic solution, that Aristotle could be reconciled with divinely revealed truth, and that the realm of nature, to which the one referred, and the realm of supernature, to which the other referred, were two supplementary parts of one whole, either was not understood or had for certain reasons not commended itself to the Latin Averroists. The outcome was that they believed that nature and supernature were two unrelated parts of life; whereas the Thomistic view, and of course also that of Hooker, had been that nature and supernature were supplementary parts of life; each requiring a special mode of cognition but incapable of contradicting one another, since the law that pervaded the latter was also the cause of the law by which the former was regulated.

Marsilius, who had been educated under the influence of Latin Averroism in Padua, and who remained a life-long friend of the

does that he adds '. . . cum philosophice procedamus . . .' P. Mandonnet, *Siger de Brabant et L'Averroisme au Latin XIII siècle*, Louvain, 1908, Pt. II, p. 164. And in his *Quaestiones de Anima Intellectiva*, Mandonnet, op. cit., Pt. II, p. 154, he says: '. . . Philosophus senserit aliter quam veritas se habeat et per revelationem aliqua de anima tradita sint, quae per rationes naturales concludi non possunt. Sed nihil ad nos nunc de Dei miraculis, cum de naturalibus naturaliter disseramus.' St. Thomas did not follow the argument. On his assumption that there was one world of nature and supernature and hence only one truth, he could but conclude that Siger taught that faith teaches falsehoods because it contradicted reason. *De Unitate Intellectus*. Ch. VII, ad finem. The above quoted texts from Siger seem to contradict Gilson's interpretation of Siger, who thinks that the latter merely wanted to explain what the philosophers said but admitted that they may be wrong and that the truth may be otherwise. *La doctrine de la double verité, Etudes de Philosophie Mediévalé*, Strassburg, 1921, p. 59. This interpretation may be put on the text: 'et in tali dubio fidei adhaerendum est, quae omnem rationem humanam superat.' Mandonnet, op. cit., Pt. II, p. 169; but not on ibid., p. 153-4.

[1] For a general description of the problem of double truth in religious thought see F. Betzendörfer, *Die Lehre von der zweifachen Wahrheit*, Tübingen, 1924.

most influential Averroists of his time[1], had availed himself of these presuppositions in order to reconcile a theory of complete State sovereignty over the Church with the assertion that such a State could nevertheless profess to be a truly Christian State. In fact, on the ground of this Averroistic doctrine he thought that a society could be truly Christian only if it achieved a complete divorce between those principles of conduct and law-making that spring from a purely rational consideration of the natural ends of man and those that urge him towards faith in a divinely revealed law. The latter, as something wholly spiritual and unearthly, were to be relegated to the inner life of man. They were not pertinent to man's natural life. He did not integrate the natural end with the supernatural end by saying that the former was a partial good and the latter a complete good. Instead he maintained that the natural end was itself as complete a good as the supernatural end. According to this conception the two ends existed side by side, and a complete good could be achieved by the pursuit of either end. For all practical purposes he held it sufficient to consider the natural side of life and let the spiritual look after itself. Being in fact spiritual, this side could not really affect the non-spiritual side.[2] On these assumptions Marsilius had erected his theory of the State. He took it that the community as a whole can make all the laws that are required for its well-being and that no law that was made by any other institution could have any validity. The end of society was a natural end and as such not subordinated to supernatural considerations. The institution

---

[1] For his life, his education and connexions see L. K. Brampton, *Marsiglio of Padua, Life, E.H.R.* Vol. XXXVII, 1922.

[2] 'Vivere autem ipsum et bene vivere conveniens hominibus est in duplici modo, quoddam temporale sive mundanum, aliud vere aeternum sive caeleste vocari solitum.' *Defensor Pacis*, I, 4. There is no hierarchy of ends, those of one life being subordinate to those of the other, but a complete separation: there are two sets of ends, which can be pursued independently. Marsilius and the Latin Averroists were biased in favour of the natural end, but did not exclude the supernatural end. Since full perfection could be reached by the pursuit of either end they could define the *summum bonum* and 'to live well' in both natural and supernatural terms. For an attempt to do the former see M. Grabmann, *Die Opuscula des Boetius von Dacien, Archives d'histoire doctrinale et littéraire du moyen âge*, VI, 1931, pp. 207-17.

which cared for the supernatural end of man was subject to the State as far as its dealings with man's natural life were concerned, i.e. in all practical matters. It was allowed full freedom in matters spiritual, which by definition did not affect man's outward behaviour. It was very largely for those reasons that Marsilius had commended himself from the very beginning to the Tudor State.[1] This had been no accident, since the reasons for which Marsilius had attacked the Papacy had also been the reasons for which Henry VIII had attacked it. And it is important to note how the Averroistic tendencies of the one were tacitly taken over by Elizabeth so that one can speak of a sixteenth-century *Tudor Averroism*. In this sense the recurrence of the medieval situation which we have noted in the previous chapter is even more complete than was indicated there. For now we find also the third party, the Latin Averroists, on the scene. And Hooker by his own choice had inherited the part played by St. Thomas in the thirteenth century: he fought against the Puritans on one side and against the Tudor State on the other.

6

His opposition to the Tudor State did not take the form of an open criticism but was an attempt to reinterpret it in his own terms as we have described above. The Church-State relationship which was implied in the Averroistic Marsilian theory of the Tudor State was, at first sight, as unacceptable to Hooker as to the Puritans. He had therefore endeavoured in general outline to draft a scheme in which the Tudor Constitution could be reconciled with the basic requirements of the Thomistic theory of the relationship between State and Church. But when Hooker came to the details of Tudor practice, he found that the brute facts were too strong for him. He could not do justice to it without introducing Marsilius.

[1] Cp. A. F. Pollard, *Henry VIII*, London, 1913, p. 329; A. F. Pollard, *William Marshall* in *D.N.B.* and F. W. Maitland, *English Law and Renaissance*, Cambridge, 1901, pp. 14, 60, 61, for Marshall's translation of the *Defensor Pacis* sponsored by Cromwell.

There were several reasons why Hooker in the end was compelled to take account of Marsilius and to incorporate his ideas into the last part of the *Laws of Ecclesiastical Polity*. The first and most compelling reason was the obvious correspondence between Marsilian theory and Tudor practice: no political theory fitted the Tudor State so well as this fourteenth-century adaptation of Aristotle.[1] Its main feature, the theory of the origin of all valid law as an expression of the will of the society could be taken as an exact justification of Parliamentary sovereignty in England. The second reason was that Marsilius had argued against the supremacy of the Pope. Now the claims put forward by Boniface were based on the same assumptions as those put forward by the Puritans.[2]

These assumptions were that the secular State, being nothing but the expression of man's depraved reason, ought to be placed under the direct tutelage and direction of the ecclesiastical institution which was believed to be in possession of the true divine law. Marsilius had opposed this claim against a Pope; Hooker opposed it against a Puritan congregation. It can therefore be assumed that there was something in Marsilius's theory itself which commended itself to Hooker and made the former appear a useful ally, for both Hooker and Marsilius were determined to vindicate the right of the secular State against ecclesiastical domination.

There remained the fact that Marsilius had tried to vindicate, against the extreme ecclesiastical claims, the absolute autonomy of the State as a secular institution; whereas Hooker had committed himself by his theory on reason and faith to vindicate, against the same claims, a well-balanced relationship between Church and State. By adopting Marsilius, therefore, Hooker was,

[1] de Lagarde suspects that Marsilius went beyond Aristotle in his claim that human law should be completely autonomous and not be subject to natural law. *Une adaptation de la Politique D'Aristote au XIV siècle. Revue historique de droit français et étranger*, 4th series, Vol. XI, 1932, p. 246. There could be observed a similar tendency in the Tudor Parliament. And the definition of the absolute sovereignty of a 'multitude of free men' by Sir Thomas Smith, *De Republica Anglorum*, Bk. I, ch. x, is very similar to Marsilius's theory that final sovereignty is vested in the 'universitas civium', *Defensor Pacis*, I, 12.

[2] We shall show in the next chapter the connexion between Boniface and the Puritans. It is possible to trace the direct connexion between the man who drafted Boniface's bulls and English Puritanism.

perhaps unwittingly at first, driven into a position that was no longer consistent with his initial thesis. And this brings us to the third reason why Hooker followed Marsilius: why was it possible for a man with Hooker's intellectual acumen to be driven into such a position? The answer is that it was the nature of his own argument which tempted him into this position. There is indeed in Thomistic philosophy an incipient naturalism and, it will be remembered, St. Bonaventure and the other more orthodox Augustinians were aware of this fact and had warned St. Thomas of it.[1] St. Thomas himself had understood the problem only too clearly and therefore had guarded himself against Aristotelian naturalism, which he would have considered an error. But Hooker did not heed the warning: as we have seen in the previous chapter, in philosophy he succumbed to the temptation. From there it was only a short step to a similar move in political theory. The basic decision was that reason could competently deal with all human concerns, and that these dictates of reason were not only consistent with divine law because they flowed from the same source as divine law, the *lex aeterna*, but were actually equivalent to it. This decision once made, it was easy to reach the conclusion that a body representative of all members of the commonwealth could govern and make law as they thought fit in both Church and State. This body could be thought to avail itself of reason. It was then in the last instance the naturalism incipient in Thomistic philosophy which prepared the way for Hooker's approach to the political theory of Marsilius. The basic Aristotelian elements were common to St. Thomas and Marsilius; they differed exactly in that one took up the second and the other the third type of Christian political philosophy. And in Hooker we find the curious phenomenon of an attempted combination of the two types.

For these reasons we find that Hooker's description of the Elizabethan State shows in almost all decisive points a remarkable correspondence with the theories of Marsilius.[2] How close that

---

[1] Cp. Ch. II. p. 59.

[2] Hooker's debt to Marsilius has been noted by A. P. d'Entrèves, *Riccardo Hooker*, Torino, 1932, pp. 57 ff.; R. Scholz, *Marsilius von Padua und die Idee der Demokratie, Zeitschrift für Politik*, Vol. I, p. 91; C. W. Prévité-Orton, *Marsilius of Padua, Proc. of the Brit. Academy*, Vol. XXI, 1935, pp. 165 ff.

correspondence was can be gauged from the following summary of the main points.

The primary assumption on which the rest of the theory depends is that assent of the citizens as a community is the true cause of the validity and effective power of all laws.[1] With this doctrine a definition of the nature of valid law is given. There is only one source of public authority, the people; and all power is derived from them. No rule which has not received their consent can be a valid law. The legislative power resides therefore entirely in the community as a whole; but majority rule, i.e. pure democracy, is limited by Marsilius by the well-known phrase *vel valentior pars*, and by Hooker in the English rendering of that phrase which expresses so well the difference between the terse Latin style of Marsilius and the baroque English of Hooker: '. . . though happily some one part may have greater sway in that action than the rest'.[2] Kings are instituted for the sake of better government by human law. But since men owe the power to establish human law to God, Kings that have been thus established rule ultimately by divine right.[3] This theory clearly illustrates the naturalistic dangers of Thomist philosophy. Both Hooker and Marsilius start with the Thomistic conception of man as the 'coadjutor of God'. God has given man the faculties for the making of human law; hence a monarchy established by human law is in the last analysis established by God. But whereas St. Thomas always laid the emphasis on God, Marsilius stressed the human element and thus relegated the divine element in law to a very insignificant position. When Hooker used the theory, he could in all sincerity maintain that at least on this point St. Thomas and Marsilius looked as if they were in perfect agreement.

The supreme authority which Kings have thus received from the community must be exercised by them over the whole community, i.e. over both clergy and laity. For a Christian society is coextensive with the Church, and both clergy and laity are its

[1] I. x. 8; I, 12; The first reference is to Hooker, the second to Marsilius's *Defensor Pacis*.

[2] VIII. vi. 6; I, 13.

[3] VIII. ii. 6; I, 9; The power of the King is derived 'a Deo tamquam a causa remota, qui omnem principatum terrenum etiam concedit'.

members.[1] And it must be exercised in matters secular and in matters spiritual.[2] Within any one territory this authority must be monopolized: there ought to be no division of sovereignty or a variety of conflicting jurisdictions.[3] All citizens, therefore, clergy as well as laity, must be subject to the secular State. No one part of the body politic can overrule the King who has power of dominion thus derived from the citizens.[4] It follows that the State is the supreme head in all matters of Church government. It helps the Church as a master, not as a servant.[5] The clergy, if they should venture to make laws of their own, are guilty of high treason against the human legislator. Neither congregation nor bishop nor Pope can overrule the King whose power is derived from the human legislator.[6] In matters ecclesiastical it is only wise and proper that the clergy, as experts, ought to give their advice as to the framing of the necessary laws. But these laws can derive legal validity and coercive authority only from the lay-assent of the human legislator.[7] In consequence all ecclesiastical jurisdiction can only be a delegation.[8] And similarly no decision of a general council can be valid unless it has received the assent of the sovereign ruler.[9] The clergy, in short, although their spiritual powers are derived from God, must obtain the permission of the secular ruler to exercise them.[10]

From all this it appears that Hooker followed Marsilius fairly closely. The Aristotelian natural state was accepted in its entirety; and it was not felt necessary to give it a supplement in the form of an institution which represented those rules that were of a direct divine origin and that were known by revelation. The State was Christian only in so far as the officials of which it availed itself for the spiritual guidance of its citizens administered the Christian sacraments rather ,than, e.g. Orphic rites. It was never doubted that the human legislator might be a competent judge in all matters of human conduct both private and public. This State

---

[1] VIII. i. 2; II. 17.

[2] VIII. ii. 14; II, 4; III, 2, 5.

[3] VIII. iii. 1; I, 17.

[4] VIII. ii. 3; II, 5.

[5] VIII. iii. 4; II, 21.

[6] VIII. ii. 3; II, 23.

[7] VIII. vi. 11; II, 5, 6, 10, 21, 27.

[8] VII. xv. 2; II, 2, 4, 6.

[9] VIII. vi. 9; II, 21.

[10] VII. xv. 2; II, 17.

was Christian, however, on the assumption that Christian religion was so entirely spiritual that it could have nothing whatever to do with any earthly problems; its rewards and punishments, in fact its whole efficacy was relegated to the world beyond the grave and completely divorced from the natural part of human existence. Hence the clergy could be compelled to enforce a truth which might be quite inconsistent with the supernaturally known truths of divine law. Marsilius's State was true to Aristotle in that its citizens were urged to act as if the end of human life lay within the socially assessable terms of natural life; and it was Christian in that it was based on the Latin Averroists' doctrine of the double truth.

All this fitted the Tudor State admirably. And by making use of Marsilius, Hooker had indeed brought his interpretation of the Tudor Constitution down to earth. He had now stated his ideas in very concrete terms and nobody could object that the State thus described did not represent a correct picture of the Tudor State. But at the same time Hooker's difficulties were revealed: he had set out to interpret the Tudor State in terms of a Christian philosophy and had thus endeavoured to show that a true Christian could not find fault with it. In order to carry that interpretation, however, to a successful conclusion he had been obliged, by various factors, to avail himself of a political theory which was diametrically opposed to the principles of the Christian philosophy which he had expounded in the earlier part of his work. These principles had been based on the second type of Christian philosophy; whereas through his adoption of Marsilius he had later espoused the third type of Christian philosophy. Where then did Hooker stand? And what did he make of this peculiar situation? Before we can attempt to answer these questions, we shall have to note another significant feature of Hooker's political philosophy.

7

Hooker, although he looked upon himself as an apologist and defender of the *status quo*, did not merely justify existing conditions

—as we have had occasion to note before. He was always intent on interpreting these conditions in terms in which they would become acceptable to his general philosophical outlook. And he did that by drawing attention to neglected factors and diverting it from those that seemed less pleasing. In short his method of defence was not a stubborn apology for what was, but an attempt to avoid revolution or violent disturbances by shifting the emphasis from the undesirable to the desirable elements of the *status quo*. It was in this sense that he saw in the Tudor State, among other things, the rule of law and a constitutionally limited monarchy.[1]

To such ideas Hooker was led by the very requirements of his Aristotelian assumption that the end of the State is the true happiness of its members.[2] Natural and divine law between them cover all the needs of man. But in so far as he is living in a society, he must make special human laws to meet all special cases and circumstances.[3] These human laws must be 'deducted by way of discourse as conclusions from the former, divine and natural, serving for principles thereunto'.[4] In this way Hooker was obliged to formulate a number of constitutional principles which limited and defined the scope of royal power in order to ensure that it would be exercised for its proper end. He had to make certain that human laws were not made and administered according to an arbitrary will. In order to do so, he used certain legal maxims that had been well known in English legal and constitutional thought for many centuries.[5] There can be little doubt that he considered them, if not directly part of natural law, derived from natural law *per modum determinationis*.[6]

---

[1] His general prejudice in favour of such a view has been noted by Holdsworth, *History of English Law*, London, 1924, Vol. IV, p. 212.

[2] I. x. 2; VIII. i. 4.

[3] VIII. vi. 5; St. Thomas, S.Th. I, II, 108, 2.

[4] St. Thomas, ibid.

[5] R. A. Houk, *Hooker's Ecclesiastical Polity, Book VIII*, New York, 1931, pp. 50 ff., believed that the eighth book is on the whole a product of the law schools and written under the influence of Hooker's friend Sandys.

[6] 'The English law of reason seems to have had the same close relation to custom that the old law of nature had formerly borne to the *ius gentium* . . .' Ch. H. McIlwain, *The High Court of Parliament*, New Haven, 1910, p. 105.

As the King ruled by the will of the people for 'their own most behoof and security' it followed that he was *maior singulis, universis minor.*[1] And similarly it had to be granted that *quod omnes tangit ab omnibus tractari et approbari debet.*[2] And the Aristotelian principle that a multitude requires one ruling principle to preserve the *bonum publicum*[3] implies that the king derives his power from the people whom he is appointed to govern. The 'original influence' of power from the body into the king is cause of the 'king's dependency in power upon the body.'[4] Hence *Lex facit regem* and not vice versa; and *rex nihil potest nisi quod iure potest.*[5] Finally Hooker quotes with great approval Bracton's famous maxim that the King, though not under man, is under God and under the law.[6] He certainly believed that all these maxims followed directly from the principles of natural law as it manifested itself in the Aristotelian theory of society that man was by nature a social animal and that every society evolves naturally a form of government fit to attain the proper end of society, to live well.

Of royal power itself, Hooker did not have a very exalted view. He referred his readers to Luke xi. 17 for the observation that 'without order there is no living in public society, because the want thereof is the mother of confusion, whereupon division of necessity follows and out of division inevitable destruction'.[7] Order he defined as a 'gradual disposition' of society where each member kept his proper place.[8] And power is but the 'instrument of this order'[9] i.e. the ability and duty vested in the King to see that law and order are kept. As to the original derivation of this power, Hooker always uses the Aristotelian theory that power is inherent by nature in society as a whole[10]. Therefore it is 'the whole body politic [that] makes laws, which laws give power unto the king'.[11] Nevertheless he thinks that power once granted cannot

---

[1] VIII. ii. 7.
[2] VIII. vi. 8.
[3] VIII. iii. 1.
[4] VIII. ii. 9.
[5] VIII. ii. 13.
[6] VIII. ii. 3.

[7] VIII. ii. 2.
[8] Loc. cit.
[9] Loc. cit.
[10] I. x. 8.
[11] VIII. viii. 9; VIII. vi. 11.

be revoked[1] and therefore advises that it ought to be limited before it be granted.[2] But he warns against the mistake of limiting it too much so as to render the King's power ineffective. Not 'the most, but the best limited power is best'.[3] Hooker was acutely aware of the immense danger of any discretionary power. The temptation to commit crimes is very strong for ordinary human beings who know that they are going to be punished. How much stronger must be the temptation for a King who has no fear of punishment?[4] And so it was that already at a very early stage of his work he defined the necessity for a strict rule of law. To live by one man's will, he explained,[5] becomes the cause of all men's misery. Therefore men have to agree upon laws wherein all men might see their duties beforehand and know the penalties for every offence.[6] And as a conclusion to Hooker's argument we may quote: 'Where the King does guide the state and the law the King, that commonwealth is like a harp or melodious instrument, the strings whereof are tuned and handled all by one, following as laws the rules and canons of musical science.[7] The King who does not follow these maxims becomes a tyrant. Hooker thus puts himself in line with the great tradition of medieval political thought that found its earlier representatives in John of Salisbury, in St. Thomas Aquinas and in Fortescue. It is the tradition that has earned for its most eminent exponent, St. Thomas, the epithet of 'the first Whig'.

---

[1] VIII. ii. 10.

[2] Ibid.

[3] VIII. ii. 12.

[4] VIII. ix. 1.

[5] I. x. 5.

[6] We find the same argument in Marsilius: 'Nam perversa iudicantis affectio, ut odii vel amoris aut avaritiae desiderium iudicantis pervertit. Haec autem a iudicio prohibentur: ab his praeservatur, dum fuerit iudex seu principans determinatus secundum leges ferre iudicia, propterea quod lex omni caret affectione perversa, non enim facta est ad amicum aut inimicum utilem vel, novicum, sed universaliter ad agentem civiliter bene aut male.' *Defensor Pacis*, I, 11. It seems that Hobbes found his refutation a generation before he wrote. For according to Hooker Hobbes's sovereign, with his unlimited powers, would defeat the very end for which he was created.

[7] VIII. ii. 12.

And it was indeed this aspect—and this aspect alone—of Hooker which found its way into the thought of Locke and hence into modern constitutional thought.[1]

One can hardly be surprised therefore to find that Hooker always pronounced in favour of the rule of law and against the exercise of the royal prerogative. And even if the latter had to be exercised at all, Hooker considered it defined and granted by the law itself—a view which could not have pleased Elizabeth very greatly. Personally the King, he maintained, is always subject to divine law and his public acts are subject to the law of the state.[2] As far as the royal supremacy over the Church was concerned, Hooker was no less unequivocal: The Elizabethan Act of Supremacy lays down the law of the Church under which the Queen was to exercise her supremacy.[3] There could for him be no question: the royal supremacy was not one of the 'mysteries of kingship' and was not inherent in royal power.[4] It is only by the laws of this realm that ecclesiastical power is annexed to the crown.[5] And in the Church itself 'all decisions of things doubtful, and corrections of things amiss, are proceeded in by order of law . . . it is neither permitted unto prelate nor prince to judge and determine at their own discretion, but law has prescribed what both shall do.'[6]

And finally through the channel of Hooker's deep constitutionalism, some of the basic ideas of the conciliar movement found their way into the last book of the *Laws of Ecclesiastical Polity*. Hooker explained expressly that just as the true and original power to make civil law resided in the whole body of the commonwealth, so the true natural power to make laws for the

[1] For Locke's debt to Hooker see Appendix D.

[2] VIII. ii. 17.

[3] VIII. ii. 17.

[4] Although in other places he comes fairly close to the Marsilian conception that royal power, once granted, implies *eo ipso* a supremacy over the Church since the Church is in no different position within the commonwealth than other societies. To Constantine and the Jewish kings he would grant supremacy over the Church out of the nature of the case.

[5] VIII. i. 1.

[6] VIII. viii. 9.

Church resided in the entire body of the Church.[1] Neither Gerson nor Cusanus could have expressed their fundamental thesis more concisely.

According to Cusanus the general body of the Church was the true subject of the Church's mandate and right.[2] Therefore in the Church as well as in the State, all authority is based on voluntary consent.[3] The community thus bestowed the coercive authority upon the clergy; God contributed only grace.[4] There can be no coercion in the Church any more than in the State except through consent. The law is based on the 'concordantia subiectionalis eorum qui per eam legem ligantur'.[5] The community therefore is the source of all the powers of jurisdiction and administration conferred upon the ecclesiastical hierarchy.[6] The latter stand like the King above individuals but are inferior to the people as a community.[7] We can presume therefore, since there is not a single one of these ideas which we have not found in one part or another of Hooker's work, that his thought followed lines similar to those exemplified in the conciliar movement. One could always substitute 'King' for 'Pope' in the conciliar theory, since Cusanus had expressly declared that the latter derived his powers from the community through election,[8] that his power was limited by the canons and decrees of councils[9] and that he could even be judged and deposed;[10] a reservation which Hooker would not make even in regard to a King.[11] And then, if we remember Hooker's principal premiss,

[1] VIII. vi. 1. That Hooker was well acquainted with Cusanus is shown by his reference to him in I. viii. 3.

[2] I, 12–17. The references to Cusanus are according to the description of Cusanus's ideas in O. Gierke, *The Development of Political Theory*, London, 1939, pp. 189–90, n. 25.

[3] Ibid., II, 13–14.

[4] Ibid., II, 34.

[5] Ibid., II, 8–12.

[6] Ibid., II, 2, 13–15.

[7] Ibid., II, 34.

[8] Ibid., II, 13–14, 34.

[9] Ibid., II, 9–10.

[10] Ibid., II, 17–18.

[11] VIII. ii. 10.

that in England Church and Commonwealth were coextensive and thus indistinguishable, we can surmise the final drift of his argument: if Church and Commonwealth are one, Parliament which represents the one must also be held to represent the other. And since the subject of the Church's right is the whole community one can infer from that the right of Parliament to act as Cusanus would have the General Council act. A Council to the latter represented both clergy and laity—it was in fact the precise equivalent of Hooker's 'Parliament with Convocation annexed thereunto', the highest authority in the Church. Looked at in this light, Hooker's adoption of Marsilius becomes much more than a mere concession to the Aristotelian-Erastian tendencies of the Tudor State: it becomes a natural conclusion from the two premisses that (a) the Church can only be ruled by a law to which it consents and (b) in England Church and Commonwealth are one. The complete supremacy of the human legislator does not mean to Hooker a simple supremacy of the secular State over the Church; it assumed a double character. In matters ecclesiastical the human legislator acts *qua* Church; as a General Council would in the theory of Cusanus. And in matters civil, it acts *qua* Commonwealth; as the Tudor Parliament in fact did act.

8

Hooker did not, however, tie up these loose ends in this way. He left the last three books of his work unfinished. He must have become conscious of the hopelessness of the effort to reconcile the various standpoints. We have noted already the contradictions between his Thomism and his Marsilian theory of the State. And to this we must add the awkward position in which he found himself when he had developed his constitutionalism: Elizabeth and her statesmen would most certainly have been offended by his treatment of her prerogative. Elizabeth had always avoided putting forward any clear definition of her ideas as to a proper constitution. She was too diplomatic to pronounce unequivocally on such knotty and tender questions. Within the ecclesiastical sphere there were apparently no limits to royal authority, for papal jurisdiction had been transferred to the King, and the Pope's powers had been unfettered. The extent to which the Queen was bound by law in temporal matters was doubtful and it was even more doubtful in spiritual matters. In any case, we know from her practice that Elizabeth's notions on these matters did not differ very much from those of James, and we can imagine how much she would have resented Hooker's defence of her government had the last book been published during her lifetime. It defended the Tudor State in fact for the very characteristics Elizabeth disliked most and which she would gladly have abolished. How obnoxious Hooker's ideas on these matters must have been to her is revealed by the following example. Bancroft, in his sermon at Paul's Cross, on February 9th, 1588,[1] officially denounced the treasonable theories of the *Vindiciae contra Tyrannos*, of *De iure regni apud Scotos* and the *De iure Magistratuum in subditos*. All these sixteenth-century works are expressions of a most fervent constitutionalism; and, to choose only one example, they all subscribe to the doctrine that the king is *maior singulis, minor universis*.[2] The *Laws of Ecclesiastical Polity* contained precisely the lines of thought Bancroft was denouncing, including the maxim just quoted.[3]

Hooker therefore must have been concerned when he discovered that he was no longer a real apologist but had become a critic. On the other hand, if he had decided to omit his constitutional ideas, he could never have hoped to reconcile his adoption of Marsilius with his Thomistic philosophy. So the deeper he got into the problem of practical politics, the more he found himself involved in difficulties. The work slowed down, and when he died in 1599 he left it unfinished. The notes were left in the hands of his friends and only published many years after his death under circumstances that have given rise to doubts as to their authenticity. At first his wife, who was presumed to have had Puritanical leanings, was suspected of having tampered with the manuscript in order to assist the Puritan cause. But the researches of Houk[4]

[1] Op. cit., p. 297.
[2] *Vindiciae*, Qu. III; *De iure regni*, pp. 79 ff. *De iure Magistratuum*, Qu. 5 and 6.
[3] VIII. ii. 7.
[4] *Hooker's Ecclesiastical Polity, Book VIII*, New York, 1931.

have shown that there is no reason to doubt the authenticity of these books, and more recently Prof. Sisson[1] has produced evidence which completely exonerates Hooker's wife from that and many other more personal charges. In fact, after having noticed all the conflicting viewpoints in the last three books we can imagine that there was a certain temptation to tamper with them not only for Puritans, but for defenders of the royal prerogative, as well as for some High Churchmen who had good cause to find fault with Hooker's adaptation of conciliar theories. After the work of Houk and Sisson there is nothing to be added to this problem from a bibliographical point of view. But from the above arguments, and the well-known conjectures of Hallam and Coleridge that the High Church party cast doubt on the authenticity of the three last books because they disliked their contents[2], there emerges one clear fact. Disagreement with Hooker, by the time he had come to the writing of the last three books, was no longer confined to the Puritans. The High Church party and the Tudor State might have objected to some of his views had they known them. Especially the former, in the person of Hooker's friend Andrewes, had, it seems, a better opportunity to interfere with his work and to delay its publication than had the Puritans.[3] All this shows that Hooker was in the end not as successful an apologist for the *status quo* as he had hoped to be. When he had said what he had wanted to say, he had criticized not only the Puritans—but the extreme High Church party and the Tudor State as well. In this fact we must seek the reason for the peculiar condition in which the last three books have come down to us. They are unfinished with a number of loose ends which do not meet, not because someone has tampered with the manuscript, but for a different reason.

When Hooker had first set out to write his work, he had believed that he would eventually be able to give a satisfactory account of the Tudor Constitution by showing how it satisfied the demands of what he considered to be true philosophy. He started his work with philosophical and theological questions and

[1] *The judicious Marriage of Mr. Hooker and the Birth of the Laws of Ecclesiastical Polity*, Cambridge, 1940.

[2] *Literary Remains of S. T. Coleridge*, London, 1838, Vol. III, pp. 19-20.

[3] C. J. Sisson, op. cit., pp. 107-8.

with some vague and undefined notions about the political aspects of the problem. But when he actually came to the writing of the last three books which were to deal with political matters more directly than the preceding books, he discovered that the task he had set himself was more difficult than he had anticipated. The Tudor Constitution showed features which were not easily compatible with the principles of Thomistic philosophy to which he had declared his adherence in Book I. Hooker therefore began to hesitate. The work slowed down, and although there is reason to suppose that work on these three books was well in hand by 1593[1] he left them in an unfinished state when he died seven years later. This curious fact can only be explained by assuming that Hooker had not been able to make up his mind as to what to say. He knew that it would be almost impossible to reconcile such features of the Tudor State as the royal supremacy, the sovereignty of the Queen in Parliament, etc., with the theory about nature and supernature and the doctrine of natural law. And so it came about that, by the logic of the theories expounded in the first books, he was forced to give a theory of politics in the last which was more than a description of the *status quo*. On the other hand, if he had given a description of the *status quo*, it would not have been possible to justify it on the grounds that it met the requirements of a sound philosophy. Hence his hesitation and the slow progress. But he kept on trying to do the impossible and achieved a curious result: to make the ends meet, he went from St. Thomas to Marsilius; from Tudor sovereignty to the idea of a sovereignty limited by law; and from Erastianism to the conciliar movement. It is likely that he felt none too happy about this result, and it appears that his friends, for different reasons, did not either.

There is little doubt to-day that the last three books are authentic but it is no accident that their authenticity should have been doubted. We can discern a certain discrepancy between them and the first books, and gauge Hooker's own dissatisfaction with the shape his work was taking from his consequent inability to bring it to a final conclusion. Hooker was too honest and deep a thinker to succumb to the temptations he must have felt often during

---

[1] Houk, op cit., pp. 91 ff., thinks there is good reason to suppose that they were then as finished or unfinished as we know them to-day.

those seven years when his work was making little progress, to force either his ideas or the brute facts of politics into the Procrustean Bed of a systematic treatise, the completion of which would probably have given him a good deal of personal satisfaction. But Hooker was not sufficiently a propagandist to do such a thing. Nor was he willing to sacrifice either his philosophical convictions or his deep belief that the *status quo*, as the work of divine providence, could not be altogether objectionable. Had he given up his philosophy he would have become an uninteresting conservative; had he given up his faith in divine providence he would have become a revolutionary and furnished a blueprint for the reform of England. But Hooker would do none of these things. He hesitated. And it is just this hesitancy which is the noblest and most lovable feature of his mind. Like most thinkers who understand the real issues of their age, he lived in that tension between fact and idea which is at the core of all human existence. To sacrifice either would have meant to abandon oneself to drift: for it is just this combination of the one with the other which provides the necessary discipline in human thinking. Facts alone are indifferent; and ideas by themselves, fantastic. To overcome the tension one has to have a prophetic nature like Marx or Plato. But men like Hooker, whose strength lies in their intellect and in their balance of temper, hesitate and thereby reveal their unflinching personal integrity.

CHAPTER FOUR

HOOKER AND ARISTOTLE

THE central problem of sixteenth-century political thought
was to find a theory in terms of which one could account
for what historians are wont to call the 'New Monarchy'.
That name is not too good a description of the facts of the situation, for it is incorrect to look upon the Tudors in England,
Ferdinand and Isabella in Spain, and Louis XI in France as the
initial stage of a new phase in the history of government. Especially French historians have pointed out that monarchy and feudalism were two diametrically opposed systems of administration;[1]
that the expression 'feudal Monarchy' really contains a contradiction in terms and that the history of government from the
eleventh to the seventeenth century is the history of the struggle
between monarchy and feudalism. Nor can we see in the sixteenth
century the culmination of that struggle—for feudal elements
continued to survive everywhere and were often not even
destroyed by the French Revolution. And yet, in that long-drawn-
out process, the sixteenth century shows certain features which
do not make the name 'New Monarchy' for its most prevalent
system of government seem wholly inappropriate. It was especially in regard to ecclesiastical organization that the monarchy
achieved an outstanding triumph in the sixteenth century: this,
taken together with the exhaustion of both France and England
through civil and feudal warfare, assured for both monarchies
an ascendancy over the feudal elements which far surpassed any
of its previous victories. In addition to these negative factors there
were positive conditions which favoured the evolution of strong,

[1] See esp. Ch. Petit-Dutaillis.

more centralized monarchical government: commercial considerations and the growing importance of the middle classes gave the monarchy a hitherto unknown opportunity. And the best argument in favour of the theory that the sixteenth century does represent a special period in the development of the modern centralized and unitary state is the fact that for the first time in the history of Western thought all political theory was concerned with the discussion of that form of government.

The two outstanding and well-known figures in this connexion are Machiavelli and Bodin: and equally important are those writers who attacked the New Monarchy on the grounds of medieval constitutional arguments and who thereby revealed themselves as reactionaries, as Hotman and the author of the *Vindiciae contra Tyrannos*. But less well known and more misunderstood in that connexion is that group of thinkers who were too deeply preoccupied with theological problems to bring to bear on this matter a purely legalistic argument and only political considerations. And just the fact that they occupied such a large part in the theoretical and controversial literature of the sixteenth century reveals once more the curious dual character of that period: its central problem could be discussed in the terms of both past and future: it was as thoroughly medieval as it was modern.

The second group of thinkers consisted in fact of those who availed themselves of Aristotle's political theory in order to cope, critically or apologetically as the case may be, with the problem of the modern, sixteenth-century state. To all those whose main preoccupation was religious and who could see the problem only in terms of theology, the advent of the New Monarchy in the sixteenth century represented a problem which was exactly analogous to the problem which had been created in the thirteenth century by the impact of the newly discovered Aristotle. In both cases, Christian thinkers had to face a body of facts and truths none of which was due to Christian revelation but which claimed validity on the ground that they were natural and due to human propensities and human reasoning. When faced with that situation one could observe the formation of the three broad types of Christian thought outlined in the first chapter. And when the

113

problem recurred in the sixteenth under the guise of the New Monarchy, the classification naturally repeated itself. There were those who denied to the New Monarchy the right to legislate for or govern Christians altogether—since the New Monarchy could not derive its authority from revelation. Secondly there were those who dealt with the New Monarchy exactly in the manner in which St. Thomas had dealt with Aristotle: they Christianized it on the basic assumption that nature and supernature represent two independent but complementary spheres. And finally there were those who accepted the New Monarchy in the sense in which Siger of Brabant and Marsilius of Padua had accepted Aristotle. These latter were the *Tudor Averroists* whom we have described above.[1]

Among the theologically-minded thinkers the opponents of the New Monarchy consisted of the representatives of the first type of Christian philosophy. Their arguments, unlike those of Hotman and his school, were not based on legal and constitutional considerations but on the assertion that none but divine law could compel the obedience of Christians, and that the proclamation of divine law through Christ had superseded all corrupt and merely human, natural law. This in brief was the Puritan or extremist Protestant outlook; as an argument it had nothing whatever in common with the argument of the *Vindiciae contra Tyrannos*;[2] except that its propounders belonged to the same camp as the French Huguenots in that they all denied the authority of the New Monarchy and were intent on obstructing its administration. This was clearly recognized by so astute an observer as Bancroft when he mentioned them all in one breath as opponents of the New Monarchy.[3] The so-called reactionary political thought of the sixteenth century had two poles, a constitutional one and a theological one.

[1] For details of *Tudor Averroism* see Appendix C.

[2] I do not think that Hooker wrote in order to refute the *Vindiciae contra Tyrannos* as suggested by Prof. Laski in his Introduction to the *Vindiciae*, London, 1924, p. 54. He was in agreement with the constitutionalism of this work, as explained in Chapter III. And his argument was only indirectly opposed to the line of reasoning employed by the author of the *Vindiciae* in that it denied the right of resistance.

[3] Op. cit., p. 297.

The basis of all sixteenth-century Monarchomachist thought was the positive law of European states whereby authority was exercised under the principle of *mutua obligatio*.[1] The source of Monarchomachist theory was therefore the actual practice of medieval government. Hooker supporting the Tudor monarchy was writing in opposition to the Monarchomachi, and he had discerned unfailingly that their arguments could best be met by ignoring the constitutional practice of the Middle Ages—except in those cases where its survival in the English constitution was too obvious to be passed over in silence—and by building up the theory of the State on a purely Aristotelian basis. For, though an Aristotelian theory would not directly contradict the notion of *mutua obligatio*, it attributed a sufficiently slight importance to it to make it lose its revolutionary implication. Instead Hooker put forward the idea that the natural existence of society implied the establishment of a magistrate, and that once the magistrate was established there was no possible ground on which one could get rid of him.

In this way Hooker's Aristotelianism countered the two trends of anti-'New-Monarchy' political thought of the sixteenth century. The arguments of the theological school were refuted by emphasizing the doctrine that Society and State are the products of a nature that is supplemented but not set aside by grace, and the arguments of the legalistic school were met by an appeal from the positive constitutional law and practice of the Middle Ages to the wider and more general theory of Aristotle.

It appears then that one-half of the sixteenth-century political thought, though obviously occupied with exactly the same problem as the other half, was Aristotelian or anti-Aristotelian, as the case may be, in its orientation. In so far as it was anti-Aristotelian it was reactionary in its opposition to the modern state; but progressive in that it linked up most naturally and conveniently with the vast sixteenth-century movement to dethrone Aristotle and to undermine the position of authority which he had occupied in so much of the thought of the preceding two and

[1] Cp. K. Wolzendorff, *Staatsrecht und Naturrecht in der Lehre vom Widerstandsrecht des Volkes*, Breslau, 1916, pp. 123–179. This is also true for Calvin: see C. Bohatec, *Calvin's Lehre von Staat und Kirche*, Breslau, 1937, pp. 239 ff.

a half centuries.[1] This is again another instance of the view propounded earlier that the new is rarely produced through the death of the old but seems rather to grow through an intensification of the old: it is indeed doubtful whether seventeenth-century science could have freed itself from the fetters of Aristotelianism if Aristotle's authority had not been rendered suspect in the sixteenth century,[2] by that most unscientific and almost anti-scientific of all emotional habits of mind, the exclusive reliance on the revealed word of God. Those who prepared the way for modern science by undermining the authority of Aristotle would have looked with even greater suspicion on such products of the human brain as scientific knowledge. It is therefore wrong to think that Aristotle succumbed before the progress of rational enlightenment. True, the development of independent inquiry in the sixteenth century, though no new factor[3], was very marked, but the main decline of Aristotelianism was due to the rise of Protestantism and Platonism. To Protestants Aristotle appeared as the bulwark of scholastic philosophy and as the symbol of that synthesis between Judaism and the ancient world which they rejected. Furthermore, he stood as he had stood to the Middle Ages, as the personification of human reason[4] and was as such suspect to the Christian who relied on the pure and direct word of God and who regarded reason as the snare of the Devil, the vain pride of a corrupt and depraved human nature. Aristotle was despised and came to be neglected; so that Hooker when taunted with his Aristotelianism could reply to the Puritans that they were very lucky men to know so little of so corrupt a philosopher.

[1] The terms 'progressive' and 'reactionary' are used in a neutral sense. They designate what proved to be victorious in the future or what came to be defeated, respectively.

[2] The work of Peter Ramus is an example. Ramus was not modern: but his anti-Aristotelian influence paved the way for the reception of Cartesianism. Cp. St. d'Irsay, *Histoire des Universités Françaises et étrangères*, Paris, 1895, Vol. II, p. 38.

[3] It dates in fact back to the rise of Nominalism in the early fourteenth century. See P. Duhem, *Etudes sur Leonardo da Vinci*, II, Paris, 1909, p. 412; and K. Hammerle, *Von Ockam zu Milton*, Insbruck, 1936, passim.

[4] Cp. Cl. Bäumker, *Platonismus im Mittelalter*, in Beiträge, Münster, 1927, Vol. 25, pp. 140 ff.

Partly coupled with and partly antagonistic to this trend, we find a decline of Aristotle's influence through the development of sixteenth-century Platonism.[1] The return to Plato had started with Petrarch and the appeal was very largely an aesthetic one. But the philosophical implications of the rejection of Aristotle and the return to Plato were clearly understood. And no matter what the causes of the movement were, its effects were clearly apparent throughout the sixteenth century in both camps. Whether Catholic or Protestant, the sixteenth century endeavoured to throw off the yoke of Aristotle in order to breathe more freely the air of the pure word of God or the less numbing philosophy of Platonism as the case may be. Anti-Aristotelianism has thus been considered the dominant note of the intellectual history of the sixteenth century. That there were many Aristotelians left nobody denied: but they were looked upon as a forlorn hope.

And yet there took place in the sixteenth century a real revival of Aristotelianism. It was only too obvious that Aristotle's theory of the natural origin of society and the State could be used to account for the facts of political organization of the sixteenth-century Monarchy. And according to what one thought about Christian philosophy, one would use either St. Thomas's or Marsilius's version of Aristotle. The most outstanding example of the latter use is Marshall's translation of the *Defensor Pacis* in the reign of Henry VIII; and both Barclay and Widdrington made use of Marsilius's Aristotle in order to explain the character of the sixteenth-century State.[2] And finally we ought not to forget that Hooker himself, in spite of his Thomism, was driven towards Marsilius when he came face to face with the brute facts of the Tudor Constitution. It is difficult to say whether these examples can be classed as a definite revival of Aristotelianism, though they undoubtedly bear witness to the importance and fruitfulness of Aristotle in an age when he was considered with suspicion,

---

[1] Though the Platonic tradition was continuous through the Middle Ages as shown by R. Klibansky, *The Continuity of the Platonic Tradition*, London, 1939, there can be no doubt that it became intensified after the second half of the fifteenth century.

[2] *Auctarium Bellarminianum*, Supplement aux Oeuvres du Cardinal Bellarmin, Paris, 1913, p. 361 f.

bitterness and often with derision. The Aristotelian revival proper, however, took place in connexion with the Thomistic Aristotle.

The chief significance of Thomistic philosophy in the thirteenth century had lain in the fact that it had defined the place of divine grace in the Universe without detracting from the efficacy of nature and of natural causes. In all spheres of philosophical speculation the angelic doctor had elaborated that theory with great subtlety and perfection; only in political science he had been satisfied with a few cursory remarks. There is no doubt that here, as elsewhere, he was true to Aristotle; and if one considers the nature of his philosophical speculation one can supply the necessary details and envisage what he would have said on this matter had his remarks been more specific. His ideas on these matters represent in political theory a decisive break with the general Augustinian speculation about the sinful origin of the State and the supersession of all law by the revealed word of God. To St. Thomas there was nothing sinful about the State and human society which it ordered. Both State and Society were the natural products of natural and human propensities and the ends which they served found their exact and proper place in the great hierarchy of ends, the apex of which was the beatific vision. The natural-human sphere has its own independent ends and operates according to its appropriate means; only as a whole, however, is it subordinate to the higher, supernatural end of human existence, which ultimately transcends the realm of nature. 'Ius autem divinum, quod est ex gratia, non tollit ius humanum, quod est ex naturali ratione'.[1] Church and State, as the guardians of natural and divine law respectively, are to co-operate without denying each other the complete efficacy of their respective modes of operation: reason and faith. Such are the general principles of Thomism in regard to this problem. Through them and the general character of his philosophy St. Thomas had furnished a framework on which a definite political theory could be established. St. Thomas himself, however, confined himself to a few general remarks and left his one work *De Regimine Principum*, which was to have dealt with the matter, unfinished.

[1] S.Th. II, II, 10, 10.

This proved of enormous consequence: for the meaning of the Thomistic synthesis in politics was probably not understood for another two centuries. No matter how much St. Thomas's adaptation of Aristotle in philosophy proper was used and applied, in politics it was not appreciated. For we find that, instead of elaborating his general principles, his followers and disciples merely toyed with them and failed to see the obvious point, i.e. that Society and State are natural products of natural propensities,' and thus that the fact that they can exist independently of the Church or of revealed divine law in no way detracts from the justice that is inherent in them as products of nature. It was rare that the twin principles of Thomistic philosophy were ever understood together. There were many theories, during the two centuries succeeding St. Thomas, of the natural state and of natural society. And Durandus of Saint Pourçain, though not a Thomist in the strict sense, for instance, expressed the conviction that the order of nature and the order of supernature 'nullam oppositionem vel repugnantiam habent'.[1] But the fourteenth and fifteenth centuries failed to evolve a theory of the proper relationship between ecclesiastical and secular political organization on the basis of these two fundamental principles. Those thinkers who like Durandus of Saint Pourçain had grasped the second principle, did not arrive at a clear notion of the complete efficacy of the natural propensities of man which resulted in the formation of Society and the State. More often than not they saw in these propensities merely a force subsidiary to the true end of man, to supernature and were wont to compare it to the art of making colours— which is of itself of no use and only valuable in that it is subsidiary to the art of painting. On such a basis they could not possibly arrive at any theory of a natural society and a natural state; for the test of such a theory, as we shall see later, is whether it provides a purely natural standard of justice and hence a valid criterion of judgement; and whether it is therefore possible to treat heathen societies as real societies. The potentialities of Thomism in politics were not realized during these centuries.

That this is true will become even more apparent when one analyses the theories of those thinkers who tried to grapple with

[1] *De origine Jurisdictionum*, Qu. II.

the concrete political conditions of the earlier part of the fourteenth century. By this time the secular State had shown itself to be too powerful a factor not to be given special consideration in political theory. Again and again we can detect therefore a tentative approach towards an Aristotelian theory of politics. But it is significant that neither Giles of Rome nor James of Viterbo nor any of their contemporaries availed themselves of the Thomistic method of dealing with Aristotle. Perhaps they had not understood it as far as political questions were concerned, or perhaps they did not wish to understand it; but in fact they often reveal that they followed Aristotle. But at the crucial moment when they would have had to discuss the relationship between secular and spiritual authority, they unquestioningly abandoned Aristotle and stated categorically that all power, in order to be just, must be derived through the Pope from God. Alvarius Pelagius (d. 1352), for instance, quoted Aristotle almost verbatim: 'Homo enim naturaliter animal sociale.'[1] He claimed that the Pope therefore had no authority 'in imperio'[2] and ought to occupy himself only mediately with temporal affairs.[3] But he leaves these arguments like loose ends—for in his theory of justice he shows, as we shall see presently, that he either does not wish or is not able to understand Aristotle and the Thomistic version of his philosophy.

The case of Giles of Rome (d. 1316) is even more startling. In his early work *De Regimine Principum*, he showed himself so thoroughly an Aristotelian and so unperturbed by the ecclesiastical point of view that it has been said that not even an Averroist could have found fault with him.[4] The treatise is a definite exposition of the theory of society as the product of man's natural inclinations. But later, when Giles was faced with the urgent demands of a political crisis, he could not see that it was possible to combine Aristotle with the requirements of a Christian society; he forsook Aristotle and probably regretted that he ever

---

[1] *De Planctu Ecclesiae*, I, 41, G.

[2] Op. cit., I, 37, T.

[3] Ibid., I, 40, C. It was probably on the strength of these passages that Bellarmine later tried to claim Pelagius for his party.

[4] R. Scholz, *Die Publizistik zur Zeit Philipps des Schönen*, Stuttgart, 1903, p. 116.

had toyed with him. He certainly did not see the possibility of a Thomistic compromise or synthesis and must have regarded Aristotle in his later years as dangerous. For once, he thought, the natural right to authority of the secular State was admitted, he could not see how God and man's supernatural destiny could be granted their legitimate claims. And so Giles of Rome reverted to a theory of society and of authority which denied that lawful authority could ever have any basis in natural, human inclinations.

A similar, unresolved conflict between the 'either-or' of Aristotle and a Christian philosophy can be detected in the works of James of Viterbo (d. 1308). He understood the Thomistic doctrine of grace as a perfection, not a destruction, of nature; and nevertheless added that 'human power as it exists among the faithful is not formed and perfected until it has been approved and ratified by the spiritual power'. [1] He could no more than Giles of Rome see that if grace does not destroy nature, it is in perfect harmony with Christian doctrine to ascribe a complete efficacy to second natural causes and thus to believe that there is justice in natural society. He looked upon society as a natural product but could ascribe a moral value to it only after it had received the direct divine sanction. Society as a product of nature can never be a good society, because moral perfection can be found exclusively in a Christian society. He expected Christianity not only to add to natural society the orientation towards supernature but also those elements that are required to make social authority lawful; and thereby clearly shows that he is capable of envisaging a natural society which can exist without Christian sanction. The same inadequate approach towards Aristotle is shown when he says that the temporal *regnum* exists by natural instinct and consent. Its laws are sufficient for an orderly life and for happiness in this world. But the perfect society exists only when the natural *regnum* is either subject to or replaced by the spiritual *regnum*.[2]

A very much weaker attempt at a theory of a natural State

[1] Quoted by A. Gwynn, *The English Austin Friars*, London, 1940, p. 61.
[2] *De Regimine Christiano*, in R. Scholz, op. cit., p. 142.

can be found in Augustinus Triumphus (*d.* 1328). He distinguished between human law, which can be made and unmade by men; natural law, which has been made for men and angels but can never be unmade; and the *lex aeterna*, which is neither made nor unmade and is divine law.[1] He knew such a law as *iustitia naturalis* which he said is violated whenever men are subject to restraint and compulsion; for, since men are born naturally with a free will, every tyrant violates nature. But what he really meant by 'nature' is explained immediately by the statement that therefore 'tyranni a Papa sunt puniendi . . .'.[2] Again he recoiled from the admission that there are any natural standards of justice independent of divine law as administered by the Pope or the Church.

These persistent attempts to make use of Aristotelian ideas bear witness first to the enormous influence of Aristotle[3] even over those who were partly at least avowed opponents of Thomism and secondly to the fact that by the beginning of the fourteenth century the political structure of the Western world was such that society and the secular State could no longer be looked upon as something that had to be superseded by divine law. The

[1] *Summa de Potestate Ecclesiastica*, Romae, 1584, Qu. 44, III ad Resp.

[2] Op. cit., Qu. 26, IV.

[3] Grabmann has collected very much material for the study of Aristotle's influence on political theory during the later Middle Ages. But his interpretation of it is inadequate. He simply lists authors under two headings as to whether there was an Aristotelian influence or not. (*Studien über den Einfluss der aristotelischen Philosophie auf die mittelalterlichen Theorien über das Verhältnis von Kirche zu Staat.* Sitzungsberichte der bayrischen Ak. d/. Wissenschaften. Philos-Philol. Klasse, München, 1934.)

Many authors merely used Aristotelian logic and certain principles of Aristotelian metaphysics but did not so much as mention Aristotle's theory of the natural origin of society and the state. In this sense we find that Ptolemy of Lucca in his *Determinatio compendiora de jurisdictione imperii*, 1281, Ch. VII, uses an Aristotelian concept: the Pope must use the Emperor as an instrument, as the soul uses the body as an instrument. And similarly Alvarius Pelagius, *De Planctu Ecclesiae*, I, 40, K. The principle of Aristotle's metaphysics that in every species there must be one object which serves as 'metrum et mensura' (*Metaphysics*, Bk. 10) is used by Dominicus Venetus in his *De Potestate Papae* (Grabmann, op. cit., p. 112) to prove that there must be one power to serve as measure and norm for the others. Also Rodrigo Sanchez de Arrevalo makes use of Aristotle (*Metaphysics*, XII, 10): there must be one guiding principle to preserve order and to avoid conflict. Hence Pope and Emperor cannot be

modern State under Philip le Bel, Edward I and Louis of Bavaria was too potent a factor not to be recognized in its own right. It is obvious that its outspoken defenders such as John of Paris, Nogaret and Marsilius should have accepted it without divine sanction. But what is significant is that even its avowed opponents felt that they could no longer afford to brush its claims aside and to condemn it outright as the product of sin. Nevertheless the authors whom we have discussed, did not understand the meaning of the Thomistic synthesis sufficiently clearly to make full use of it. Instead they paid a mere lip-service to the important Aristotelian influence and under the pressure of the political battle reverted to the pre-Thomistic idea which has become known as political Augustinianism.[1] The basic idea of political Augustinianism was that justice is a supernatural and not a natural concept, and that therefore the degree of justice present in any society is exactly proportionate to the degree to which that society is subject to the Church. Nevertheless the post-Thomistic stage of political Augustinianism, is, with notable exceptions of course, though hardly less extreme in its claims for the Papacy than the pre-Thomistic stage, characterized by the attempt to take greater

equal. (*De Anima*, Bk. 2–3) St. Antoninus uses Aristotle in this way: *Summa Theologica* III, iii, §11; and Scott-Pearson has noted a similar influence of Aristotle on Cartwright in his *Church and State*, Cambridge, 1928, Ch. VI.

All this may be of great interest to the historian of pure philosophy but proves nothing in the history of political thought. For the one principle of Aristotelian philosophy which wrought a change in the long tradition of political Augustinianism, the natural theory of society, was not accepted by any of these authors. What one should note therefore is the absence of a general Aristotelian influence rather than the presence of certain metaphysical concepts of Aristotle.

At the same time it escaped Grabmann that just the theory of natural society, so important from the point of view of the history of political thought, was present in Alvarius Pelagius, op. cit., I, 41, G. Grabmann simply quoted the judgement of the editor N. Iung to the contrary. If one does not notice this Aristotelian influence in fourteenth-century Augustinianism, one cannot do justice to its exponents and must fail to notice the important distinction between pre- and post-Thomistic political Augustinianism.

[1] For political Augustinianism see H. X. Arquillière, *L'Augustinisme Politique*, Paris, 1934 and E. Bernheim, *Mittelalterliche Zeitanschauungen in ihrem Einfluss auf Politik und Geschichte*, Tübingen, 1918.

account of the purely natural features of the secular State and to avail itself for that purpose of Aristotle's *Politics*. But they did not understand how they should use Aristotle in the Christian sense: and so we find that after having toyed with him for some time they dropped him like a hot brick as soon as they approached the question of the relationship between Church and State.

2

It was indeed left to the sixteenth century to realize the potentialities of a Christian Aristotle in political thought. Some sixteenth-century thinkers described the sixteenth-century State in terms of Aristotelian politics and at the same time recognized in that State not a final end in itself, but brought it into a co-operative relationship with the Church and thus ordered it in regard to the hierarchy of ends. This revival of Aristotle was very largely the work of Richard Hooker in England and of Cardinal Bellarmine on the Continent. Francisco Suarez followed along the same lines and gave a more systematic exposition of the theory of law connected with these ideas. The connexion between Hooker and Suarez has been noted,[1] and though historians have been aware of this late sixteenth-century natural-law school, they have generally failed to see it in its correct historical setting. This revival has always been looked upon as the beginning of the great natural-law schools of thought which culminated both in the jurisprudence of the following and in the Deism and rational enlightenment of the eighteenth century.[2]

[1] Cp. N. Sykes, in Hearnshaw ed. *The Social and Political ideas of some great thinkers of the sixteenth and seventeenth centuries* 1926; J. W. Allen, *Political thought in the sixteenth century*. London, 1928, p. 188.

[2] Cp. W. Dilthey, *Weltanschauung und Analyse des Menschen seit Renaissance und Reformation*, Leipzig, 1921, p. 103; and O. v. Gierke, *The Development of Political Theory*, London, 1939, p. 73; A. Lang, *The Reformation and Natural Law*, in *Calvin and the Reformation*, New York, 1909, explains how the Protestants who had started by denying natural law were driven back to natural law when they realized that a further appeal to revelation on their part would remain ineffective, for it stood against someone else's appeal to revelation. So they fell back on the medieval tradition, the *ius naturale* of St. Thomas. Lang

There can be little doubt that Grotius owed a great deal to the Spanish Thomists and that Hooker exercised a very strong influence on English rationalism and enlightenment. But this must not blind us to the fact that all this was purely accidental; that the sixteenth-century natural-law school does not represent the first sign of rationalistic enlightenment, but the last great flowering of scholasticism; and that Richard Hooker was one of its chief representatives. And yet, just because both Suarez and Hooker proved so influential during the succeeding centuries, we must state once more that the modern world was not born through the decay and failure of medieval thought and thus as a reaction against the Middle Ages; but evolved out of the very fullness of the best that medieval thought had to offer.

The work of Bellarmine and Suarez was the direct result of the revival of scholasticism which had been initiated in Spain by Vittoria and his school. Aware of and perturbed by the fact that the spread and popularity of Occam and of Nominalism had paved the way for Protestantism[1], these Spanish philosophers could see in Thomism the safest defence against Protestantism. It is very much more difficult to explain the revival of Thomism in England. There is little evidence that Hooker was unusually perturbed by Nominalist tendencies and therefore no ground for

sees in Hooker and Grotius the protagonists of this development. To this I would reply that nothing can be gained by classing Hooker as a Protestant, especially since there were Protestants left by the end of the century who denied the validity of natural law, and that the similarity between Grotius and Hooker is more apparent than real. To Hooker natural law is part of the divine fabric of the universe; or rather the structure that sustains the universe. It is grounded directly on the conception of God as the creator of that universe. In Grotius, natural law is derived from the dictate of right reason and the principles of self-evidence and does not stand in need of a divine will or reason, as he himself pointed out. W. K. Jordan, *The Development of Religious Toleration in England*, London, 1932, Vol. I, p. 232, accepts uncritically the view of Buckle that Hooker's rationalism, as all rationalism, implied scepticism; and that Hooker must therefore be regarded as a force making for religious toleration. Buckle was not aware of the fact that to Hooker rationalism did not mean scepticism because he understood reason in the wide sense. Cp. Chapter II.

[1] For Occam as a preparation for Luther, see Hermelink, op. cit., pp. 96, 133. Cp. F. X. Arnold, *Die Staatslehre des Kardinal Bellarmin*, München, 1934, p. 1.

supposing that he simply followed the Spanish example. And there was nothing in the curriculum of Oxford University beyond the usual tradition of scholasticism which might have influenced him extraordinarily.[1] Little that might be of any help is known of his early college days at Corpus Christi, and the only decidedly Aristotelian influence in Oxford during the latter part of the sixteenth century was that of John Case, a Catholic.[2] After the resignation of his fellowship, Case had obtained permission from the University to hold classes in his home and he published several works on Aristotle's philosophy. But it is unlikely that Case was a factor in a larger movement, nor is it probable that he ever came into any close contact with Hooker. Failing any other explanation, the historian can but conclude that Hooker had enough intellectual acumen and insight to strike out on a new path—once his analysis of the situation had shown him that that was the right path. The fact that he did not constantly quote St. Thomas or ever expressly discuss the significance of the latter's adaptation of Aristotle, also seems to indicate that Hooker did not think of himself as part of a larger movement which was striving consciously for a Thomistic revival; but rather felt that he was merely promoting a philosophy which was in itself adequate and reasonable.

3

Nulla potestas nisi a Deo is the key-principle of all Christian political thought. No man, according to Christian doctrine, can be coerced in any way unless the coercion takes place with the sanction of God. St. Thomas, through his adaptation of Aristotle, had shown how it was possible to look upon such a purely natural process as the formation of a society and the establishment of governmental authority, provided it was ordered in regard to the higher, supernatural end of human existence, as the work of God.

[1] For Hooker's education and the influence of Oxford see A. P. d'Entrèves, *Riccardo Hooker*, Torino, 1932.
[2] For John Case's life and teaching see *D.N.B.* and W. R. Sorley, *History of English Philosophy*, Cambridge, 1920, p. 8.

And these potentialities of Thomist philosophy were for the first time fully and consciously exploited by Hooker. His theory in that respect is completely identical with that of Bellarmine and Suarez; but to him belongs greater credit because he forestalled his great Jesuit contemporaries and because, unlike them, he could not draw upon an unbroken tradition of Thomist philosophy. Confronted with such a powerful institution, bursting with vitality, as the Tudor State, Hooker's thoughts were naturally directed towards Aristotle, and, because he was a Christian, towards the Thomistic Aristotle.

The essence of Aristotle's political theory is that man is by natural inclination a social animal; and that he needs his fellowmen in order to provide for the needs of his material as well as of his intellectual life. To achieve well-being, men must live in society. But if men are to live together in societies, there must be an institution which organizes societies in such a way that they will not harm one another. That is to say, the establishment of a government or of some form of public authority, is the natural consequence of man's social nature. In this way it is possible to deduce the necessity and justification of public authority from human nature. There is no mention of any form of contract or of any voluntary submission. There was, on the assumption that men were by nature social animals, no need to introduce the notion of contract at all. The formation of society and the establishment of government was as natural a process as the growth of an apple. We find these ideas explained in *The Laws of Ecclesiastical Polity*, Book I, chapter x; in Suarez' *De Legibus ac Deo Legislatore*, Book III, chapter i; and in Bellarmine in *De Laicis*, chapters 5 and 6, and in his *De Potestate Summi Pontificis*, chapters 3 and 5.[1] From all this it follows as a corollary that, by natural law, all power resides in the community as a whole.[2]

It appears then that that theory is based upon the intimate connexion between the existence of society and of the State which governs it. Society and State are not based upon a contract in natural law, but are due to the working in man of the very same

[1] See also his *De Verbo Dei*, III, 9.

[2] Hooker, op. cit., I. x. 8; Suarez, op. cit., III. ii. 3, 4.

efficacy which he, as a created being, exercises owing to the goodness of God.[1] God of course is the primary cause of everything that happens; but owing to the fact that in His generosity He has enabled human beings to function naturally, He is only the indirect cause of all the things they do; when they follow their natural instinct and when they discover the law of reason, they are performing natural operations which depend on God only in the second instance. State and society, just like the dictates of reason, are the creation of God through the medium of man's natural inclination and his natural reason. Thus the right of society, and the authority which it exercises, are vindicated as natural and suitable to the condition of man as created by God.

The New Monarchy had thus found one of its many possible justifications. But just because ultimately the functioning of the natural faculties depended on God, the secular State was through the very nature of its origin and its mode of existence ordered with a view to the higher, supernatural end which God had appointed to man. There could be no conflict between the secular State and the organ of government which regulated that part of human existence which concerned the salvation of man's soul, the Church. On this theory, the two could work together; each in its proper sphere, enabling man to exercise his efficacy as a second cause, i.e. to lead a natural life—and yet to live in such a way that the salvation of his soul would not be endangered. The New Monarchy was thus put into a relation to the Church which would assure to the former a full, if limited, freedom to exercise its vitality with vigour, and which at the same time would safeguard the place of the latter in the *Respublica Christiana*.

Bellarmine and Suarez objected to the theory of direct papal power in temporal matters. They asserted that the end of temporal society is *bonus sed non ultimus*. In other words: the secular State has a function of its own but needs to be supplemented by the Church. So far they agreed with Hooker. They differed merely in their conception of the Church. But it is important to remember that Hooker too looked upon the Church as a supplement to the State. He was no Erastian and would have disapproved of the Erastian tendencies of Anglicanism after Laud.

[1] Cp. Chapter II. p. 52.

Bellarmine achieved this result by developing his theory of the *potestas indirecta in temporalibus*.[1] Hooker achieved the same result by putting forward the apology of the Tudor Constitution which we have discussed in the preceding chapter. The two theories are of course quite different and in certain points even contradictory; but the important point is that both were developed with the help of Thomistic philosophy on an Aristotelian basis. Hooker and Bellarmine realized the potentialities of Thomism in different ways. But if they had not been able to avail themselves of the Thomistic method of dealing with Aristotle they could only either have rejected the right of the modern State to an independent existence and followed in the footsteps of previous Christian political thought which ultimately sacrificed natural to revealed law; or have accepted the modern State and left Christian requirements to look after themselves in the fashion of Machiavelli or the sixteenth-century adaptations of Marsilius. The Thomistic theory of the efficacy of second causes, and the Thomistic conception of reason operative in man who thus participates in the divine nature and who makes thus the *lex naturalis* strictly dependent—just as divine law itself—on the *lex aeterna*, was taken up by both Hooker and Bellarmine. It enabled them to develop the political ideas of which St. Thomas had only furnished the very rudiments and which his disciples and followers had not been able to interpret in this way until the stress of sixteenth-century circumstances compelled them to take a stand in the matter.[2]

The issue was joined with the representatives of the first type of Christian philosophy which we have discussed in the first chapter and which historians have called political Augustinianism. It is a moot point to what extent St. Augustine himself was the founder of political Augustinianism.[3] But there can be very little

---

[1] For a full exposition of this doctrine see F. X. Arnold, op. cit.

[2] For Hooker's theories see Chapter II; for Bellarmine see F. X. Arnold, op. cit., and for Suarez, H. Rommen, *Die Staatslehre des F. Suarez*, München-Gladbach, 1926.

[3] Cp. J. N. Figgis, *The Political Aspects of St. Augustine's City of God*, London, 1921, and the criticism of C. H. McIlwain, *The Growth of political thought in the West*, London, 1932, pp. 157 ff.

doubt that the influence of St. Augustine's teaching often countenanced the doctrines which have been called political Augustinianism. There is, moreover, an obvious connexion between political and philosophical Augustinianism; for both types of thought tend to deny the efficacy of second causes and to ascribe all truth and goodness that can be found in man and nature to the direct workings of divine grace. With St. Augustine himself, the tendency to absorb natural law in supernatural justice and the right of the State in the right of the Church was only one of many tendencies; but with his followers in the Middle Ages this tendency became a fixed doctrine; largely owing to the prevalence of philosophical Augustinianism.[1] It was this tendency in Augustinian thought against which Hooker, Bellarmine and Suarez directed their attacks and against which they vindicated the right of the secular State against the Church; and the function of natural law against divine law. It is therefore not really correct to look upon this criticism as a reaction against the apotheosis of divine law achieved by the reformers.[2] This criticism was rather the first attempt to stem the tide of political Augustinianism by arguments other than those used by Marsilius. It was certainly neither a Protestant reaction to early Protestant thought nor a Catholic reassertion of Thomism against Protestantism. To understand the movement correctly it is necessary to abandon altogether the idea that the intellectual world was divided into two hostile camps, opposed to one another in all issues.

The movement for the exposition of a Thomistic Aristotle cut across the conventional boundaries of Protestantism and Catholicism: defenders and opponents were to be found on either side. This throws also an important light on the whole question of whether it is correct to cling too rigidly to the conventional division of the Western world into Protestants and Catholics; the boundary was set up on the basis of a purely political distinction, i.e. according as to whether a man accepted the Papacy or not. But for purposes of the history of ideas the distinction does not hold good. There were ideas and religious attitudes which

[1] See H. X. Arquillière, op. cit., pp. 4–5.

[2] This is the view of A. Lang, op. cit., which is also accepted by Prof. A. P. d'Entrèves, *The Medieval Contribution to Political Thought*, Oxford, 1939.

were both defended and opposed in either camp. In this sense Hooker's attack was directed against the Puritans; and Suarez' and Bellarmine's against the exponents of political Augustinianism proper. But that Puritanism and political Augustinianism proper amounted to one and the same thing is shown by the fact that sixteenth-century Puritan political doctrine was essentially the obvious descendant of political Augustinianism. From the point of view of pure political thought, there was very little difference between the attacks of the Puritan Cartwright and of the ultra-Catholic Carerius on the independence and autonomy of the secular State, besides the fact that the one looked upon the Congregation and the other upon the Papacy as the true source of divine law.

The direction of Hooker's arguments has been described in a previous chapter. Let us now glance at the analogous trend of thought in Suarez. Suarez begins by listing the arguments which are adduced in favour of the view that all human authority and government is born of sin and therefore bad; and that therefore God is the only true and sovereign ruler.[1] It is firstly alleged that Lucan thought Alexander to have been nothing but a fortunate freebooter[2] and that this was also the meaning of St. Augustine.[3]

Secondly it is stated that St. Augustine said that God gave man dominion over fish, fowls and beasts[4] but not over men.[5] Gregory the Great too said that all authority of man over man was introduced through sin and acquired by usurpation.[6] And finally people are fond of quoting Isaiah, xxxiii. v. 22: 'The Lord is our judge, the Lord is our king, the Lord is our lawgiver.' On these authorities the defenders of these views conclude that the advent of grace has superseded all natural efforts to establish a just form of government, to exercise authority on purely rational grounds, and has rendered any form of natural law superfluous through the revelation of divine law.

---

[1] *De Legibus ac Deo Legislatore*, III. i. 1.
[2] *The Civil War*, Bk. X.
[3] *De Civitate Dei*, IV, 4.
[4] *Genesis*, v. 26.
[5] *De Civitate Dei*, XIX, 15.
[6] *Moralia*, Bk. XXI, Ch. XI; *Regulae Pastorales*, Pt. II, Ch. 6.

As a result, Suarez wrote, these people think that all public authority ought to be derived from the Pope, and that no kind of government that is not directly subject to the Church is a lawful government.[1] As the particular defenders of this theory he mentioned among others St. Antoninus,[2] Pelagius,[3] and Augustinus Triumphus.[4] On the whole the arguments of these men are based on numerous papal decrees, on quotations from the Scriptures, on the practice of the great medieval Popes and finally on the argument that unless there is one supreme Head in all Christendom, there would be dissension.[5]

Bellarmine's political philosophy is a conscious criticism of exactly the same theories; but being a greater controversialist than Suarez, his criticism is more elaborate and the sweep of his attack covers a wider field. It is especially noteworthy that he included the Anabaptists among the special opponents of political Aristotelianism,[6] for they taught that the true Christ has no need of magistrates, and that since the revelation of divine law all natural law and its institutions, such as the secular State, have become obsolete. He also pointed out that the Anabaptists themselves had quoted Gregory the Great's *Moralia*, Bk. XXXI, Ch. XI—the very same passage to which Suarez was to take exception in connexion with the extreme claims on behalf of the Papacy. But Bellarmine went further and traced these ideas—on the Protestant side at least—back to Wycliff's theory that all dominion is based on divine grace and that without grace, i.e. on purely natural grounds, there can be no lawful dominion at all.[7]

On the Catholic side, Bellarmine, criticized [8] the denial of the natural-law state in Hugo of St. Victor[9] and in Bernard of

[1] *Defensio Fidei*, III. v. 4.

[2] S.Th. Pt. III, Tit. XXII, Ch. V. §§13-17.

[3] *De Planctu Ecclesiae, passim.*

[4] *Summa de Potestate Ecclesiastica, passim.*

[5] *Defensio Fidei*, III. v. 5.

[6] *Antitheses Christi, veri et falsi*, No. 7, Albae Juliae, 1568.

[7] *De Laicis*, Ch. 8.

[8] *De S. Pontif*, lib. 5. Ch. 5.

[9] *De Sacramentis*, I, 2, Pt. 2.

Clairvaux,[1] and in the preface of his treatise *De Potestate Summi Pontificis* he expressly referred to a large number of political Augustinians, the most important of which are Augustinus Triumphus,[2] Alvarius Pelagius,[3] and Giles of Rome.[4] He found the very same ideas in the writings of his Catholic contemporaries, and among them he singled out A. Carerius and Th. Bozius[5] for special criticism. Especially against the former, Bellarmine carried on a vigorous polemic and characterized his position thus: 'Pagina prima scribit, apud eos qui vivebant in lege naturae, fuisse dominium usurpatum.'[6] Carerius in fact denied the efficacy of second causes: temporal kings, he argued, have no power at all except in so far as they derive it from the productive principle of spiritual things. Hence the Pope alone can be the true source of all temporal power.[7]

Suarez' and Bellarmine's polemic against the Augustinian tendency to absorb natural law into supernatural was carried out on the conviction that Thomistic Aristotelianism was correct. It was carried on for the benefit of the New Monarchy which was fighting its last and decisive round with the Papacy in the sixteenth century. Suarez and Bellarmine realized that nothing could be gained for Catholicism if the Papal claims were pressed to such an extreme that they could not be reconciled with the most powerful factor on the sixteenth-century political scene. It was better, they thought, to defend a moderate position and thus to put forward a theory which would enable the New Monarchy to preserve its self-respect and at the same time to continue its allegiance to the Papacy. For, needless to say, the defenders of

[1] *De Consideratione*, lib. 4, Ch. 4.
[2] *Summa de Eccl. Potestate*, Qu. I, art. I
[3] *De Planctu Ecclesiae*, I, 13.
[4] *De Eccl. Potestate*, I, 30.
[5] Th. Bozius, died 1610; *De signis Ecclesiae Dei*, Rome, 1591; *De Iure Status*, Cologne, 1594; A. Carerius *De Potestate Romani Pontificis adversus Impios Politicos*, Patavii, 1599.
[6] See le Bachelet, *Auctarium Bellarminianum*, Paris, 1913, pp. 428 ff.
[7] For the whole controversy between Bellarmine and Carerius see J. Brodrick, *The Life and Work of Blessed Robert Francis Bellarmine*, London, 1928, Vol. I, pp. 258-9; For Bellarmine's theory of the efficacy of second causes see his *De Potestate Summi Pontificis*, Ch. 14.

political Augustinianism insisted on the direct power of the Papacy in both temporal and spiritual affairs and denied the secular State, based on a purely natural law, its right of existence. Against this Suarez and Bellarmine asserted the independent right to legislate of the secular State, postulating for the Pope a mere indirect right to interfere in matters temporal. The justice which they thus claimed to be inherent in the secular State without Papal sanction was due to the fact that the secular State was based upon natural law. Or rather, both the secular State and natural law were the products of man's natural ability to find the path appointed to him by God; the one being discovered by reason and the other being the result of man's natural inclination towards a social life.

With Hooker the polemic was exclusively directed against the Puritan upholders of political Augustinianism; but this meant merely a shift in emphasis, for they only substituted the congregation with its presbyters for the Pope. The underlying idea was the same: a State which existed for natural reasons only, and was neither controlled nor sustained by the vitalizing force of divine law as interpreted by the congregation, could not be a just State and had therefore no claim on human obedience.

It is useful therefore to recall briefly the history of political Augustinianism in order to observe how its sixteenth-century Catholic and sixteenth-century Puritan argumentation had sprung from the same Augustinian roots. The central question was the place of divine grace in human life. The further question, whether the channel through which this grace flowed into the world was the Pope or the congregation's interpretation of the Bible was philosophically only of secondary importance: for more often than not it was decided by purely accidental historical circumstances. What is important for the historian of ideas is that both Cartwright and Carerius agreed in their opinion that the secular State could claim a Christian's allegiance only if it were the handmaid of the Church.[1] They themselves at the time

---

[1] Cartwright was too circumspect ever to pronounce this doctrine so bluntly, because it was too obviously seditious. But both Hooker and Whitgift took it that that was what he meant. Carerius could afford to be more frank, for he had the Pope's protection. For a while Bellarmine's work against Carerius was put on the index.

would certainly have maintained that the most important issue was the one on which they differed, i.e. Pope or congregation; but looking backwards the historian to-day can discern in both the same basic ideology of political Augustinianism.

According to the conception of political Augustinianism the revelation of the divine Word had split History into two. Before the revelation, man, depraved by sin, had led a life according to the instincts of his corrupted nature. With such a life and the social organization that was appropriate to it, he could not hope ever to reach the beatific vision. But when God in His infinite goodness had revealed the divine law through which man could by supernatural means be led to life eternal in spite of the corruption of his nature—a new leaf had been turned over in History. Henceforth the only true authority to be recognized by men was that of the divine law; to persist in following the authority of reason or the law of nature was not only superfluous but downright sinful; for it meant to refuse willingly the chance which God had offered to man for the salvation of his soul.

To St. Augustine therefore there were two kinds of men: those who lived *secundum spiritum vel Deum* and those who lived *secundum hominem vel carnem*. Through Christ the *Civitas Dei* had been established as the Church.[1] One could be a member of the *Civitas Dei* only by being a member of the Church, for the Church is 'umbra quaedam et imago civitatis huius'.[2] *Iustitia, Pax* and *Humilitas* are the characteristics of the *Civitas Dei*. St. Augustine does not exactly deny the possibility of the presence of the first two in the *Civitas Diaboli* but says that, if at all, they are only very imperfectly present. *Superbia*, however, in the *Civitas Diaboli* corresponds to *Humilitas* in the *Civitas Dei*. But in any case, true *Iustitia, Pax* and *Humilitas* are spiritual virtues and as such different from the purely rational concepts of a similar nature in pagan philosophy.[3] They must therefore be presumed to flow from the law administered by the spiritual authority. The purely natural system of society cannot possess them; and thus it follows that a State

---

[1] Cp. E. Bernheim, op. cit., p. 18.

[2] Scil. 'supernae sanctorum civitatis'; *De Civitate Dei*, xv, 2.

[3] See *De Civitate Dei*, xix, 21, where St. Augustine criticizes Cicero's purely rational concept of justice.

which is not under the direct control and supervision of the Church is not a just State—for such a State is merely a bad contrivance of man's depraved nature. The State itself, though of pagan and natural origin, could become a Christian State only by its submission to the Church, because *Iustitia* has become a spiritual concept. St. Augustine himself might have hesitated to state these last conclusions categorically. But his disciples and intellectual heirs did not hesitate. And, since *ex nihilo nihil fit*, it is probably legitimate to assume that St. Augustine's thoughts were moving in that direction.

In all this there is not a single idea which we shall not meet again in sixteenth-century Puritanism. For the fact that for many centuries the Church came to be identified with the Pope is from the standpoint of these ideas themselves a historical accident. The development of these ideas has been treated adequately by many historians[1] and there is no need to go over the same ground again. It is well to remember, however, that the ambitions of Gregory VII, Innocent III and Boniface VIII were not so much inspired by pure statecraft as by grandiose designs to satisfy the political convictions of the majority of medieval men who, as far as they thought at all, thought in terms of Augustinian philosophy. The plan for Papal supremacy grew out of the idea of the primacy and sole efficacy of the spiritual, and of the denial of the natural law right of the secular State to be autonomous even in its own sphere.

During the thirteenth century with the adaptation of Aristotle to Christian philosophy, however, political Augustinianism itself seemed at first to undergo a slight change. As we observed above, there is scarcely one among the major defenders of the Papacy during the great struggle of the early fourteenth century who did not recognize the strength and cogency of the Aristotelian argument as to the social instinct of man. The decisive feature of post-Thomistic political Augustinians, then, is not so much that they consider the State in itself the product of sin, but that they do not manage to avail themselves fully of the Christian Thomist Aristotle. When the crucial moment arrived they could see no other way for the preservation of the primacy of the spiritual power

[1] See E. Bernheim, op. cit.; H. X. Arquillière, op. cit.; J. P. Whitney, *Hildebrandine Essays*, Cambridge, 1932.

than a straight return to the original tenets of political Augustinianism.

We have had occasion before to note the Aristotelian elements
in Augustinus Triumphus. At times this author managed in fact
to draw a distinction between the powers exercised by Emperor
and Pope and to assure each an independent sphere of action.[1]
But he could not proceed with such arguments; for when he came
to the point where he had to assert as a Christian, 'ut animalis et
temporalis, seu carnalis homo per spiritualem examinatur et pro-
batur. . .'[2] he does not succeed in showing as St. Thomas had done
that an examination by reason may in itself be an examination by
God, for 'signatum est super nos lumen tui vultus, Domine'.[3] Augustinus Triumphus instead was compelled to revert to the simple and
more naïve conception: everything that is just depends on divine
reason, i.e. on the *lex aeterna*. Hence all law has to conform to the
lex aeterna; and as the *lex aeterna* is divine reason, the Pope as vicar
of God is the only judge of what is just law. 'Unde nulla lex populo
christiano est danda nisi ipsius Papae auctoritate.'[4] The quintessence
of Augustinus Triumphus's theory is the distinction between
tyrannical and political dominion. The former has existed ever
since Cain and is a punishment for sin;[5] and the latter is derived
from the *sacerdotium* and exists as a *remedium peccati*.[6] And from

[1] Op. cit., Qu. 26, IV, ad Resp.; Cp. also Pelagius, op. cit., I. 37, T: 'in
imperio ius habere papam negatur' and ibid., I, 68: 'Distincta autem quantum
ad hoc . . . sunt officia romanorum pontificum et imperatorum.'

[2] Op. cit., Qu. 41, III.

[3] Cp. also Pelagius, op. cit. I, 40, C: '. . . nam totus homo Christianus spiritualis
est', and he concluded therefore that the spiritual power alone must be supreme.

[4] Op. cit., Qu. 44, I, ad Resp.

[5] It is important to note that this theory was also put forward by Luther
and has become since one of the characteristic doctrines of so-called Lutheran
Protestant thought. During the present century it was put forward by the
Protestant Gogarthen. He supported the Nazi régime in Germany because it
was so tyrannical and therefore such a good punishment for Germany's sins.

[6] Op. cit., Qu. 36, I, ad Resp.: This was repeated almost verbatim by St.
Antoninus almost two hundred years later. Cp. his *Summa Theologica*, III. v.
xxiv. For the rest, St. Antoninus seems to have been more of a Thomist; cp.
ibid., I, xi ff. But he could not integrate Thomist ideas properly. He simply
quoted Augustinus Triumphus because he could find nothing in St. Thomas
on the subject.

these premisses there followed all the other propositions put forward by Augustinus Triumphus on the complete supremacy of the Pope.[1]

James of Viterbo showed a greater ingenuity in dealing with these problems than any of his predecessors, Giles of Rome included. He had understood Aristotle sufficiently well to see that there was nothing wrong with a society and a State that had resulted from the natural propensities of man. But, unlike St. Thomas, he failed to integrate the natural end of man provided for by natural society with the supernatural end of man provided for by the Church, in a hierarchy of ends. To James of Viterbo, the laws of the temporal *regnum* existed by natural instinct, and dominion was exercised 'communis consensu communitatis hominum'. These laws were sufficient for an orderly life and for human happiness in this world. But to this natural society James of Viterbo contrasted Christian society, the laws of which guide men towards their true and final destination, the salvation of their souls. In such societies power is not derived from the natural propensities of men, but from God, i.e. from his vicar, the Pope.[2] He thus showed that he fully realized the strength of the Aristotelian argument that the State is not the result of or the punishment for sin. But he failed to elaborate a theory in which State and Church are made to collaborate. In his view a society is either natural or Christian; he could not bring himself to the understanding that it could be both. The view that nature itself could possess as a second cause a complete efficacy and yet be the 'coadjutor' of God—in the Thomistic sense—he could not for one reason or another accept. That he was, in the last analysis, living in the ideology of St. Augustine is clearly shown by the following argument: the *regnum* is the most perfect of all types of community. But its real properties are only present in the Church. Hence the Church is the *regnum* par excellence; and therefore Cicero's definition of the *respublica*, as we find it in St. Augustine, applies really only to the Church.[3]

[1] Op cit., Quaestiones 36–45.
[2] *De Regimine Christiano*, II, 3.
[3] Op. cit., I, 1–6.

As is well known, the most drastic example of the two conflicting theories of society is to be found in the writings of Giles
of Rome. In his great treatise, *De Ecclesiastica Potestate*, written
twenty years after his attempts at Aristotelianism, all he could
get himself to admit was that a certain amount of temporal power
existed so that laymen would not lose their self-respect completely.[1] But the most significant part of this work is the section which
deals with the right to exercise dominion and the right to possess
property. Through sin, Giles argued, men have lost all right to
the possession of property. Only when men have been partly
regenerated through the rites of the Church are they again
worthy of possessing property.[2] Therefore it is actually only the
Church which has a universal dominion and a right to property.
All human right to possession is thus derived through the Church.[3]
A natural right to property and to the exercise of authority is not
a lawful right.

It is difficult to imagine a more radical statement of political
Augustinianism and of the denial of the validity of natural law.
Giles of Rome was one of the most influential teachers of the
Augustinian order and among his fellow-friars his doctrines
found a ready and wide acceptance.[4] It was in fact through the
English Augustinian friars that these ideas were spread in Oxford
towards the end of the fourteenth century, and it was their work,
notably that of Fitz-Ralph, which is 'the essential link in the chain
which unites Wyclif's *De Civili Dominio*, published in 1367, to the
De Ecclesiae Potestate which Giles of Rome had written in Rome
seventy-five years before that date'.[5] It seems indeed that the

[1] II. xiii.

[2] Op. cit., II. viii.

[3] Ibid., II, vii.

[4] See R. Scholz, *Unbekannte kirchenpolitische Streitschriften*, Rome, 1911,
Pt. I, pp. 16–17.

[5] A. Gwynn, *The English Austin Friars*, Oxford, 1940, p. 71. Cp. Richardi
Radulphi *Summa in Quaestionibus Armenorum et Graecorum*, first published in
Paris, 1512, Ch. 4, Bk. 10: all *dominium* is based on divine grace and without
that grace there can be no *dominium*. In 1390 Woodford had pointed out that
Fitz-Ralph was responsible for Wyclif's doctrine: *Wodfordus adversus Joh.
Wiclefum*, ed. Brown, London, 1690, I, pp. 237, 240; Thomas Waldensis was of
the same opinion, lib. 2. *Doctrinalis Fidei*, Ch. 81 ff. And Bellarmine also knew
it: *De Laicis*, Ch. 8.

Oxford Austin friars gave strong support to Wyclif during the early part of his career[1] and only parted company, and then half-heartedly when he challenged the dogma of transubstantiation.[2] At this point the movement of political Augustinianism split into two over issues which were themselves quite irrelevant to political Augustinianism. And so we find the two branches, one Catholic, the other Protestant, in the sixteenth century, both bearing clear witness to the roots from which they had sprung. Neither Calvin nor Cartwright on the Protestant side, nor any of the most extreme defenders of Papal supremacy on the Catholic side, added anything essential to the theory. They all held fast to the positions developed in Giles's second treatise and generally speaking maintained all those ideas which were completely untainted by any Aristotelian influence.

4

In the sixteenth century we meet the two branches of political Augustinianism in the forms of Presbyterianism, Calvinism or Puritanism and of ultra-Catholicism. We have no concern with the latter beyond noting that its political theory was based on a philosophy identical with that of Puritanism. But we must briefly trace the arguments of the Protestant side, for they had provoked Hooker's reply.

There are places where Calvin actually paid lip-service to natural law.[3] But this natural law is to Calvin not the dictate of right reason; in fact, since the human cognitive faculties have been destroyed or at least corrupted by the Fall, it cannot be known at all. But 'finis legis naturalis est, ut reddatur homo inexcusabilis'.[4] This is well in accordance with Calvin's theology: man cannot know the law; but if he disobeys it, he must suffer punishment—or rather, since he will disobey it, he is a sinner and can only be

[1] A. Gwynn, op cit., p. 234.
[2] Ibid, p. 262.
[3] *Institutes*, II, 2, 12; II, 213; II, 8, 1.
[4] Op. cit., II, 2, 22.

saved by God's grace. The complete denial of any natural law by Cartwright was then only a corollary to Calvin's teaching. The divine law of Moses was to be made the basis of the whole legal system of a society. The common law which was incompatible with it was to be abolished; lawyers were to throw away their textbooks and the clergy were to be considered experts in law.[1]

The State and the society which it ordered could therefore not be the work of nature either. To Calvin the State is the result of sin. If men were not sinful, no State would be necessary. The State was instituted by God in order to obliterate some of the worst effects of sin. And in that sense, it is 'ordo a Deo institutus'.[2] The great example of the correct secular order was the Jewish theocratic State under the judges.[3] The lex Mosis was perfect and immutable because it had been revealed by God Himself.[4] The Old Testament—as the direct revelation of divine law—yielded the true norm of the State; and hence it was imperative to establish a political order on this direct basis of divine law. And since the Church is the institution which is in possession of divine law, the State must conform in all particulars to the requirements of the Church.[5]

The secular State was therefore not looked upon as an institution which had grown in order to meet the natural social needs of men. To begin with, there was no obvious reason why God should not simply have abolished all magistrates when He revealed His law. Calvin at any rate, found it necessary to explain explicitly why they had continued to exist,[6] for there was no function or end proper to the secular State to fulfil. The State had the duty of the

---

[1] In Whitgift's *Works*, Parker Society, Vol. I, p. 273; Wyclif had expressed the same idea. See R. Seeberg, *Dogmengeschichte*, Leipzig, Vol. III, pp. 613 ff.

[2] Calvin's *Works*, Corpus Reformatorum, Vol. 57, p. 535. All references to Calvin's works are to the edition in the Corpus Reformatorum.

[3] Ibid., Vol. 52, p. 605; Vol. 54, p. 310.

[4] Ibid., Vol. 73, p. 174.

[5] Cartwright, in Whitgift's *Works*, Vol. III, p. 189.

[6] Op. cit., Vol. 64, p. 626.

'cura publicae honestatis'.[1] Its real purpose is 'ne idolatria, ne in Dei nomen sacrilegia ne adversus eius veritatem blasphemiae aliaeque reli gionis offensiones publice emergant ac in populum spargantur'.[2] Calvin could not imagine a real distinction between a crime against human law and an offence against divine law, for the former was to him completely absorbed by the latter. And so he could ask: 'unde inter fidei violationem et alia malificia discrimen nisi ex cerebro suo?'[3]

As a consequence, sixteenth-century Presbyterianism evolved the famous doctrine that the secular State was really only the handmaid or servant of the Church.[4] The Church is considered the only true and real society; and those of its members who are charged with serving it by enforcing the divine law are known as magistrates. But the magistrate, or in the case of England the Queen, will always remain a member of the Church; and for contravening its law she can be excommunicated. As a secular

---

[1] Ibid., Vol. 80, p. 267; Vol. 81, pp. 139, 143 ff.

[2] *Institutes*, last chapter; the same idea is expressed by the early medieval author, Jonas of Orléans, Reviron ed., p. 145.

[3] *Defensio Orthodoxae Fidei*, written against Servet.

[4] Calvin's *Works*, Vol. 68, p. 707; Vol. 29, p. 242; Vol. 53, p. 644, etc.— The princes are the *vicarii*, *legati*, lieutenants of God: Vol. 2, p. 1096; Vol. 25, p. 634; Vol. 26, p. 312; etc.—The princes are *Officiers de Dieu*: Vol. 25, p. 634; Vol. 26, p. 117, etc.—Magistrates are the instruments of God, Vol. 135, p. 152, but by using them He has not given up His own power: Vol. 25, p. 644. Travers, *Full and Plain Declaration*, 1574, p. 185; Cartwright, Whitgift's *Works*, Vol. I, p. 390.—And for medieval sources of the same idea see Isidor of Seville, *Sententiae*, lib. III, Ch. 51 in Migne, *Patrologia Latina*, Vol. CCCIII, Coll. 723-4: 'Ceterum intra ecclesiam potestates necessariae non essent, nisi ut, quod non prevalet sacerdos efficere per doctrine sermonem, potestas hoc imperet per discipline terrorem.' And Jonas of Orléans, Reviron ed., p. 145: 'Regale ministerium est populum Dei gubernare et regere cum equitate et iustitia . . .' To understand this passage correctly, it is necessary to remember St. Augustine's meaning of *Iustitia* as explained by Bellarmine: 'Idem Augustinus, *De Civitate Dei*, 19, 21, dicit apud infideles non posse esse iustitiam nec verum populum aut rempublicam. Sed vocat veram iustitiam et vera iura, quae ducunt ad vitam aeternam.' *De Laicis*, Ch. 8; and Alvarius Pelagius, *De Planctu Ecclesiae*, I, 39: 'Imperator . . . servus ecclesiae . . .' and the same author's *Speculum Regum* in R. Scholz, *Unbekannte kirchenpolitische Streitschriften*, Pt. II, p. 518.

authority which serves the natural needs of the community, she has no valid dominion at all. [1]

There is a never-ending controversy as to whether Calvin believed in the existence of natural law or not. Some historians have answered the question in the affirmative,[2] others in the negative.[3] Each side is able to produce a large selection of quotations from the voluminous writings of Calvin in support of their thesis. Little or no progress can be made if the question is put in this way—for it must appear from the fact that the documentary evidence is so conflicting that Calvin himself did not attribute much importance to the answering of that question. If one examines one of the passages most relevant to the question, one will find that Calvin's exposition of the subject is far from unequivocal: there are no sharp distinctions drawn between the meaning of nature and the meaning of grace, and he seems to withdraw with one hand what he has just granted with the other.[4] This points in a writer of such clarity as Calvin to the conclusion that he was not greatly interested in furnishing a definite answer to the abstract problem whether there was a valid natural law or not. We must therefore assume that the question which has puzzled historians has proved so intractable because it was an unhistorical question: historians have attempted to answer on behalf of Calvin a question which he himself had never asked— at least not in that form. Hence one cannot find a clear answer to it in his writings.

[1] For an exact definition of her duties as the servant of the Church see Cartwright in Whitgift's *Works*, Vol I, p. 386, and Scott-Pearson, *Thomas Cartwright and Elizabethan Puritanism*, Cambridge, 1925, p. 96, and the same author's *Church and State*, Cambridge, 1928, pp. 32–33. For medieval ideas on these lines see St. Ambrose, in Migne, *Patrologia Graeca*, Vol. VI, Coll. 1018AB: 'Imperator enim intra ecclesiam . . .' and Alvarius Pelagius, *De Planctu Ecclesiae*, I, 39; '. . . Imperator . . . filius est ecclesiae . . .'

[2] E. Doumergue, *J. Calvin*, Lausanne, 1917, V, p. 469; G. Gloede, *Theologia Naturalis bei Calvin*, Stuttgart, 1935, pp. 178 ff.; J. Bohatec, *Calvin's Lehre von Staat und Kirche*, Breslau, 1937, pp. 20–35; E. Brunner, *Justice and Social Order*, London, 1945, p. 233.

[3] K. Holl, *Gesammelte Aufsätze zur Kirchengeschichte*, Tübingen, 1927, I, 492; Hausherr, *Der Staat in Calvin's Gedankenwelt*, pp. 10, 60 ff.; H. Baron, *Calvin's Staatsanschauung*, Berlin, 1924; A. Lang, op. cit.

[4] *Institutes*, II, 2, xi–xv.

One will get a clearer view of the situation if one takes as one's point of departure a sixteenth-century criticism of Calvin's political thought such as that of Hooker. Hooker refused to see any significant difference between the ideas of Calvin himself and those of the Anabaptists and the English Puritans. To him the quintessence of their teachings was their Bibliolatry and their consequent denial of the justifiability of the purely natural State. It was therefore that problem, i.e. the question as to the justice inherent in a State which was the product of man's social inclinations, which occupied the foremost place in the discussion, and which we must also presume Calvin to have attempted to answer. The abstract question, as to the nature of natural law, was of minor significance and rarely found an unequivocal answer. But to the former question Calvin did give an unequivocal answer, which was taken up and applied by the various schools of English Presbyterianism and which did not differ very much from the Anabaptist views: Calvin was incapable of visualizing a State which was the natural product of man's natural inclinations. He was prepared to recognize existing States whether they were actually controlled by the Church or not: but only because the Scriptures affirmed that Kings reigned by the providence of divine wisdom;[1] i.e. not because human nature demanded it. This theory laid itself open to Hooker's criticism in that it was based upon an exclusive reliance on Scripture and thus on a denial of the efficacy of natural causes.

Once this was determined it was of comparatively little significance whether people followed the anti-revolutionary teaching of Calvin himself or inclined towards the subversive theology of the Anabaptists. What Hooker clearly saw was that Calvin's inability to recognize the inherent justice of the secular State, and his exclusive reliance on the efficacy of divine grace for the establishment of a just government, gave a blank cheque to anybody who for one reason or another decided to find fault with the Tudor Monarchy. It is in this sense that we must understand Calvin to occupy a position diametrically opposed to that of Hooker; whereas on the question of natural law proper Calvin's standpoint was not only not clearly defined but in some respects

[1] *Institutes*, IV, 20, vii.

144

resembled that of Hooker. So he explained for instance that certain things are always forbidden, but the special circumstances of time and place require the methods of enforcing obedience to this law to be changed.[1]

As far as Calvin's place in the history of political thought is concerned, the historians who have placed Calvin in direct opposition to Hooker by denying that he believed in natural law were, as far as the spirit if not as far as the letter is concerned, correct. For on the point which, to judge by the decisiveness with which Calvin pronounced on it, was really vital to the discussion, his theory is in direct contradiction to that of Hooker. Only in the matter of abstract natural law it is impossible to determine precisely the relation of the standpoints of Hooker and Calvin respectively.

With these ideas the development of political Augustinianism had reached its climax. And it was at this point that the first well-reasoned replies in the shape of a Thomistic Aristotelianism were brought forward by Hooker and Bellarmine. We cannot agree that all the problems were proposed and developed during the great controversy of the early fourteenth century. We have seen that these authors were still groping in the dark in that they did not really manage to formulate the problem clearly. For the problem was whether to accept the Thomistic Aristotle or not. Because of the failure of the fourteenth-century authors to avail themselves of St. Thomas's adaptation of Aristotle, they had been pushed by the force of circumstances, as upholders of Papal claims, towards political Augustinianism. And thus the ultimate shape of the problem remained obscured. It was only in the sixteenth century that the problem was clearly formulated. Then the great political controversy raged round Aristotle in the sense in which the great philosophical controversy of the thirteenth century had raged round him.

This revival of Aristotelianism in politics was the work of Suarez, Bellarmine and Hooker. Hardly known to each other, these men had joined forces and brought about a new heyday of Thomism towards the end of the sixteenth century. It was on the crest of this wave that the greatest intellectual achievements of

[1] *Institutes*, IV. 20. xi; *Laws of Eccl. Polity*, I. x. 6.

the Middle Ages, such as the belief in reason and the conception of a universal higher law, rode into the following century and became the basis for a new development in political thought in Grotius and Locke. Had the seventeenth century understood Bellarmine and Hooker more correctly as a Thomistic revival, they might have shied off these ideas. But as it was, Hooker and Bellarmine were taken at their face value, reinterpreted in terms of the then current philosophy and given their proper place in the history of the modern intellect. Looking backwards now, we can discern the transition from medieval to modern ways of thought just in that last great revival of Aristotelianism in the sixteenth century. Modern ways of thought, at least in this respect, did not grow on the ruins of the Middle Ages but on the last great flowering of medieval philosophy.[1]

[1] See Appendix D.

CHAPTER FIVE

HOOKER AND PLATO

IF TO some modern philosophers there is little to choose between the 'errors' of Platonism and Aristotelianism[1], the historian must lay special emphasis on the gulf which separated Plato from Aristotle and which divided for many centuries all thinkers into two main classes, namely into Platonists and Aristotelians. At all times there were many important cross-currents between these two chief groups; but, in spite of these cross-currents which often wiped out any clear line of demarcation, the historian can always ultimately recognize the different and opposing points of view; for in the last analysis the two philosophies are incompatible with one another and together exhaustive of philosophical thought. There are, on one side, the doctrine of innate ideas, the theory of intuitive knowledge, and the consequent stress of the ecstatic and emotional aspects of intellectual work in Plato; and there are, on the other side, Aristotle's cautious empiricism, the theory of the slow and gradual acquisition of knowledge through definition and classification and a corresponding emphasis on the more sober and certain, if more pedestrian, features of human intelligence.

The key-point in Aristotle's opposition to Plato is his criticism of the Platonic version of the theory of ideas. And it was largely because of the plausibility of that criticism that St. Thomas espoused the cause of Aristotle and accepted all its consequences and in turn criticized the Platonic basis of Augustinian philosophy.[2]

[1] Both Plato and Aristotle are condemned by the vigorous modern approach to philosophy. Cp. B. Russell, *History of Western Philosophy*, London, 1946; and R. K. Popper, *The Open Society and its Enemies*, London, 1945.

[2] See Chapter II.

147

Hooker for reasons which we have discussed in an earlier chapter fell back upon St. Thomas; and thus committed himself to the latter's Aristotelianism and took an uncompromising stand against Plato. Hooker's theory of knowledge corresponds in fact exactly to the Thomistic version of Aristotelianism.

According to Hooker and St. Thomas, only angels have complete and full knowledge in the highest degree; for they know through innate ideas without the help of sense-experience. Since they have no body, their intellect does not start its work of cognition with sensation.[1] Men can attain such complete knowledge as angels have from the very beginning, only after a long life of intellectual labour.[2] For the human intellect works in a manner completely different from that of the angels. 'The soul of man is like a book, in which nothing is, and yet all things may be imprinted.' The human intellect, being imperfect, is basically passive. It is a *tabula rasa*, capable of receiving knowledge. The human intellect is an *intellectus possibilis*: it is in potency to all intelligible things.[3] There are no innate ideas in the human intellect: both Hooker and St Thomas accepted the Aristotelian doctrine that 'nihil est in intellectu quod non prius fuerit in sensu'. Nevertheless the human mind is not entirely passive. Elementary forms, which are very close to matter, cannot reach beyond matter. But animals obtain knowledge through their senses.[4] And man himself can reach even higher than unto sensible things. For his soul, the form of his body, resembles spiritual substances. He can therefore know the spiritual and the abstract.[5] This process of acquiring knowledge takes place in the following way: to begin with, the human soul just stores up images which later 'serve as instruments unto the knowledge that is greater'. The process begins with knowledge acquired through the senses.[6]

[1] In the following notes the first reference is to the *Laws of Ecclesiastical Polity* and the other references are to the works of St. Thomas—I. vi. I; S.Th. I, 55, 2 ad Resp. and ad Ist.

[2] I. vi. I; S.Th. I, 62, 5 ad Resp.

[3] I. vi. I; S.Th. I, 79, 2 ad Resp.; S.c.G. II, 59 ad Per demonstrationem.

[4] I. vi. 2; S.Th. I, 76, I.

[5] I. vi. 3; S.Th. I, 76, I.

[6] I. vi. 3; S.Th. 76, I.

But through that sense-knowledge the soul can proceed to more abstract knowledge. The *intellectus activus* raises through its power of abstraction mere images to intelligible forms.[1] Images themselves—if we may expound Hooker's brief references with the help of Thomistic doctrine—become intelligible only through the active intellect. Hence our knowledge, though caused by sense-experience, ultimately transcends it.[2] We can think of corporeal things only with the help of analogy with other corporeal things.[3] Pure spiritual substances think of the corporeal by analogy with the incorporeal; men do exactly the opposite.[4] As long as we are living on this earth our intellect cannot enable us to know pure spirits in themselves.[5] The human intellect works by abstracting general concepts from the initial sense-data; but it can never know anything in any other way. Not even the most abstract and general idea, God, is known intuitively and directly *qua* God, but is known to the human mind through a gradual process of abstraction from, and an analogy with those images that are known through the senses, i.e. by the method by which anything can be known at all by the human mind. Consequently both Hooker and St. Thomas showed themselves strict Aristotelians even in their theology. We can know nothing about God, they maintain; for He is no *species* and has no *differentia* and no *genus*.[6] Such matters as the doctrine of the Trinity are mysteries of faith, beyond human understanding.[7]

Thus the anti-Platonic outlines of Hooker's philosophical standpoint are quite clear. He denied that the human mind could know anything through innate ideas or that it could have a direct intuitive understanding of any object or concept which had not entered the mind through one of its senses. The mind, in short, is a *tabula rasa* and neither through *anamnesis* nor through special

[1] S.Th. I, 79, 3.
[2] S.Th. I, 84, 6.
[3] S.Th. 84, 7 ad 3rd.
[4] S.Th. I, 85, 1.
[5] S.Th. I, 88, 1.
I. ii. 2; S.Th. I, 3, 4 ad Resp.; S.c.G. I, 24, 25.
I .ii. 2; Comp. theol. I, 36.

divine illumination does it ever grasp abstract and general notions. Abstract notions have to be arrived at through a painstaking and laborious process of the human intellect. Once this is understood, we can see Hooker's position in regard to the main and most powerful currents of sixteenth-century philosophy.

As is well known, and as we tried to indicate in the preceding chapter, these currents were always of an anti-Aristotelian character, and nearly always tended towards some form of Platonism. There is a large variety of reasons for the wide popularity of Platonism in the sixteenth century. It is very likely that people turned towards Platonism in order to extricate themselves somehow from the philosophical débacle of Nominalism. The weakened realism of Aristotle and St. Thomas was powerless to stem the sweeping tide of Nominalist arguments; but the out-and-out realism of Plato himself was at least a strong and dogmatic counterblast to any Nominalist criticism. And so we find the curious phenomenon that Platonism was especially welcomed by those radical Protestants who owed their own background and conviction almost entirely to the influence of Nominalism.[1] But Protestantism itself had, through its revival of St. Augustine, an even more direct connexion with Platonism. For St. Augustine was foremost a Platonist and some of the basic presuppositions of his thought are Platonic.[2]

The belief that only ideas are real and that the sensible world is ephemeral is entirely Platonic. And the Augustinian tendency towards the first type of Christian philosophy, as outlined in the first chapter, must be partly, at least, traced back to the conception of Plato that a certain stigma attaches to the natural and sensible world, and that it is less noble than the world of ideas. This was only one side of Plato's thought—as we shall see later—

---

[1] Puritanism 'needed a stick to beat the dog of Nominalism' because a world made up of concrete entities which conformed to no collective terms, to no laws or rules conceived by men, could never serve as the scene for the drama of salvation. Perry Miller, *The New England Mind*, New York, 1938, p. 147.

[2] St. Augustine, however, took up only one aspect of Platonic thought: he was more interested in Plato's religiosity and his transcendentalism than in the philosophy of the Symposion or the Phaidros. Cp. C. Bäumker, *Platonismus im Mittelalter*, in Beiträge, Münster, 1927, Vol. 25, p. 166.

but, emphasized through hundreds of years by the vogue of an Augustinian Platonism, it became one of the corner-stones of philosophically inclined Protestantism and was directly responsible for the sixteenth-century failure to preserve the dual poles of the Christian conception of the universe in a proper equilibrium. And there were other Platonic doctrines, such as that truth and the certainty of it are innate in the human mind, or that God can be apprehended directly with the spiritual eye: they were taken up by St. Augustine[1] and came to be intimately connected with Protestant thought. The doctrine of the certainty of regeneration through faith with its notion of the direct contact between the divine and the human and its disparagement of an intellectual or moral effort in that direction, could certainly find a better inspiration in Platonism than in an Aristotelian empiricism.

2

There is no reason to suppose that Hooker was very much concerned with the Platonic basis of Puritanism. But through his allegiance to St. Thomas he was led to reject Platonism by implication; and we have seen that his attitude in this respect was perfectly clear and consistent. He did not argue against Platonism because it proved an inspiration for Puritanism; but he took a firm stand against his contemporary English Platonists who, when he was writing his *Laws of Ecclesiastical Polity*, had gained a fairly firm foothold in the University of Cambridge, because they were endeavouring to undermine Aristotelianism and Thomism. His sole reason for doing so was that his own arguments against Puritanism stood and fell with St. Thomas's Aristotelianism. We shall refer to these Platonists at Cambridge as Ramists: because they were supporters of Peter Ramus it is necessary to distinguish them clearly from the famous school of Cambridge Platonists of the following century, with which they had nothing whatever in common.

From a philosophical point of view, the most significant figure

---

[1] Cp. v. Hertling, *Augustin*, Mainz, 1902, p. 43.

in late-sixteenth-century Protestantism was the French philosopher Peter Ramus. He taught for many years both in France and Germany and established his powerful influence in both countries through his prolific writings. He was finally killed, the victim of professional jealousy, during the massacre of St. Bartholomew in Paris in 1572.[1] To begin with, Ramus represented the typical Protestant reaction against Scholasticism and Aristotle.[2] He held the latter responsible for the barrenness of fifteenth- and sixteenth-century philosophy and outdid himself in accusing him of a sterile formalism. In logic he considered Aristotle a sophist, and in metaphysics an atheist, since his conception of God allowed neither for providence nor for creation. On these grounds he sustained his famous thesis 'quaecumque ab Aristotele dicta essent, commenticia esse' in 1563; and wrote: 'I think that this recent darkness, i.e. scholasticism, should be cast away as far as possible and the ancient light brought back.'[3] He thus suggested repeatedly a return to the golden age of Christianity.[4] He wanted to abolish all idle logic and all barren disputes and go back to the language of the Holy Spirit.[5]

On the positive side, Ramus endeavoured to bring about nothing less than a complete revolution in education and a reform of all logic. The quintessence of his argument was that human reasoning must follow the natural inclination of the human mind and therefore take as its standard criteria not the artificial and formal rules of Aristotle, but the great examples of the good writers of antiquity. He believed that man ought to follow natural dialectics, and that formal doctrine, *ars*, can only imitate the latter and that all exercise in logic must be guided by man's natural instinct.[6] He probably meant that human speech does not

---

[1] For his life, doctrine and writings see Perry Miller, op. cit.; F. P. Graves, *P. Ramus and the Educational Reformation of the sixteenth century*, New York, 1912; H. Ritter, *Geschichte der Philosophie*, Hamburg, 1850, Vol. IX; Ch. Waddington, *Ramus*, Paris, 1855; for the meaning of his philosophy see H. Höffding, *A History of Modern Philosophy*, London, 1900, p. 186.

[2] G. Saitta, *La Scolastica del Secolo XVI*, Torino, 1911, p. 40.

[3] *Comm. de Religione Christiana*, I, Preface.

[4] Op. cit., I. 6. 25; II. 9. 165; IV. 17. 338; etc.

[5] Ibid., IV. 18. 343.

[6] *Dialecticae Institutiones*, Praef.

really aim at formal proof of propositions but at persuasion. The rigid technicalities of the syllogism carry therefore only a very limited amount of conviction compared to the striking appeal achieved by the natural flow of language of a trained rhetorician. There is no need to go into the details of Ramus's scheme for the reform of logic: but it is well to remind ourselves that it has been suggested that Ramus simply failed to understand the difference between logic and rhetoric. He believed in fact that dialectics was *l'art de bien disputer* and tried to prove it by showing that both λογίζεσδαι and διαλέγεσαι were derived from one and the same root: λόγος.[1]

He meant the ultimate outcome of his teaching to be a reform of the aims of education. He wanted those things to be taught which would enable a man to dispute well. He wanted to free the curriculum from all the cumbersome technicalities which were of no practical use. He strove for simplification and common sense so that the fruits of education might be enjoyed not only by the professional scholar but also by the man engaged upon the practical affairs of everyday life. Knowledge was to be applied in practice, and philosophical terminology was to be made more like everyday language. He never tired of criticizing those who had studied philosophy but could not apply it. So he chose his examples from the ancient writers with a view to their practical usefulness and dispensed altogether with instruction in formal logic.

Behind Ramus's philosophy there had always stood Plato. He had first been influenced in that direction by his teacher Sturm, from whom he had learnt more than from the set curriculum of the Paris schools.[2] Plato was to him the God and Homer of philosophers[3], and of all pagans he was the most pious. One can indeed easily detect the Platonic presuppositions behind Ramus's reasoning. There is first of all the idea that formal logic is only an imitation of the natural bent of a dialectical argument. What really matters is the spontaneous play and counter-play of

[1] *Dialectique*, 1555, p. 1.

[2] Ritter, op. cit., Vol. IX, p. 472.

[3] *Dialecticae Institutiones*, Basel, 1556, p. 50; *Animadversiones Aristotelicae*, Paris, 1556, III, p. 88.

propositions. And everything that was important in that respect had in fact been invented by Plato and had only been confused by Aristotle.[1] The Socratic method, rather than the Aristotelian syllogisms, could guide the human mind towards true understanding. This argument was significant in itself; because it meant not only a rejection of the whole scholastic method but an attack on the very subject-matter of Thomistic Aristotelianism. To take only one example: formal deduction plays a very important role in the Thomistic theory of natural law. Without it, the vital distinction between the *modo determinationis* and the *modo conclusionis* breaks down. Or, in Hooker's words, 'merely' and 'mixed' human law will be confused with one another.

But Ramus's Platonism went even deeper than that: he accepted the theory of ideas in its full Platonic sense. If the art of logic is to be conceived as an imitation of nature, the rules of logic and such notions as universal concepts must be embedded in nature herself and are not merely artificial constructions of the human intellect, invented in order to facilitate discourse. 'The art of Logic is in the thing', as a seventeenth-century commentator put it.[2] Names cannot be attributed arbitrarily to objects; but our language reflects the structure of the world: the art of discourse mirrors the relationships that exist in the natural world of objects. We find thus in Ramus a very strong Platonic realism and by implication a criticism of Aristotle.

On the Continent the teaching of Ramus spread like wildfire.[3] Towards the end of the century it had gained a firm foothold in most French and German universities and its attack on Aristotle paved the way for the reception of Cartesian philosophy. It established itself in Scotland, through the teaching of the Scottish reformers[4] and it became almost the official philosophy of the Puritans in New England.[5]

[1] *Animadversiones Aristotelicae*, I, pp. 9 ff.

[2] Quoted by Perry Miller, op. cit., pp. 146 ff.; cp. also Ritter, op. cit., Vol. IX, p. 490; and Graves, op. cit., p. 111.

[3] St. d'Irsay, *Histoire des Universités Françaises et étrangères*, Paris, 1935, Vol. II, p. 38.

[4] A. Grant, *The Story of the University of Edinburgh*, London, 1844, Vol. I, pp. 68, 80.

[5] Perry Miller, op. cit., *passim*.

In England itself there appeared in the seventies and eighties a considerable number of editions and translations of Ramus's works.[1] In Oxford, dominated as it was by the more conservative elements, his teaching found no real supporters—though even there the merits and demerits of his ideas were debated.[2] But in Cambridge Ramus gained a wide popularity through his appeal to the English humanists and more particularly through the open support of men like Ascham, Sidney, Harvey and Temple; so that by the end of the century Cambridge was renowned even abroad as a seat of Ramist philosophy.[3]

In his *Schoolmaster*, Ascham had actually expressed an unfavourable opinion of Ramus's philosophy. He thought that in religion it might lead to dissension and in politics to faction. It appears that he chiefly disliked Ramus's unqualified attack on Aristotle.[4] But in a letter to Sturm he defined his attitude more clearly. 'Ex animo profecto', he wrote, 'faveo Ramo.'[5] Nevertheless he considered Ramus's attack on the many bad Aristotelians more appropriate than his attack on Aristotle himself. He agreed with Ramus's ideas on Christian doctrine and with his conviction that much of Aristotle's doctrine was obscure and useless.[6] Thus the ground for a reception of Ramism was prepared by one of the greatest English humanists whose influence and prestige was very great in Cambridge. Nevertheless it was at first difficult for Ramism to find official recognition. Aristotelianism was the dominant note in the set curriculum of the University, and in England the foundations of peripatetic philosophy had never been really challenged from a philosophical point of view although there had been much criticism of Aristotle during the sixteenth century by both natural scientists and mathematicians.

So we cannot be surprised to find that Gabriel Harvey, another

---

[1] For details see Hardin Craig, *A Contribution to the Theory of the English Renaissance*, *Philological Quarterly*, 1928; Perry Miller, op. cit., Appendix.

[2] See John Case, *Speculum Moralium Questionum*, Oxford, 1585, Preface.

[3] Th. M'Crie, *Life of Melville*, Edinburgh, 1819, Vol. II, p. 306; W. Dillingham, *Vita Chadertoni et Usserii*, Cambridge, 1700, p. 15.

[4] Ed. Mayor, p. 101.

[5] *Rogeri Aschami Epistolarium Libri Quatuor*, Oxoniae, 1703, p. 45.

[6] Loc. cit.

eminent humanist and supporter of Ramus, met with much hostility and opposition in Cambridge. It appears that in 1573 he was nearly refused admission to the M.A. degree because of his outspoken criticism of Aristotle. And it is unlikely that the University authorities were very much impressed or placated by his defence that he was merely following Ramus and other moderns.[1] It would be wrong to suppose that Harvey's difficulties at Cambridge were entirely due to his agreement with Ramus; but there can be no doubt that the fact that he was an avowed Ramist confirmed many people in their dislike for him and labelled him officially as a representative of a dangerous new philosophy. 'Ut pulcherrime philosophatur Ramus . . .', he wrote.[2] Ramus to him was the chief master in theology and arithmetic.[3] And as Galenus was a sophist, not a physician, in comparison to Paracelsus, so Aristotle was a sophist in comparison to Ramus.[4] So we can discern in the violent quarrel between Nashe and Harvey which excited Cambridge during the eighties the opposition of Aristotle to Ramus, which was soon to become one of the most fundamental intellectual issues of the time. Harvey made little headway, chiefly because he was a very difficult person to get on with. But official opinion towards the end of the eighties began to swing round and espoused the cause of Ramus when it was put forward and defended by a more able philosopher such as W. Temple of King's College.[5]

Temple's attack was directed against the teaching and influence of Digby, a fellow of St. John's College and a very popular lecturer in philosophy in the University. Digby was neither very original in his thought nor very enlightened. In his writings there are traces of Neo-Platonism, Aristotelianism, Jewish and Christian mysticism and a strong belief in what we to-day might call Black

---

[1] Cp. *The Letter Book of G. Harvey*, Camden Society, 1884, p. 10.

[2] *G. Harvey's Marginalia*, collected and edited by G. C. Moore-Smith, Stratford-upon-Avon, 1913, p. 207, line 16.

[3] Ibid., p. 195, lines 19–24.

[4] Ibid., p. 155, line 7.

[5] Cp. F. R. Johnson, *Astronomical Thought in Renaissance England*, Baltimore, 1937, p. 191.

Magic.[1] He had lectured on philosophy during the seventies, and even his great adversary Temple admitted that there had been a considerable revival of interest in philosophy through the teaching of Digby.[2] What concerns us at the moment is that Digby, in spite of his eclecticism, taught an Aristotelian theory of knowledge and was a staunch defender of the formal Aristotelian logic. Formal logic was to him the science of all sciences and the art of all arts.[3] And he maintained that logic was to the other sciences like rational speech to chattering; and like life to a corpse.[4]

He denied that the human intellect could know anything, by a simple act of intuition, of the first principles and of the universal concepts from which everything else could be deduced. On the contrary, he maintained, the first and most general principles are for us the last to be known. The human intellect begins with the apprehension of sense-data and with particular sensations and proceeds from them through abstraction to the universal first principles.[5] 'Sensus est initium notitiae nobis prioris.'[6] The soul notes images of objects, and from these images the intellect, through abstraction, forms its general concepts.[7] Digby, however, was not a Nominalist, but a realist in the weak sense; for he said that the general concept is contained in the particular, and that it is only in the human mode of knowledge that the cognition of the particular precedes the cognition of the universal. The universal is not a human artefact but a true property of the nature of things.[8]

In the beginning then, the soul is a *tabula rasa*.[9] Neither concepts nor ideas are innate but are formed through the activity of the intellect, which is no passive recipient of images but an *intellectus agens* in the Thomistic sense. And without the activity

---

[1] Cp. J. Freudenthal, *Beiträge zur Geschichte der englischen Philosophie*, *Archiv für Geschichte der Philosophie*, Berlin, 1892, Vol. V, p. 597.

[2] *Mildapetti Admonitio*, Frankfurth, 1589, p. 16.

[3] *Theoria Analytica*, p. 377.

[4] Ibid., p. 378.

[5] *De Duplici Methodo*, I, Ch. 16.

[6] *Theoria Analytica*, pp. 62 ff.

[7] Ibid., p. 116.

[8] *De Duplici Methodo*, I, Ch. 19; *Theoria Analytica*, p. 393.

[9] *Theoria Analytica*, pp. 54 ff.

of the intellect our sense-impression would never attain to the level of real knowledge.[1]

It is easy to see how closely Digby moved along the lines of the Thomistic, Aristotelian tradition of scholastic philosophy. He in fact merely reiterated St. Thomas's epistemology as expounded in *Summa Theologica*, I, 84, and found himself therefore completely at one with Hooker. Digby believed that Aristotle had a divine intelligence[2] and thought that any departure from his perfect philosophy was some form of heresy.[3] And in the preface to his *Theoria Analytica* he is full of abuse for those who forsook the certain fruits of the tree for the newly invented ideas of Ramus which only served to increase error, ignorance and confusion.

Against this philosophy Temple raised his protest in the name of the modern age and of progressive enlightenment.[4] There was no sense, he wrote, in the blind veneration of Aristotle[5] and though we owed much to him, he was only human and therefore liable to err.[6] Hence it is perfectly legitimate for Ramus to claim to have improved on Aristotle and to have surpassed all the works produced by the Aristotelian schools.[7] Philosophy, after all, was a search for truth and not a blind worship of Aristotle.[8] It is a real tragedy in philosophy that all new ideas, no matter how true they are, are rejected, and that every thinker is simply expected to abide by Aristotle.[9] The modern scholastics live in the shadow of Aristotle's authority and have invented some logical sophistry

---

[1] *Theoria Analytica*, p. 57.

[2] *Theoria Analytica*, p. 99.

[3] *De Duplici Methodo*, I, Ch. 19.

[4] His first attack was published anonymously: *Francisci Mildapetti Navarreni ad Ever. Digbeium Anglum Admonitio de unica P. Rami Methodo*, London, 1580, reprinted in Frankfort, 1589. His second attack appeared under his own name: *Pro Mildapetti De unica Methodo Defensione contra Diplodophilum commentatio Gulielmi Tempelli*, London, 1581, reprinted in Frankfort, 1584; quoted as MA and MD respectively. The references are to the Frankfort editions.

[5] MD, p. 27.

[6] MD, p. 175.

[7] MD, pp. 25, 28.

[8] MD, p. 64.

[9] Loc. cit.

in order to be able to lie[1] 'Non ego alicuius Aegidii quotidianum loquacitatem sine usa, nec e Thomae schola exilem aliquam et absonam cantilenam requiro.'[2] Thus Temple defined his position: he was reasonable in his criticism of Aristotle and, like Ascham, more intolerant of Aristotelians than of Aristotle himself.

For the rest he admittedly only wished to propound the principles of Ramist philosophy in England, without wishing to make any contribution himself.[3] He argued that logic, which is the *ars bene disserendi*, must follow nature. During the Middle Ages, however, logic had been degraded to being the servant of sophistry and of futile verbalism.[4] He showed himself a true Platonist in that he maintained that philosophy and science were only interested in the universal and the necessary.[5]. And that therefore the only proper method of obtaining knowledge was to proceed deductively from universal principles[6] which were apparently either innate or known intuitively. In any case, he rejected the empirical method defended by Digby and propounded a typical Christian Platonism: universal concepts are not purely subjective concepts, but are the essences of things. The idea or form imparts being to every particular object. This form, created by God out of nothing, is the essence of things. And man is what he is, not through matter, but through his form, the soul.[7] The universal idea contains the causes of particular things and is needed by us in order to understand them. The particular cannot be known at all without the universal.[8] But the universal, on the other hand, can be known without the particular, in the way in which Plato thought it could be known. Hence the proper method of obtaining knowledge begins by a grasping of the abstract universal and then deduces from it the particular; and not *vice versa*.[9] The particular which is known through the senses in the Thomistic-Aristotelian way is not an object of knowledge at all.[10] In all this we can find the traces not only of a very thoroughgoing exemplarism but

---

[1] MA, epistula dedicatoria.

[2] MD, p. 77.

[3] MD, p. 25.

[4] MA, p. 3 f.

[5] MA, Ch. 6 and 8; MD, pp. 53 f, 78.

[6] MD, p. 130, 151.

[7] MD, p. 180.

[8] MD, p. 103.

[9] MD, p. 130 f.

[10] MD, p. 80.

also a typically Platonic contempt for the world of individual objects and knowledge through sense-experience.

One could hardly wish for a more determined expression of Platonism and rejection of Aristotelianism. Temple took his stand against Digby during the eighties; and towards the end of the controversy, it became clear that Ramism had carried the day in Cambridge. Digby had become increasingly unpopular in his College and in 1588 was deprived of his fellowship and ejected from the College.

In appearance Digby was expelled from St. John's for irregular behaviour.[1] But an examination of the documents reveals that there was more to the expulsion than a mere breach of discipline such as blowing a horn. For when Whitgift and Burghley as visitors of the University insisted on an inquiry, Whitaker, the Master of St. John's, wrote back to say that he objected to an inquiry only because Dr. Legge, who had as Vice-Chancellor of the University been appointed one of the commissioners of inquiry, was himself suspected of being a Catholic. And then Whitaker came to the point: if Digby was restored by superior authority, he wrote, many other insolent people in Cambridge would be encouraged. 'It is a pity and unspeakable grief that the state of this most excellent University should be such, many very good, but never so many bad. Papistry does secretely increase and namely in this College.'[2] And in the same letter he went on to say that Digby was 'notoriously suspected of Papistry' and encouraged papalist opinion in the College.

On April 4th, 1588, Whitaker wrote again to Burghley on this matter and appended a long list of Digby's offences.[3] And here it was explicitly mentioned that Digby was of corrupt religion and that he inveighed in open disputation against Calvinists, that he had tried to influence others in favour of Catholicism and that he had been mixing freely with Papists. Nevertheless the bulk

---

[1] This is the impression given by J. B. Mullinger, St. John's College, London, 1901, p. 79.

[2] See his letter to Burghley of 18th February 1588, printed in The Eagle, October Term, 1906, p. 11. The editor gives the date as 1587 according to the old calendar.

[3] The Eagle, October, 1906, p. 13-4.

of the offences listed are breaches of discipline such as the blowing of the horn in the College. Notwithstanding these charges the
visitors finally decided in favour of Digby. Thereupon the Master
asked the Earl of Leicester to use his influence with Whitgift
to have Digby's expulsion confirmed. Leicester wrote two letters
to Whitgift on behalf of Whitaker. In the first, dated April 30th,
1588, he merely mentioned that he had received many bad reports
of Digby and urged Whitgift to reconsider the matter. When
this remained unsuccessful he wrote again on May 6th of the same
year and this time was more explicit: he called Digby a lewd
fellow who had corrupted the youth of the College and who
therefore ought to be removed for the sake of religion.[1] With
Leicester's aid the expulsion was finally confirmed.

All this looks like a curious conspiracy. The main emphasis
in the case against Digby was obviously laid upon the breaches of
discipline. And the modern historian of St. John's College related
the case with that emphasis.[2] But if one looks at these documents
more closely one cannot fail to discern that the breaches of discipline were not the decisive points, and that Whitaker knew that
they were not; and when pressed admitted, just as Leicester had
done, that the real issue was Digby's religion and philosophy.
But the case against Digby could not stand on the breaches of
discipline and was therefore, when examined in this light alone,
decided by the commission of inquiry in favour of Digby. The
real explanation of Whitaker's reluctance to bring a case against
Digby on purely religious grounds must be sought in the great
controversy with Temple which had preceded Digby's expulsion.
Any discussion of doctrine and philosophy would inevitably have
led to a reference to the Ramist controversy. And here, though
Temple had the support of all progressive humanists, Digby could
cite in his favour the traditions and the curriculum of the University. Whitaker and his friends would have revealed themselves to
the authorities as dangerous innovators and supporters of a really
Protestant philosophy. To do so during the years that led up to
the passing of the Conventicle Act would have been extremely
imprudent. So they endeavoured to get rid of Digby and his

---

[1] For both letters see *The Eagle*, October, 1906, pp. 18, 21.
[2] See J. B. Mullinger, loc. cit.

vigorous and able defence of Aristotle quietly in order to purge the University and open it to Puritan influences.

Hooker's work appeared a few years after this controversy, and was conceived and written while this dispute was still the great event in the learned world of England. It need not surprise us therefore that he should have made his standpoint in regard to these issues very clear and left no doubt as to his agreement with Digby. He did not refer to Digby or the controversy by name; but that he should have found it necessary in a treatise on political philosophy to state in detail the grounds for his rejection of the Platonic theory of knowledge and his criticism of Ramus, is ample proof that he was fully alive to the implications of the Digby –Temple controversy. Temple's victory was not only a triumph for philosophical Puritanism; but also an attempt to undermine the whole edifice of scholastic and particularly of Thomistic philosophy upon which Hooker's own arguments against Puritanism were based. It must have become clear to Hooker, as he was writing while the controversy was in progress, that Puritanism was a danger not only in its blatant and crude statement of Augustinianism as described in the beginning of Chapter II, but also in its more philosophical, Platonizing aspects. The triumph of Platonism—even though in a Ramist guise—would mean a triumph for the Protestant-Puritan elements in St. Augustine and at the same time undermine the influences of Hooker's Thomist-Aristotelianism which he considered so essential to the maintenance of the second type of Christian philosophy. We must therefore look upon Hooker's criticism of Plato as a conscious pronouncement against the Ramism which was in the ascendancy at Cambridge in the eighties and nineties of the sixteenth century.

3

Once Hooker's position in regard to Platonism has become clear we can understand his relationship with the main current of English humanism at his time. Hooker stood aloof from it, if he was not actively hostile, and certainly repudiated any connexion with it. Hence the strange fact that there are so few references to contemporary English thinkers in his work. The main current of English humanism was indeed Platonic; and of Platonism Hooker disapproved. Spenser and Champan[1] were avowed Platonists; Sidney wrote on the theory of poetry in a truly Platonic vein and began to translate de Mournay's Platonic philosophy into English.[2] The connexions of these men tell their own story: Spenser was a close friend of Harvey; Temple was secretary to Sidney; and Ascham was a great friend of J. Sturm, the German Platonist and teacher of Ramus. In all these men Hooker could see, if not active promoters of Puritanism itself, the opponents of the philosophy which he had chosen to combat Puritanism and which he thought to be the most effective weapon to do so. That he never suspected any Nominalist influence behind Puritanism is shown by the fact that he turned so exclusively towards St. Thomas's Aristotle; for he could not have remained blind to the fact that if Puritanism was based on Nominalism, Ramus's naïve but strong realism might prove an effective counter-argument. But his unhesitating and unqualified rejection of Ramus and of Platonism showed in which direction he suspected the enemy.

But it was not only the theoretical issue of Platonism in philosophy which put Hooker into opposition to the main current of late sixteenth-century thought in England—whether that thought was strictly speaking Puritan or not. There was another, more practical, issue which revealed once more the nature of Hooker's temperament and through which we can study again the transition in the scale of values from medieval to modern man. Hooker shared, at the bottom of his heart, with so many medieval men, the belief that contemplation was the final aim of knowledge; and that knowledge in the wide sense ought to be acquired because it led man towards contemplation and therefore enabled him to become a better man. Knowledge, according to this view, was to be sought for the moral value it entailed.[3]

[1] Cp. J. Schoell, *Etudes sur l'humanisme continental en Angleterre*, Paris, 1926.

[2] F. R. Johnson, op. cit., p. 149; Perry Miller, op. cit., p. 178.

[3] For the conflict between such a view and the stress and demands of modern life in Archbishop Laud see H. R. Trevor-Roper, *Archbishop Laud, History*, Vol. XXX, 1945.

The sixteenth century, however, grew more and more dissatisfied with the purely contemplative ideal and opposed to it the ideal of an active life. As a result it questioned the cumbersome and over-theoretical educational methods of the medieval university. People began to understand that the world was not static but constantly changing; and that in a changing world success would come to those who managed to adapt themselves most thoroughly to these changing conditions. But adaptation and adjustment are the result of intelligence and applied knowledge. Hence the dissatisfaction with an educational ideal which set up as the final aim of perfection the ideal of the contemplative life. While the world and the social pattern were being transformed, men began to understand that the acquisition of knowledge was the most useful and the most efficient method of achieving mastery over nature and man. Knowledge could no longer be regarded as an end in itself—but was looked upon as an instrument. And it was considered nothing but common sense that that instrument should be fashioned to serve its purpose in the most efficient way possible.[1] In this way the ground was prepared for Bacon's famous re-formulation of the aim of education and of the acquisition of knowledge: men seek knowledge in order to gain power and control over nature. The acquisition of knowledge held out to man the promise of power, comfort and wealth, provided the knowledge acquired was the right kind of knowledge.

The revolt against the cumbersome and verbalistic methods of education had begun during the early part of the sixteenth century as an appeal to a devout religious spirit which refused to

[1] For the encouragement given by Puritanism to a more utilitarian type of education see Perry Miller, op. cit. pp. 66 ff.; L. Wright, *Middle Class Culture in Elizabethan England*, Chapel Hill, 1935, p. 63; M. James, *Social Problems and Policies during the Puritan Revolution*, London, 1930; R. K. Merton, *Puritanism, Pietism and Science. The Sociological Review*, 1936. The last mentioned author lays special stress on the fact that the Puritans were bent on an explanation of nature for the greater glory of God. But it seems to me that the utilitarian motive of Bacon to explain nature for 'the relief of man's estate' was of greater significance. Merton can explain by his thesis the rise of science under Puritan influence; but he cannot explain its markedly utilitarian and practical characteristics which found their strongest expression in the spirit in which the Royal Society was founded.

allow true religiosity to be buried under a mass of sophistry. It had proceeded as the dictate of common sense with the demand for simplicity, clarity and intelligent appreciation rather than continuous memorizing of abstract rules which most people never understood. But all the time it was fed by the growing consciousness that knowledge was actually being sought for an entirely new purpose. It was that new purpose which Hooker disliked; and it was for that reason that he explicitly dissociated himself from the movement of English humanism with its strong plea for greater simplicity and for a practical application of the knowledge acquired. For it was this as much as theoretical Platonism which Ascham, Harvey, Temple and Sidney had in mind when they endeavoured to introduce Ramus's philosophy in Cambridge.

Hooker had understood that the early criticism of the scholastic method, as expressed for instance by Erasmus, was fully justified. In fact one can take Hooker himself as the best example of the way in which this type of criticism had borne fruit towards the end of the sixteenth century in the scholastic camp itself.[1] The syllogistic method and the formality of the *quaestiones* had been dropped completely. He did not burden his treatise by cumbersome quotations of useless authorities but proceeded clearly from point to point without pedantry or hair-splitting. Nevertheless he retained all the good features of the formal, scholastic method and incorporated them into his modern style of writing.[2] As far as actual practice goes, Hooker is therefore as modern as the most ardent advocates of the new method could wish. But he was aware of the kind of spirit which fed the revolt against the scholastic method. And since he disapproved of that spirit he pronounced emphatically against the method and the theory which

[1] Hooker was completely free from the pedantry of Jewel and Harding who had continuously argued about their opponents' lack of learning rather than about the issue itself. He refused to split hairs, III. xi. 7; and considered it childish 'to lurk under shifting ambiguities and equivocations of words in matters of principal weight', VIII. i. 2.

[2] 'The mixture of those things by speech which by nature are divided is the mother of all error', III. iii. 1; and stressed that 'not in the communication of names, but in the confusion of things, is error,' VIII. iv. 3.

sustained it. He was thus compelled to refer to his learned contemporaries and to the English humanists as men 'full of tongue
and weak of brain'. As there was for him no question that knowledge was an end in itself and concerned with the moral improve-
ment of man, he was driven to expose the new method as the
result of idleness and of the desire to acquire without work or
effort in three days what should take three-score years to be
acquired. He simply dismissed Ramism as an 'art which teaches
the way of speedy discourse and restrains the mind of man that it
may not wax overwise.'[1] To Hooker the acquisition of knowledge was a long and laborious process which required much
education and instruction.

He thought that it was through instruction in the art of reasoning that man's natural faculty of reason would be improved to
judge rightly between truth and error, good and evil.[2] He was not
at all anxious that men should as quickly as possible finish with
their education so that they should be able to get on with the 'real
business of life' and apply their knowledge; to him the 'real
business of life' was just that slow process of increasing one's
knowledge and understanding, and apart from idleness and sloth-
fulness he could see no reason why one should want to hurry along
with it and decrease its quality by cutting it short. St. Thomas said
indeed that the length of man's life depended on his mode of
knowledge. Because it was so difficult for man to acquire knowledge, he had been given a long life to do so: 'Homo secundum
suam naturam non statim natus est ultimam perfectionem adipisci
sicut angelus: et ideo homini longior vita data est ad merendum
beatitudinem quam angelo'.[3] The view that the acquisition of
knowledge was a gradual progress from sense-impression through
abstraction to the formulation of general concepts had thus determined both aim and method of education. And it need not surprise
us that Hooker with his Thomistic epistemology should have rejected the new methods and that Ramus and his followers, on the
other hand, should have given up the old epistemology

[1] I. vi. 4.

[2] I. vi. 5.

[3] S.Th. I, 62, 5 ad Resp.

because it would have contradicted their aims and methods of education.[1]

Ramus and his followers did not think that the art of acquiring wisdom or knowledge was very long; for they had shortened it, so that it would not take up an undue proportion of man's life.[2] From Hooker's point of view, this was a very mercenary utilitarianism.[3] But from the point of view of modern man it was but common sense to confine the acquisition of the instruments for living to a due proportion and not to allow them to make an end of themselves. To spend a life-time in the acquisition of knowledge was absurd to a man who saw in knowledge not the end but the means of life. Again we find a fundamental clash between two opposed conceptions of the value of human life. There does not seem to be much room for argument between the two views. The issue was never joined between Hooker and his opponents. He condemned them from his standpoint; and they from their standpoint must have considered such a condemnation both pedantic and unreasonable. Only the modern historian is at an advantage, for he can see, looking backwards after three hundred years, that the clash lay really in the two standpoints. But while, as a historian, he is no more capable of deciding which is the

---

[1] Behind this dispute we can discern the changing social pattern. During the sixteenth century there took place if not the first, some very decisive, changes which brought about during the nineteenth and twentieth centuries the downfall of that social system which gave certain classes sufficient leisure to think of the acquisition of knowledge as a life-long process. But it was inevitable that a more just distribution of wealth and income should deprive men of that leisure and make it imperative for everybody to regard the acquisition of knowledge primarily as an instrument with which he could contribute to the production of the goods he consumed. The modern attitude towards knowledge is strictly determined by the social pattern we are hoping to achieve. In this sense we are to-day prejudiced against a Thomistic epistemology not for philosophical but for social reasons.

[2] Cp. Ritter, op. cit., Vol. IX, p. 480.

[3] Hooker here repeated the current criticism which had nicknamed Ramus *usuarius*; had called him an *ignoramus* and had said that he wished to teach his pupils to fly without wings. Cp. Schlegk, *Hyperaspites ad epistolam P. Rami*, pp. 4 ff.; Ursinus, *Bedenken ob Rami Dialecticae in Schulen einzuführen*, Heidelberg, 1586.

better standpoint, he can discern very clearly that here was another point at which Hooker's argument lost much of its strength: for it was obviously not very reasonable from the humanist point of view to insist on the maintenance of an old and outmoded method in philosophy and on an educational curriculum which was concerned with perpetuating it. Hooker's appeal must therefore have been limited to those who shared his standpoint, i.e. to those who agreed with him anyway. The others could but shrug their shoulders at his stubborn conservatism.

Thus Hooker had cut himself off from the broad current of English humanism. And conversely, it was thus that English humanism favoured the cause which Hooker opposed.

4

Sixteenth-century Platonism, however, drew its strength and support not only from the Protestant interest in Augustinianism. There was another broad stream of Platonism in the sixteenth century, which was determinedly anti-Protestant. It grew under the influence of the Italian Platonists and more particularly through the work of Marsilio Ficino. Ficino reacted against medieval Aristotelianism; but not for the reasons for which Ramus had reacted against it. To him, medieval Aristotelianism had been responsible for the growth of Averroism[1] and as such had proved sterile from the point of view of Christian philosophy. Hence a return to Plato was imperative and promised to be fruitful. But the Plato to which these thinkers returned was not the Plato behind St. Augustine. They took up and emphasized those doctrines of Plato which were opposed to the Augustinianism of the Protestants. Nevertheless the channel through which they approached Plato was their study of St. Augustine and a revival of interest in his personal philosophy. St. Augustine had throughout the Middle Ages been one of the chief sources of Platonism. It was through him that Plato's ideas were known and it was

[1] For the growth and influence of Averroism in Italy see Rashdall, *Medieval Universities*, Oxford, 1936, Vol. I, p. 263 f.

through his favourable judgement of Plato that the latter was held in such high esteem.[1] But the Florentine Platonists were not interested in St. Augustine's doctrine of sin and grace and predestination. They were influenced by his Platonism rather than by his theology.[2] They were led to Plato through St. Augustine: but in the Platonic Eros they found the theory of the innate, good propensities of human nature and thus repudiated any Augustinian or Protestant doctrine of the complete depravity of human nature. We find here another type of Renaissance Platonism, stressing the optimistic features of Plato's thought and attributing high value to aesthetic experiences which play such an important role in Platonic philosophy.

Through the teaching of Colet, Erasmus and More this Platonism gained as much ground in early sixteenth-century England as the other, more truly Augustinian, Platonism gained in late sixteenth-century England. The early Platonism was also most certainly a strong ingredient in the humanism of Ascham, Spenser and Harvey in spite of their adherence to Ramism. When Colet had returned from Italy in 1496 he had been very strongly under the influence of Ficino and it is likely that his approach to the Scriptures and his attempt to understand them in their religious sense rather than in their dogmatic rigidity, was due to the influence of Cusanus's scepticism.[3] Grace to him meant an expression of divine love; and since to be elect was to love God, the fact of election could not be a divine decree imposed upon man, but a natural human urge. And that man should

---

[1] Cp. M. Grabmann, *Mittelalterliches Geistesleben*, München, 1936, Vol. II, pp. 8 ff.; The Florentine Academy derived their Platonism from the study of St. Augustine: see M. Heitzmann, *Etudes sur l'Académie Platonicienne de Florence. Bulletin international de L'Académie Polonaise des sciences et lettres, Classe de philologie, d'histoire et de philosophie*, 1932, pp. 18 ff., 1933, pp. 35 ff.; cp. also R. Klibansky, *The Continuity of the Platonic Tradition*, London, 1939, p. 46.

[2] Cp. P. O. Kristeller, *Augustine and the Early Renaissance*, Review of Religion, 1944, p. 356.

[3] Cp. F. Seebohm, *The Oxford Reformers*, London, 1869, pp. 29 ff.; E. Cassirer, *Die Platonische Renaissance in England und die Schule von Cambridge*, Leipzig, 1932, pp. 75 ff.

have this urge was certain proof that his nature was not really depraved.[1]

To Erasmus Christianity was not an annihilation of the human will and the human in general—but an education of man and a completion of the human level of existence. The natural bent of man, he believed, is towards philosophy and right conduct. And, with but a slight effort of his own, man will be able to follow that for which he has been created.[2] Or, in other words, supernature is not a substitute for but a supplement to nature.

The Platonism of the Oxford Reformers amounted therefore to a special emphasis on the Platonic doctrine of human nature and of the innate inclinations of man towards beauty, goodness and truth. The other current of Platonism was based on an emphasis of the theory of ideas and the natural advantages of Platonic dialectics as opposed to formal logic. The real significance of the Platonism of the Oxford Reformers was therefore that it presented in a new guise and with a new connotation the quint-essence of St. Thomas's Christian humanism. This humanism furnished through its view of the relationship between nature and supernature a Platonic basis, as opposed to St. Thomas's Aris-totelian basis, for the second type of Christian philosophy dis-cussed in the first chapter. Through its Platonism this trend was both more important and more influential for the development of the modern world than the statement of the second type of Christian philosophy on an Aristotelian basis: for Platonism was a more widespread and more active factor in the thought of the

---

[1] Seebohm, op. cit., p. 37 note; there is no doubt that Colet was not an Augustinian Protestant who believed in depravity and predestination; but Cassirer seems to make too much of his opposition to St. Augustine. After all both Colet and Erasmus cared a good deal for St. Augustine. Cp. J. H. Lupton, *A life of Colet*, London, 1887, p. 57. Cassirer thinks it necessary to stress Colet's dislike of Augustine in order to make the former appear a better Platonist. But this necessity disappears once we understand that Ficino himself had derived much of the Plato he liked from his study of St. Augustine. Erasmus said that he preferred Origenes and Jerome to Augustine. Seebohm, op. cit., p. 437, and *Opus Epistolarum*, ed. P. S. Allen, No. 844, Vol. III, pp. 330 ff. But in his youth at least Erasmus owed much to St. Augustine and con-sidered him important enough in 1528 to publish a critical edition of his works.

[2] D. Bush, *The Renaissance and English Humanism*, Toronto, 1939, p. 67.

sixteenth century than Aristotelianism. Its arguments were more modern and its plea more cogent. And it did not have to waste its strength by contending against the just accusation that its philosophical method was cumbersome and its chief representatives too fond of quibbling.

Thus we can see that the earlier English Platonists, with their conception of human nature and with their belief in human reason, had fought Hooker's battle. Why then did Hooker not refer to his predecessors and consciously think of himself as a continuation of the Erasmian tradition in English thought? Such an alliance with the Erasmian tradition would have been mutually beneficial: if Hooker had appealed to the very Platonism of his opponents he would really have come to grips with contemporary English humanism. And he would thereby have furnished the now missing link between the Oxford Reformers and the seventeenth-century Cambridge Platonists. As it was, the Erasmian tradition was swept aside by a wave of Puritanism. And when Henry More and Cudworth took up their fight against the Calvinistic dogma of predestination and of the impotence of the human will, they remained heroic but isolated figures in the world of English thought.

The explanation of Hooker's failure to become this link must be sought in Hooker himself. He was too much absorbed in medieval philosophy and its problems to understand the real significance of Renaissance Platonism and its enormous value in the battle for the conception of human nature he believed in. He missed a unique opportunity and his strategical error was almost fatal. For had he avoided it, the position of Erasmus and More would have found a firmer place in the English and Anglican tradition, and the Cambridge Platonists of the following century would not have remained isolated. But to Hooker, living in a thoroughly medieval world, Platonism only meant what it had meant to St. Thomas in the thirteenth century: an erroneous doctrine of ideas with a consequent tendency to extol in Christian philosophy the divine at the expense of the natural and the human. With this conviction in his mind, his attitude to any form of sixteenth-century Platonism was a foregone conclusion. He rejected it implicitly by siding with St. Thomas in all those questions where the latter had rejected it, and explicitly by his strong and out-spoken criticism and contempt for Ramus and thus also for the better part of English humanism. His knowledge of Platonism was one-sided. He had seen its Protestant tendencies and its latent Augustinianism clearly enough; but he never appreciated its other aspect, the Christian humanism of the Italian Renaissance.

As it was, English humanism remained split, because there was nobody in Elizabethan England who put forward the full strength of the Platonic argument. The so-called Platonists were absorbed by Puritanism; and the anti-Platonists, though their humanism could have proved the strongest antidote to Puritanism, had severed themselves from all progressive humanism and thus auto-matically supported the cause of the unimaginative and retro-gressive Aristotelian schoolmasters. As a result, England did not heed Hooker's arguments sufficiently: her art and her imagina-tion fell under the dead hand of Puritanism. When Matthew Arnold almost three centuries later criticized the failure of the Anglican view of life in the seventeenth century, he should have added that this failure was due to the fact that Anglicanism had failed to establish its connexion with the Erasmian tradition and had remained only a theology. It failed because Hooker could not inspire it with the spirit of sixteenth-century Platonism.[1] Angli-canism propounded as a view of life must have appeared stale in comparison to the fresher and more vigorous Platonism of the Renaissance. It was a tragedy that Hooker did not manage to find the connexion between the two, and to represent his view of life with the support of arguments drawn from a more widely ac-cepted philosophy. He had furnished all the necessary trimmings in order to save the human will and the human imagination from the Puritan onslaught. But his arguments lacked the ring of life because he failed to understand their proper connexion with the dominant ideas of the sixteenth century. Hooker became a church-man; and his significance for philosophy and the general view of life was not really appreciated.

[1] For a description of the Anglican view of life see E. Dowden, *Anglican and Puritan*, London, 1900; R. G. Usher, *The Reconstruction of the English Church*, London, 1910, Vol. I, p. 80.

5

Hooker was a baroque figure, more akin to the spirit of Cra-
shaw and Andrewes than to that of Elizabethan England. The
most obvious and the most telling characteristic of the *Laws of
Ecclesiastical Polity* which makes their author a real baroque figure,
is the style. Hooker consciously avoids symmetry.[1] His prose
style is not an Elizabethan prose-style, but a baroque prose-style.[2]
Saintsbury speaks of the architectural and even sculpturesque
character of Hooker's style and notes especially the 'adaptation
of the periodic structure of classical sentence to a large periodic
rhythm; the abrupter and more intrusive parallelism or balance,
being widened, softened and moulded out into great undulating
sweeps of phrase, rising, hovering, descending with a wing-like
motion'. This style expresses the mental attitude which lay behind
his work: an attempt to reconcile, rationally, facts and viewpoints
which are actually contradictory, and which can, however, be
grasped intuitively as so many variations of one magnificent
theme. A purely rational analysis of Hooker's thought has revealed that he could not achieve what he had set out to do. His
Thomism clashed with his adaptation of Marsilius, and his failure
to appreciate correctly the Platonic tradition rendered many of
his arguments ineffectual. He stood firmly in the Middle Ages
but was looking at modern problems and was baffled by the complexity of the resulting situation. The complexity of this situation

[1] E.g. ' . . . we were then alive in our predecessors, and they in their successors do live still.' I. x. 8.; 'Our laws do neither suffer a spiritual court to entertain those causes which by law are civil; nor yet, if the matter be indeed spiritual, a mere civil court to give judgement of it.' VIII. viii. 9.

[2] I disagree with Prof. L. C. Knights's judgement on Hooker, *Elizabethan
Prose, Scrutiny*, Vol. II, 1934. Because if it is true that Elizabethan prose-style
misses effects depending upon tone, subtlety and an exact control of tempo and
movement, then Hooker's style is not as Elizabethan as Prof. Knights thinks.
And though it is true that Hooker is at his best when he is expressing a conviction emotionally held and not when he is arguing a case, I would take this
as a further confirmation of the baroque character of his style; for the very
typically Elizabethan prose of Bancroft, for instance, is intellectually persuasive
and an excellent medium for logical argument.

made incongruous and unsymmetrical the style of the thought which had to come to terms with it. But the experience of this same complexity had taught people to appreciate the beauty of this baroque mode of expression.

But apart from this intellectual difficulty which we have observed in Hooker, the baroque was also determined by a positive vision. The generation that had progressed beyond Renaissance and Reformation could once more, in its own special manner, look upon the worldly as a reflexion of the divine and the spiritual, rather than as something to be extolled or combated, as Renaissance and Reformation had done respectively. To the new age, the divine and the worldly interpenetrated, and its art and poetry bear witness to the conscious endeavour to efface the exact boundaries between reality and illusion, between matter and spirit. In this aesthetic sense Hooker was thoroughly baroque; for no matter how much failure he admitted to himself intellectually, there can be no doubt that he was absolutely firm in his aesthetic vision of the human suffused with the divine, and of the spiritual and the temporal interpenetrating and sustaining one another as the links in the great chain of Being.

APPENDIX A

HOOKER'S DEBT TO ST. THOMAS

The following table shows the correspondence between the leading ideas of Hooker's philosophy and St. Thomas's philosophy.

HOOKER	ST. THOMAS
Everything works for an end. (II, 1.)	'Omnia quae sunt inveniuntur esse ordinata ad invicem.' (S.Th.I, II, 3; I, 21, 1; S.c.G. IV, 1.)
No certain end can be obtained unless there is a regularity in action fit to obtain it. Such a canon we term a law. (II, 1.)	
This law is given to all creatures by a superior. (II, 2.)	The lex aeterna is the source of all other law. It is the law by which God wills the universe to be governed. (S.c.G. III, 115; S.Th. I, II, 91, 1 & 93, 3.)
The being of God is a law to his own working. His law is the lex aeterna. (II, 2.)	In God, essence is identical with existence. (De ente et essentia, c. 6; S.Th. I, 3, 4, ad Resp. & 3rd.) God's law is as eternal as He Himself. (S.c.G. III, 115; S.Th. I, II, 91, 1 & 93, 3.)
We can know nothing about God. (II, 2.)	God is no species and has no difference. (S.Th. I, 3, 4, ad Resp; S.c.G. I, 24, 25; Comp. theol. I, 12.) He has no genus. (Comp. theol. I, 13; S.c.G. I, 24.) Hence, He cannot be defined. We only know what He is not and what relation everything else bears to Him. (S.c.G. I, 30.)

175

HOOKER	ST. THOMAS
God is very Oneness. (II, 2.)	As there is nothing potential in God, his essence cannot be a composite as everything composite contains both potency and act. (S.c.G. I, 18.)
The Trinity is a mystery which man cannot understand. (II, 2.)	The Trinity is a matter of faith beyond human understanding. (Comp. theol. I, 36.)
There must be a first cause in the universe. The first cause follows reason. (II, 3.)	The five proofs amount to an argument in favour of a prime mover and an intelligent guide of the universe. (S.Th. I, 2, 3.)
God is a law to Himself and to others. (II. 3.)	
Reason and Will are identical in God. (II, 3.)	As God is not a composite, Reason and Will must be identical in Him. (S.Th. I, 19, 1.)
God does nothing without cause or reason; he does things because they are good. (II, 3.)	God wills the good by the mere fact that He knows it; for He knows everything, and the good once known, becomes the object of the will. (S.c.G. I, 72.)
Nothing is perfect in this world. Though God could have made each thing perfect, He did not; but only made it perfect for one particular end. (II, 3.)	The unequal multiplicity of created things ensures the perfection of the universe as a whole. (De Pot. III, 16 ad Resp.) The highest perfection of the universe necessitates the distinction of created beings and their inequality. (S.Th. I, 47, 2 ad Resp.)
The general end of God's working is the exercise of His goodness. (II, 4.)	God's goodness is proportionate to the degree of being He possesses. (S.c.G. I, 30.)
This goodness expresses itself in the large variety of created things. (II, 4.)	The multiplicity and variety of created things is necessary to express as perfectly as possible their resemblance to God. (S.c.G. II, 45 ad Quum enim; S.Th. I, 47, I ad Resp.) Since

HOOKER	ST. THOMAS
	God wished to express His own perfection through a variety of beings, he had to use a variety of forms. But different forms are different degrees of perfection.
Nothing is created because it is good for God; but God created to show His goodness. (II, 4.)	The divine will created things as becoming to its goodness. But they are not necessary to its goodness. (S.c.G. I, 82.)
There is a reason for everything although we cannot always fathom it. (II, 4.)	
God's will is prompted by reason. This reason is the *lex aeterna* which God has made for Himself. (II, 5.)	The *lex aeterna* is the reason of divine wisdom according to which everything is worked and ordered. (S.Th. I, II, 93, I.)
The *lex aeterna* is immutable. (II, 6.)	
But God is still free because the imposition of that law on Himself was His own voluntary act. (II, 6.)	
The order which God set down with Himself and for Himself is the *lex aeterna*. (II, 6.)	The *lex aeterna* is the plan of divine wisdom according to which everything is guided to its proper end. S.Th. I, II, 93, I.)
Any rule for action is a law. Hence God's rule for Himself is a law. (III, I.)	
This law is the source of all other law. (III, I.) Nature's law Celestial law Reason's law Divine law Human law.—In all these the law eternal manifests itself. (III, I.)	This law is the source of all other laws. (S.Th. I, II, 91, I & 93, 3.)
	The law eternal manifests itself in everything that is done by created things. (S.Th. I, II, 93, 4 & 5 & 6; Hooker's own reference.)

HOOKER	ST. THOMAS
Natural agents observe the law set down for them unwittingly. Voluntary agents, because they have intellectual natures, observe it by giving their free consent. (III, 2.)	Because man is free, the *inclinatio naturalis* and the *necessitas inhaerens rebus* becomes for him a law which he freely agrees to obey. In the human act, *lex aeterna* become a *lex naturalis*. (S.Th. I, II, 91, 2.) Actions conform to laws. Those of natural agents, conform naturally; those of voluntary agents, voluntarily. Natural agents observe it *per modum actionis et passionis*. Man obeys *per modum cognitionis*. (S.Th. I, II, 93, 4 ad Resp.)
Obedience of all creatures to their law is the stay of the whole world. Disobedience results in evil. (III, 2.)	Evil is a *privatio*, the lack of something that ought to be. (S.c.G. III, 6; S.Th. I, 48, 1 ad Resp.)
Nature observes strict regularities. Natural agents always work after the same manner. (III, 3.)	We can observe regularity in the behaviour of natural agents. (S.c.G. III, 69.) The existence of these regularities has made it impossible to hold that God has created things deprived of their causality. (S.c.G. III, 69.)
Natural agents are guided by God and work because He bestows efficacy on them. (III, 4.)	Nothing can work or do anything except by virtue of the efficacy of God. (S.c.G. III, 66.)
God works through nature, using her as an instrument. (III, 4.)	There is a distinction between first and second causes. God could have done without nature; but he created natural efficacy out of the immensity of his goodness in order to make his creatures similar to Himself. (S.c.G. III, 70; S.Th. I, 22.)
As long as natural agents keep the forms which give them their being, they can't do otherwise than they are actually doing. (III, 4.)	It is not in the power of natural agents not to follow the course which is their due. (S.c.G. III, 140.) Natural agents are naturally inclined towards those actions which are becoming to them according to their form. (S.Th. I, II, 94, 3; I, 109, 2.)

178

HOOKER	ST. THOMAS
The soul is the form of man. (III, 4, *n.* 2.)	Man is a whole, composed of form and body. (De Anima, I, I ad Resp; S.c.G. II, 55 ad Omnis enim; S.Th. I, 75, 4.) The soul assigns to the body its place in the species of human bodies. The soul confers on the body the being the body has; hence the soul is the form of the body. (Ethics, X, 7, 1177, a 12.)
The soul is not sensible. (III, 4, *n.* 2.)	The soul is not a body. (S.Th. I, 77, 2 ad Resp.) It is the lowest of all intelligent creatures. (S.Th. I, 118, 3 ad Resp.)
The soul is discernible only by its effects. (III, 4, *n.* 2.)	Incorporeal things, of which there are no images, are known by us through their relation to sensible bodies of which there are images. (S.Th. I, 84, 7.)
According to their forms, things are distinguished into their kinds. (III, 4, *n.* 2.)	
There are Angels. (IV, 1.)	The perfection of the universe demands the existence of beings which have neither spirit nor body. (S.Th. I, 50, 1 ad Resp.) There must be beings which are intellectual creatures, like the soul, but superior to it in so far as they are not united to bodies. (S.c.G. II, 91 ad Natura superior.)
Angels are immaterial. (IV, 1.)	Angels are an order of pure intelligences below God and above man. If they were material they could not be pure intelligences. Their immaterialness is required by the order they occupy in the universe. (S.Th. I, 50, 2 ad Resp.)

179

APPENDIX A

HOOKER	ST. THOMAS
The number of angels is enormous. (IV, 1.)	The number of angels is enormous and much larger than that of material things. (S.Th. 1, 50, 3 ad Resp.) This is, because each angel, being immaterial, in order to be individually distinct, must be presumed to form a species of his own. (S.Th. 1, 50, 4 ad Resp.)
Angels are creatures; God has imposed a law upon them. (IV, 1.)	Angels have only a limited quantity of being. They cannot be said to be, like God, but only to have being. (S.Th. 1, 50, 2 ad 3rd.)
Angels behold the face of God directly. In this they differ from all natural, non-intellectual creatures. (IV. 1.)	Angels, in order to know, do not have to proceed from sense-impression through abstraction. Having no body, they have no senses. Hence, they, unlike men, know through innate ideas. (S.Th. 1, 55, 2 ad Resp. & ad 1st.)
Some angels have fallen through a voluntary breach of the law. As long as they saw God, they could not have seen a greater good to which their will could have inclined them. Hence their breach can only be explained by a dimming of their knowledge of God. When they looked at themselves they were so filled with admiration that their knowledge of God was drowned. (IV, 3.)	The bad angels, by a single act of their free will turned away from God. (S.Th. 1, 63, 6 ad Resp.)
God is pure act. (V, 1.)	There is nothing in God which is only in potency: He is pure act. (S.c.G. 1, 16.)
All created things are in potency. (V, 1.)	Every creature has a certain deficiency in degree and mode of its being. (De Div. Nom. c. 1 lect. 1.)

APPENDIX A

HOOKER	ST. THOMAS
Everything strives for its own perfection, i.e. to become in act what it is in potency. (v, 1.)	It is a property of all being to seek its own perfection. Intelligent beings do it by their will, animals by their appetite and nature, naturally. (S.c.G. I, 72.)
These perfections are good. And as everything can help something to become more perfect (more in act) everything that is, is good. (v, 1.)	Evil means a lack of good and of being. (S.Th. I, 48, 1 ad Resp.) It is a negative quality. It is a deprivation of something which a thing ought to be. (S.c.G. III, 6 ad Ut autem.)
All things seek the continuance of their being. (v, 2.)	It is the property of all being to seek the preservation of its own existence. (S.c.G. I, 72.)
All things seek resemblance with God in the perfection of those operations that belong to their kind. (v, 2.)	Things inferior to man (devoid of intelligence) can attain to God by participating in some resemblance to Him. To be like Him (in having being, life, etc.) is to them their final end. (S.Th. I, II, 1, 8 ad Resp.) All created things participate in or represent the Supreme God as far as becomes their nature. (S.c.G. III, 17; S.Th. 103, 2 ad Resp. & ad 2nd.)
The works of nature always aim at that which cannot be bettered.—Arist. 2 de coel. ch. 5. (v, 2.)	All nature seeks to be itself and seeks its own perfection. (S.Th. I, 12, 1.)
Man aspires to the greatest conformity with God by seeking knowledge of truth and exercise of virtue. (v, 3.)	Man must follow his nature: to bow to truth, i.e. to seek knowledge and to follow goodness as a duty. This is dictated by reason. And since a rational soul is the form of man, man follows his nature if he follows reason. (S.Th. I, II, 71, 2 ad Resp.)
Angels have complete and full knowledge in the highest degree. (VI, 1.)	Angels know through innate ideas. As they have no body, their intellect does not start with sense-impressions. (S.Th. I, 55, 2 ad Resp. & ad 1st.)

APPENDIX A

HOOKER	ST. THOMAS
Knowledge which angels have to start with, men shall obtain in the end. (VI, 1.)	Man's nature does not allow him to attain to ultimate perfection immediately, like the angel. Man needs a longer life to gain beatitude than the angel. (S.Th. I, 62, 5 ad Resp.)
The soul of man is like a book in which nothing is, and yet all things may be imprinted. (VI, 1.)	Our intellect, being imperfect is passive. It is a *tabula rasa* capable of receiving knowledge. (S.Th. 79, 2 ad Resp.; S.c.G. 59 ad Per demonstrationem.) Man has only an *intellectus possibilis*. It is in potency to all intelligible things.
Animals have knowledge through the senses. (VI, 2.)	The more noble a form is the further it can reach beyond matter. Elementary forms are very close to matter. Then come those of plants and finally those of animals. These latter have knowledge through the senses. (S.Th. I, 76, 1.)
The soul of man can reach higher than unto sensible things. (VI, 3.)	Human souls are the noblest of all forms in that they resemble spiritual substances. They can know the spiritual. (S.Th. I, 76, 1.)
To begin with, the human soul just stores up images which later serve as instruments unto the knowledge that is greater. (VI, 3.)	But they must start from sense-knowledge; (S.Th. I, 76, 1.) and only through it can the soul proceed to more abstract knowledge. The *intellectus activus* raises, through its power of abstraction, mere images to the level of intelligible forms. (S.Th. I, 79, 3.) Images become intelligible only through the active intellect. Hence our knowledge, though caused by sense-experience, transcends it. (S.Th. I, 84, 6.) We can think of corporeal things only by the aid of analogy with corporeal things. (S.Th. I, 84, 7 ad 3rd.) Pure spiritual substances think of the corporeal by

HOOKER

ST. THOMAS

analogy with the incorporeal; man does the opposite. (S.Th. 1, 85, 1.) As long as we are living on earth our intellect cannot enable us to know pure spirits in themselves. (S.Th. 1, 88, 1.)

Man, made in the image of God, resembles Him also in the manner of working. What we do as men we do wittingly and freely. Only natural agents are so tied that it is not in their power to leave anything undone. But men can choose freely. (VII, 2.)

The closer a creature is to God, the more it resembles Him. God determines Himself. Man, being close to God, is therefore free. Natural agents since they are infinitely distant from God incline to an end and are wholly determined by that inclination. (De Ver. XXII, 1 ad Resp.)

The two springs of human action are knowledge and will. The will wills the good; and the good is apprehended by reason. (VII, 2.)

In all human acts, intelligence and will co-operate. Both in the choice of the end and in the choice of the means, it is always the intellect that proposes and the will that decides to act accordingly. (S.Th. 1, II, 8-19.)

There is a difference between appetite and will. The former makes us desire a good apprehended by the senses. The latter makes us desire a good apprehended by reason. (VII, 3.)

Sensual and rational appetite differ like the two degrees of knowledge which correspond to them. (S.Th. I, 80, 2 ad Resp.) If the end is known through the senses, we are inclined to seek it through our appetite; if it is known through reason, we are inclined to seek it through rational appetite or will. (S.Th. 1, 81, 1.)

The laws of well doing are the dictates of right reason. (VII, 4.)

The will is guided by reason. Though reason may teach a thing to be good, the will will only desire it if reason also teaches it to be possible. (VII, 5.)

In every act there is an *ordo intentionis vel electionis*. Reason examines the means and decides which is best. (S.Th. 1, II, 13-15.)

HOOKER

The will of man is free. Everything good which reason sees as such has something unpleasant annexed to it. And everything evil which reason sees as such, has something pleasant annexed to it. For reason cannot see the absolutely good. Hence though we always will the good, our will is free to choose this or that. (VII, 6.)

Reason can teach a thing to be good. But as long as it does not do so with utter impossibility of it being otherwise, the will can take it or leave it. (VII, 6.)

To sin is to prefer voluntarily a lesser good to a greater good and thus to disturb the divine order; it is the result of insufficient knowledge. (VII, 7.)

Everything desires naturally the highest perfection it is capable of. So does man. (VIII, 1.)

The will inclines towards what reason judges to be good. If reason errs, we fall into evil. (VIII, 1.)

There are two ways of finding out what is good. (a) Knowledge of the cause of a thing's goodness. It is very difficult to attain to such knowledge. (VIII, 2.) (b) Signs of goodness, such as that all men account a certain thing as good. The voice of all men is the sentence of God. If all men know it they must have learnt it from nature; and nature is but God's instrument. By her we learn from Him.

ST. THOMAS

The will must incline towards that which reason proposes as good. But since reason never proposes the highest good but only a relative or partial good, the proposal is also only partial; and hence the will is free to follow reason or not to the extent to which the good proposed is only partial. (S.Th. I, II, 13, 5 ad 1st.)

As long as reason does not show that an end is necessarily good, the will can take it or reject it. The will is only obliged to will it, when reason sees the necessary connexion between the particular good and the highest good. Therefore only the clear vision of God can incline man *necessarily* towards God. (S.Th. I, 82 2.) The will is free in every state and in regard to every object.(De Ver. XXII, 6 ad Resp.)

Everythng which disturbs the divine order is sinful. (S.Th. II, II, 142, 1 ad Resp.)

All nature is striving towards its own perfection. (S.Th. I, 48, 1.)

'. . . *dupliciter aliquid cognosci potest: uno modo in seipso; alio modo in suo effectu in quo aliqua similitudo eius invenitur.*' (S.Th. I, II, 93, 2 ad Resp.)

HOOKER	ST. THOMAS
God has given reason to every man. He has illumined him. (VIII, 3.)	'*Signatum est super nos lumen vultus tui, Domine.* (Ps. iv, 6–7)'. (S.Th. I, 84, ad Resp.)
Hence we can learn the will of God by using our reason. (VIII, 3.)	The light of reason can guide our wills in so far as it is the light of His countenance. To consult reason is to consult God. (S.Th. I, II, 19, 4 ad Resp.)
Laws thus made, only appear to be made by men. In reality they are made by God and only found by men. (VIII, 3.)	As the created being is an analogue of the divine Being, so created causality is an analogue of creative causality; to be a cause is to exert a finite participation in the infinite fecundity of the creative act. (S.c.G. III, 70.) The same applies, *mutatis mutandis*, to reason. God in His goodness has thus associated man with his own divine government. (S.c.G. III, 113.) '*Dei sumus adiutores.*' (S.c.G. III, 21.)
A law is a directive rule unto goodness of operation. For voluntary agents that rule is the sentence of reason. (VIII, 4.) A law is that which reason defines to be good and which therefore must be done. (VIII, 8.)	Law is an external principle to guide our actions. And since reason directs our actions, law, the formula of that rule of reason, commands obedience, because of the demands of reason. (S.Th. I, II, 90, 1 ad Resp.)
The rule of divine operation is God's own wisdom. (VIII, 4.)	In our discursive mode of reasoning, we say that God's understanding acts upon His will. But in God, intellect and will are identical; and since nothing can be the cause of itself, there can be no relation of causality within the bosom of God. (E. Gilson, *The Spirit of Medieval Philosophy*, p. 92.)
The rule of natural agents is simple necessity. (VIII, 4.)	Natural agents follow a course of action according to the necessity of their nature. (S.Th. I, 90, 2.) They are determined by the necessity of their nature. (De Ver. XXII, 1 ad Resp.)

HOOKER	ST. THOMAS
This rule is determined by the wisdom of God. (VIII, 4.)	Sensible nature is moved by an object which it apprehends to be desirable. But it is not free to be moved or not to be moved. Animals are determined by their sensual appetite.
The rule of immaterial creatures is determined by their intuitive intellectual judgement. (VIII, 4.)	Angels do not know by abstraction but intuitively through innate ideas. (S.Th. I, 55, 2 ad Resp. & ad 1st.)
The main principles of reason are in themselves apparent. (VIII, 7.) Such as: parents are to be honoured; small difficulties to be endured for the sake of a greater good; etc. (VIII, 5 & 6.)	Natural law is the sum of all those obligations which are apprehended by reason to be natural and becoming. Such as: to avoid evil; to seek truth; not to hurt others; etc. (S.Th. I, II, 91, 2 ad 2nd & 94, 2.)
It is possible to know that there is a God and what His properties and operations are, by mere natural reason. It can be inferred from the relation in which He stands to His creatures. (VIII, 7.)	The knowledge of God which we can derive from the human mind, does not go beyond the kind of knowledge which we can derive from our senses. (S.c.G. III, 47 ad Ex his ergo.) But that much we can know through our intellect. For incorporeal things, of which there are no images, can be known to us through the relation to which they stand to corporeal things of which we do have images. (S.Th. I, 84, 7.) Worship of God is demanded by law of nature. (S.Th. I, II, 99, 3 & 101, 5 & 100, 5; S.c.G. III, 120.)
Hence we can, by natural reason, discover a good many rules regarding our duty to worship God. (VIII, 7.)	
There is no power in man or in any other creature, which can perform its function without perpetual aid and concurrence of the supreme cause of all things. (VIII, 11.)	Nothing is done or happens, except by virtue of God's efficacy. God is the principal cause of all actions performed by his creatures. (S.c.G. III, 66-67.)
As long as each thing performs the work that is natural to itself, it preserves itself. (IX, 1.)	The natural agents obey the law set down for them, they are automatically rewarded by being preserved. (S.c.G. III, 140.)

APPENDIX A

HOOKER	ST. THOMAS
Man's actions are voluntary. Hence his transgressions of and obedience to, the law of his nature, is called sin and righteousness respectively. Transgression causes evil to man in the nature of punishment. Obedience causes good to man in the nature of reward. (IX, 1.)	When voluntary agents obey the law set down for them, they are rewarded. If they do not, they are punished. There is no heteronomy; an act is not good because there is a reward; but there is a reward because an act is good. (S.c.G. III, 140.)
Take away the will and all acts are equal. (IX, 1.)	To deny free will destroys the possibility of all moral philosophy and is therefore absurd. (De Malo, 6, un. ad Resp.)
Reward and punishment come from such as can examine the behaviour. Thus God only judges thoughts and intentions. And the State external behaviour. (IX, 2.)	The State cannot watch over the thoughts of men. Hence its laws only apply to their external behaviour. (S.Th. I, II, 98, I & 91, 4 & 100, 9.)
A single man is not sufficient to himself to provide the things he needs for the life his nature desires. Hence men are naturally induced to live with other men in societies. (X, 1.) Civil society contents that nature of man more than solitude, because the benefit of 'mutual participation' is so great. (X, 12.)	Men need one another because nature has not given them the abilities to provide the things they need by themselves. (De reg. princ. I, 1.) Of all the things men need, they need other men most. (S.c.G. III, 128.) Man is by nature inclined to be a political animal and has naturally political virtues. (S.Th. I, II, 61, 5.)
Public societies exist because of man's natural inclination and through a secret or express agreement to have a certain kind of government. (X, 1.)	Man is naturally a social animal. Therefore, even before the Fall, men lived together in societies. A multitude, though, could not live socially together unless there were some form of government that looked after the common good. (S.Th. I, 96, 4.)
The end of society is the common good. (X, 1.)	The end of society is the common good. (S.Th. I, II, 90, 2.)

187

HOOKER	ST. THOMAS
All men desire to be happy in this world. They must be provided with all the necessaries for life. There must be no penury or want. (x, 2.)	It is the task of public authority to see to it that material goods are provided adequately. (De reg. princ. I, 15; S.Th. II, II, 140, I.)
Only if these things are provided for can men care for the first of their desires: the kingdom of God. It is impossible to live virtuously unless one lives. (x, 2.)	In order to lead a good life it is necessary to live virtuously; but to live virtuously, we need a secondary aid: ample material provisions. (De reg. princ. I, 15.)
When men are living together, each cares only for his private end: thus are caused envy, strife and violence. (x, 3.)	A multitude will go to pieces if left to itself; because naturally men strive and care only for their private interests. (De reg. princ. I, I.)
Hence men must subject themselves to a public authority which will promote peace and unity. (x, 4.)	In every manifold there must be one governing principle directed towards the good of the community as a whole. (De reg. princ. I, I.)
Those that are more noble and wise than others, have a natural right to govern. (x, 4.) But if everybody agrees freely, greater contentment will result. Subjection ought therefore to be freely consented to by all. (x, 4.)	Some men are naturally more wise and just than others; it would be an irrational waste if they should not rule. They have a natural right to rule. (S.Th. I, 96, 4.)
The choice of the kind of government is an arbitrary matter. (x, 5.)	There are many possible forms of just government. (De reg. princ. I, I.)
But there are certain forms of government which make things worse instead of better, e.g. tyranny. (x, 5.)	A tyrant does not rule for the benefit of a community but for his private benefit. Hence tyranny is a badly appointed form of government. (De reg. princ. I, I.)
Societies developed from families. Hence fathers were the first kings. (x, 4.)	The state developed from the family; the father naturally became king. The most natural and original form of society is the family. (Comm. in Eth. Nic. VIII, 12 ad viro autem.)

APPENDIX A

HOOKER	ST. THOMAS
Since men do not always incline towards the good, it is wise to add sanctions to laws. (x, 6.)	Not all citizens have the good will to obey the laws. Hence one needs sanctions to force men to obey. (II Sent. d 44, Q. I, 3, 4.)
The particular determination of the punishment is to be made by those who make the law. Theft is naturally punishable. But the kind of punishment is positive, and such lawful as men shall think with discretion convenient by law to appoint. (x, 6.)	Human law is derived from natural law either *per modum conclusionis;* or *per modum determinationis.* (In Eth. 5, 10, lectio 12c.)
To devise laws none but wise men must be admitted. (x, 7.)	Only wise men must make laws. (S.Th. I, II, 100, I.)
The power to make such laws belongs by natural law to society as a whole. (x, 8.)	The power to make such laws belongs to the person *'qui curam communitatis habet'.* (S.Th. I, II, 91, 3 ad 3rd.)
It is necessary to make such laws, because it is not always in every circumstance, easy to see what is the right thing to do. (x, 5.)	In order to define rules of conduct more specifically than is done by natural law, it is necessary for reason to deduce from natural law the rules for certain specific cases. (S.Th. I, II, 91, 3, ad Resp.)
Men have the power to make certain human laws for the benefit of society as a whole. (x, 11.)	A human law is a precept of practical reason promulgated for the government of a political community. (S.Th. I, II, 91, I.)
Human laws must never contradict the law of reason. (x, 10.)	A provision of human at variance with natural law is not a law but a corruption of a law. (S.Th. I, II, 95, 2.) These particular dispositions, invented according to human reason are called *leges humanae.* (S.Th. I, II, 91, 3.) They are applications of the general principles of natural law to special and concrete circumstances.

HOOKER

ST. THOMAS

There are two kinds of human law. *Mixed* human law explicitly enjoins or forbids what is enjoined or forbidden by natural law. *Merely* human law enjoins or forbids what it is expedient to enjoin or forbid but which in natural law is indifferent. (x, 10.)

Not all human law is directly deduced from natural law. Some human laws enjoin or forbid what is *bonum vel malum in se;* others enjoin or forbid what are *in se indifferentia.* (S.Th. I, II, 95, 2 ad 3rd.)

Human laws differ according to time and circumstance for which they are made. They are not less good because through the variety of human circumstances they are not universally valid. (x, 9.)

Because of the great variety of human circumstances, there is naturally a great diversity among the *leges humanae.* (S.Th. I, II, 95, 2 ad 3rd.)

Men act for ends. Each end represents a good. There are many possible ends; each is a finite good. (xi, 1.)

Man's acts arrange themselves under many headings, according to the ends of the action. (De Virt. I, 2 ad 3rd.)

Some ends are desired as means to a further end. But there must be, in order to avoid a *regressum ad infinitum,* one final end, which is desired for its own sake. (xi, 1.)

To avoid a *regressum ad infinitum* in the series of ends, there must be a final end. If there were no final end, no action would ever be carried out, for the prime mover, the final end, would be missing. (S.Th. I, II, 1, 4 ad Resp.)

Animals desire their food as their final end. This is because they are imperfect. (xi, 1.)

Animals strive with their sensual appetite for the highest end which appetite can propose to them.

What is desired as a means is desired with a strength proportionate to the end it is desired for. What is desired as an end in itself is desired with strength infinite. But only that which is an infinite good can be desired with infinite strength. This infinite good is God. (xi, 2.)

Only that, which once attained leaves nothing else to be desired, can represent the final end. But only God, being pure act and infinitely good, leaves nothing to be desired. Hence only God can be the last end of man. (S.c.G. IV, 54; S.Th. I, II, 2, 8, ad Resp.)

We cannot desire as our ultimate end anything which is not infinitely good, such as mere felicity or wealth or any other corporeal or spiritual good. (xi, 2.)

The last end of man is not a good of the corporeal order. (S.c.G. III, 32; S.Th. I, II, 2, 5, ad Resp.) Nor a good of the soul; because the soul is in potency and hence only a finite good. (S.Th. I, II, 2, 7, ad Resp.)

HOOKER

We are fully satisfied when we are united with God. In this union consists our happiness. But to this happiness we cannot attain in this life. (xi, 2-3.) For as long as we are in this world we are subject to all manner of imperfections. (xi, 3.)

ST. THOMAS

The essential and full beatitude, consisting in the vision of God, cannot be obtained in this life. For the proper object of the intellect is the sensible; and the study of the sensible is only an imperfect beatitude. But it is the only beatitude we are capable of in this world. The last end of an intelligent creature is to know God. (S.c.G. iii, 25.) The intellect attains to perfection only when it knows the essence of a thing. For perfect happiness the intellect needs to reach the very essence of the first cause. (S.Th. i, ii, 3, 8.)

Men are capable of God both by understanding and by will. (xi, 3.)

The essence of beatitude consists in an act of the intellect. The delight, which is an act of the will, is accidentally linked with it, and yet accompanies it necessarily. (S.Th. i, ii, 4, 1, ad Resp.; S.c.G. iii, 26; S.Th. i, 26, 2 ad 2nd & i, ii, 3, 4, ad Resp.)

All this joy and peace and delight is endless and everlasting. (xi, 3.)

In this lies the intellect's most enduring spiritual joy. (S.c.G. i, 5.)

No creature but man is capable of such felicity and bliss. To all other creatures perfection is what is good for them; and not what is good in itself. The perfection to which other creatures attain is no better than they themselves; but man's is. (xi, 3.)

Man is a creature living in two worlds. The one is known to him through the senses and to it he belongs by virtue of his body. But the other world is the world which he can understand by reasoning about it and by abstracting from his material sensations. In the latter world he is living by virtue of his soul and in it he is a neighbour of the angels and attains to their form of knowledge. (S.c.G. ii, 72 ad Non est autem; S.Th. i, 77, 2 ad Resp.)

Every being is intelligent in proportion as it is lacking in matter. (S.c.G. i, 44 ad Ex hoc.) Man, having an

HOOKER

ST. THOMAS

intelligent soul, is therefore proportionately intelligent and can attain to a special kind of perfection to which other creatures cannot attain.

All men naturally desire to be happy. And natural desire cannot be frustrate. (XI, 4.)

Happiness is the final end of all creatures. (S.Th. I, II, 1–5.)

Man is seeking a triple perfection:
1. Sensual: its object is the mere preservation of physical life.
2. Intellectual: its object is the pursuit of natural knowledge and virtue.

The soul has a hierarchy of three powers:
1. Vegetative: its object is the body with which it is united.
2. Sensitive: its object is a more universal object than its own body, viz. all sensible bodies.
3. Intellective: its object is more universal still: it is the whole of being. (S.Th. I, 78, 1 ad Resp.)

3. Spiritual: its object is the attainment of the divine and the supernatural. (XI, 4.)

The soul of man naturally seeks a good which transcends all the goods in this life. (XI, 4.)

A natural desire cannot be in vain. Any and every created intelligence can arrive at a vision of the divine substance. (S.c.G. III, 25.)

Hence Nature calls for a perfection which neither the sensual nor the intellectual power of man can provide. (XI, 4.)

The ultimate purpose in life is not the provision of material goods; nor the pursuit of wisdom. But the attainment of the beatific vision. (De reg. princ. I, 14.)

That perfection is in the nature of a reward. The reward is salvation. But through the Fall man's powers have been impaired. Hence he can know only through revelation what the supernatural method to be saved is. (XI, 5.) God has revealed supernatural laws in order to show us what we must do in order to be saved (XI, 6.)

APPENDIX A

HOOKER	ST. THOMAS
At the same time he has included in the revealed law certain precepts of the law of nature. Not because the latter is superfluous; but to make it easier for us to know it. (XII, 1.)	To help those that are too busy, or too weak in reason, God has included in the revealed law some things that could have been known through natural reason. (S.c.G. I, 4.)
Unto everlasting felicity we need (a) Nature and (b) Scripture, i.e. revealed law. They are jointly, and not severally, a complete guide. (XIV, 5.) We must make use of all the gifts God has endowed us with:	'*Gratia non tollit naturam sed perficit.*'

The Senses
Reason
Revelation (Grace). (XV, 4.)
Hence the laws found through *all* these faculties direct the actions of men towards salvation. (II. i. 2 & 4.)

| In this sense, all just laws are in one way or another, a manifestation of the *lex aeterna*. | All laws, in so far as they are derived from right reason, derive from the *lex aeterna*. (S.Th. I, II, 93, 3, ad Resp.) |

The references to Hooker are to Book I, unless stated otherwise.

APPENDIX B

HOOKER'S HISTORICAL SENSE

HOOKER, as no other thinker, save Burke, has helped to make Englishmen conscious of the continuity of their history which has transcended all revolutions. He has understood the two very important principles of social development; that a tradition in order to serve as a unifying force to society must be coherent, and yet must never be static. His example and his method have always worked in favour of the view that one must not force a ready-made blueprint on society but that one ought to take account of men's previous experience when one decides on further action; that politics is an attempt to adjust conflicting claims and to satisfy as many contradictory demands as possible; and that one need not press a theory to its utmost limits if a reasonable number of people are satisfied that a compromise works well and does not result in a scandalous practice. Innumerable Englishmen have been inspired by these ideas and one might conclude that Hooker, together with Burke, has had the greatest understanding of the nature of English history ever exhibited. Hooker, in short, had a historical sense. This is very remarkable for a sixteenth-century thinker, for the sixteenth century did not excel in an understanding of history. But if one understands Hooker correctly, there is nothing remarkable in this fact, because he drew the principles of his method and approach to politics from St. Thomas. Although the practical consequence of his approach is wellnigh identical with that of Burke, it is based on purely rational reflexion and shunned all connexion with Burke's essentially romantic and irrational standpoint. Burke constantly operated with the concept of 'prescription', justified institutions because they had existed for 'time out of mind' and believed that contradictions adjust themselves in practice because they are the expressions of a living spirit, and, because they never adjusted themselves in theory, he looked upon theory with suspicion. Values and institutions, to him, were not good because they could be justified by a rational and absolute principle, but because they had evolved historically.

Hooker's historical sense was anything but irrational. His understanding of law as something that has to be adjusted continuously to varying circumstances is based on the purely rational reflexion of St. Thomas to that effect.[1] He does not for one minute think of it as an expression of a living spirit.

Neither did Hooker believe that only historical study of customs and traditions can reveal what laws ought to be valid. Professor d'Entrèves has asked himself whether Hooker did not think that rational construction must always be subject to proof by historical experience and cannot contradict tradition and historical development.[2]

There can be no question that Hooker held in fact that the law of nature can be found inductively. This view might suggest itself after a cursory reading of I. viii. 3 where Hooker says that to find out what the law of nature commands we only have to find out what men have actually considered to be good.

But we must interpret this passage correctly.

(1) Hooker himself says in I. viii. 2 that there is a better though more difficult way of finding out what the law of reason commands, i.e. by an inquiry into what is good.

(2) The quotations which Hooker gives in favour of his arguments include one from Cusanus which says that one can find out truth by an appeal to the 'sana mens' of all men. True, the other quotations do not impose such a qualification; but, had Hooker expressly meant to say that the law of Nature is simply what men actually do and consider good, he would not have included the quotation from Cusanus which definitely contradicts such a view. Looking at the problem from Hooker's point of view we rather ought to say that Hooker included the other slightly equivocal

---

[1] S.Th. I, II, 97.
[2] *Riccardo Hooker*, Torino, 1932, p. 31.

quotations because he never suspected that anybody could take them to mean anything different from what Cusanus had meant.

(3) The rest of the paragraph, if interpreted in the light of Thomistic doctrine on that matter, shows what Hooker meant when he said that the law of Nature may also be discovered inductively: God has illuminated everybody with the light of reason.[1] This fact enables us to co-operate with God in the government of the universe.[2] The dictates of reason are really an obedience to the law of God. 'Dei sumus adjutores'.[3] We can therefore find out what the law of Nature commands by consulting men, the co-adjutors of God. But only in so far as they are co-adjutors is their judgement reliable.

(4) We can find this law inductively, Hooker says in I. viii. 9, because Reason has been operative everywhere all the time. But it is clear that he does not believe anything to be reasonable because men have done it.

(5) In I. viii. 11 Hooker finally criticizes those that simply accept what men have done without subjecting it to the scrutiny of reason. This is as expressive a refutation of an inductive law of nature as we find in Fortescue: 'Ratio est quae facta corrigit: sed facta nunquam mutant rationem.'[4]

Hooker therefore could look upon law as the product of history, and approach all social problems with that subtle sense for historical realities which is the result of observing a tradition rather than of a rigid theory. But, unlike Burke, he did not take this fact as an indication that the validity of law is in any way dependent on anything but its conformity with reason.

All this shows that on the grounds of medieval rationalism one could arrive at a historical sense. Only modern rationalism did not lend itself to a similar approach. In order to evolve a historical sense Burke had to appeal to irrationalism; but Hooker saw nothing irrational in his attitude towards history and tradition.

[1] S.Th. I, 84, 5 ad Resp.
[2] S.c.G. III, 113.
[3] S.c.G. III, 21.
[4] *Works*, ed Clermont, II, xxii, 137–8.

APPENDIX C

MARSILIUS IN THE SIXTEENTH CENTURY

THE special significance of the political theory of Marsilius of Padua for the Tudor Monarchy has often been noted[1] and his influence on the theory of the Tudor State has been studied.[2] There can indeed be no doubt that his theory of sovereignty and his attitude towards the Church suited the Tudor Monarchy and proved an admirable defence against ecclesiastical claims. But there is one special feature of Marsilius's theory which has never been examined in its bearing on the Tudor State and which deserves special attention.

Marsilius was fundamentally a Christian, in spite of his opponents' attempts to affirm the contrary. And as such he could not and would not deny the demands of the revealed or divine law. But, accepting the Latin-Averroists' notion of double truth and believing with them in a complete separation of nature from supernature, he could afford to place earthly life and its problems exclusively under the secular State. The spiritual aspect of life was so completely divorced from the material aspect that it could not affect the latter; and conversely: no matter what reason or the

---

[1] See F. M. Powicke, *The English Reformation*, Oxford, 1936, p. 45; A. F. Pollard, *Henry VIII*, London, 1913, p. 329: F. W. Maitland, *English Law and the Renaissance*, Cambridge, 1901, pp. 14, 60-1. F. le van Baumer, *Early Tudor Theory of Kingship*, New Haven, 1940, pp. 53-56.

[2] For his influence on Starkey, see F. le van Baumer, *Th. Starkey and Marsilius of Padua*, Politica, Vol. II, 1936; and W. G. Zeeveldt, *Th. Starkey, The Journal of Modern History*, Vol. XV, 1943, p. 168. On St. Germain, F. le van Baumer, *Christopher St Germain*, Am. Hist. Rev., Vol. 42; on Cranmer, C. W. Prévité-Orton, *Marsiglio of Padua*, Proc. Brit. Ac., Vol. 21, 1935, p. 163 ff.; on Hooker, ibid., p. 165 ff.

State commanded man to do, his well-being would be complete. There were two types of happiness, one material and earthly; the other spiritual and heavenly; and there were two methods of obtaining them which could not be integrated and might quite conveniently contradict one another.

It was this aspect of the theory that proved so suitable to the Tudor State. For on this theory Elizabeth could rule her Kingdom according to none but secular principles and yet uphold in all sincerity and seriousness that she was a Christian Queen, and did everything in her power to guide her subjects along the path of true salvation. This is not the place to discuss whether Elizabeth personally was a shrewd hypocrite or not; but it is important to remember that it was possible to take such a view of the relationship between the secular and the spiritual as to base such an attitude on good faith and earnest conviction. In that sense Tudor political theory was still Christian, and not secular and 'modern'; although it differed very considerably from the kind of political theory that had been considered Christian during the Middle Ages.

When a sixteenth-century author referred to Marsilius he might mention the latter's theory of sovereignty or of the Church; but he took it to be understood and therefore not worthy of further discussion that Marsilius's ideas were ultimately based on this special view of the relationship between nature and supernature. What Marsilius really meant to the sixteenth century, apart from his technical and legal theories, can be gauged from the following description of his basic assumptions by Albertus Pighius: 'In primis supponit actus humanos voluntarios regulari duplicibus legibus, divinis videlicet et humanis, proposita earundem transgressoribus poena. Divinarum tamen legum transgressoribus, ut dirigentium in finem futuri saeculi, nullam in hac vita vult esse poenam propositam, sed humanarum tamen. Illarum finem esse supernaturalem felicitatem, harum pacificum, tranquillum et sufficientem inter se convictum hominum. . . .'[1]

The practical consequence of this theory, which was so important to the Tudor State, was that men need not live in this

[1] *Hierarchia Ecclesiastica*, V. 8; in Roccaberti, *Bibliotheca Maxima Pontificia*, Vol. II.

world according to the dictates of divine law other than that approved of by the secular State, i.e. by man's reason. This then purported to be a Christian argument for the supremacy of State over Church. It was this implication of Marsilius's theory that made Hooker's approach to Marsilius such an unfortunate venture. And it was this implication that was seized upon by Widdrington and Barclay when they defended the taking of the oath of allegiance under James I.

Neither Widdrington nor Barclay made any express reference to Marsilius. Widdrington however pointed out[1] that Marsilius was not necessarily a heretic and also referred the reader to Azorius's *Institutes*.[2] Bellarmine, in a reply to Widdrington[3] explained that the reference to Azorius was really a reference to Marsilius, for Azorius 'Primo loco Marsilium nominat'. Azorius himself did not agree with Marsilius; but the way in which he described his opinions leaves no doubt that he too thought of the theory of the complete separation of the natural from the supernatural as the most important aspect of his teaching: 'Fuit Marsilius quidam Patavinus qui docuit duas esse in mundo potestates supremas a se invicem distinctas, Imperatoriam et Pontificiam, quarum neutra penderet ab altera. Imperatoriam quidem esse a Deo per populi electionem constitutam ad temporalia gubernanda et hanc esse ante Pontificiam . . . institutam. . . Pontificiam vero potestatem esse a Christo Domino ipsi Petro et suis successoribus traditam, et spiritualia tantum per totum terrarum orbem administranda'.[4]

Both Widdrington and Barclay availed themselves of this basic conception when they argued in favour of the oath. A perusal of their arguments makes it quite clear that their fundamental premiss was that one ought to do whatever the natural state required one to do; and that nothing so done can—being concerned with the natural or worldly end of man—have any bearing on one's supernatural destiny. For these views they were

---

[1] *A Copy of the Decree*, 1614, p. 9-10.

[2] *A Cleare, sincere and modest confutation . . . etc.*, 1616, p. 75. I have been unable to verify this reference.

[3] *Auctarium Bellarminianum*, Paris, 1913, p. 361 f.

[4] *Institutes*, II, IV, xix.

indebted to Marsilius; and Widdrington and Barclay must therefore be considered as the last exponents of the Marsilian tradition of political thought in Tudor England.[1]

It is important and most significant for our understanding of Hooker's conflict in regard to his adaptation of Marsilius that Widdrington should have expressly denied the basic Thomistic doctrine that everything is subordinated to the first efficient cause.[2] From this denial the rest of his argument follows.

The end of temporal power, he argued, is peace in the temporal commonwealth. This peace is the last end of temporal power *per se*; and of its own nature it does not refer to any other end. Any reference to a further end is purely accidental.[3] Hence Widdrington maintained that the temporal and spiritual commonwealths among Christians are *formally* two total and complete bodies. They are only accidentally united in one subject.[4] The end of civil society is a final end and it is only man's will that may refer it to a further, a spiritual, end.[5] Any subordination of the civil power to the spiritual power does not proceed from the nature of the civil power itself, but from the will and intention of him in whom the true civil power resides.[6] Spiritual ends, in fact, are given by God who is the author of supernatural grace; but he is not, in the same sense, the author of nature and of natural ends.[7] The Church, therefore, can have only a purely spiritual authority but no coercive temporal power.[8]

---

[1] There is an express reference to John of Paris who was very close to Marsilius: *De Potestate Regis et Papali*, Ch. 14 and 20: the spiritual judge can only inflict spiritual punishment. Widdrington, *A cleare, sincere and modest Confutation . . . etc.*, 1616, pp. 88–9. It is important to understand that this does not mean that any bodily punishment ought to be inflicted by the secular power at the bidding of the spiritual power; which view would have expressed the practice of the medieval Church. It means that the spiritual power has no concern with temporal affairs.

[2] Op. cit., p. 164; St. Thomas, S.Th. I, II, 1, 6.

[3] Ibid., p. 165.

[4] Ibid., p. 137 f.

[5] Ibid., p. 160.

[6] Ibid., p. 163.

[7] Ibid., p. 162.

[8] Ibid., p. 156.

By the spiritual power, Widdrington always meant the Pope. But it is obvious that the same reasoning applies, *mutatis mutandis*, to any other spiritual authority, as for instance Hooker's Church. Barclay's argument runs along similar lines. He was primarily interested in refuting the Monarchomachi[1] and in defending the unitary State. He saw in Bellarmine's indirect-power theory as great a menace to the unitary secular State as in the straightforward ideas of Bozius and the political Augustinians, and refused to draw any distinction between them.[2] Lacking the basic Thomistic conceptions of Bellarmine,[3] he could see in the latter's reasoning merely a subterfuge, and commended authors like Bozius at least on their sincerity in saying clearly that they meant the Pope to have temporal power over the civil ruler. He admitted quite frankly that his main concern was for the stability of civil rulers and that if Bellarmine or Bozius were right, rulers would be at the mercy of the Pope.[4]

His primary assumptions are again those of Marsilius. The two powers which keep the world in order, the ecclesiastical and the civil, are so by the law of God distinguished and separated that neither can by any right enter upon the borders of the other.[5] The end of civil power is the common good and a well-ordered tranquillity; the civil power is therefore, *qua* civil power, not referred to any other end.[6] The Church on the other hand is concerned only with man's spiritual end and can therefore only inflict spiritual judgement.[7] The State is all-inclusive and as far as temporal and material acts are concerned must exact obedience from laity and clergy alike.[8] The clergy must confine themselves to purely spiritual advice.[9]

---

[1] Cp. his chief work, *De regno et regali potestate . . . adversus monarchomachos.*

[2] *Of the Authoritie of the Pope*, in *Certain General Reasons proving the Lawfulness of the Oath of Allegiance*, by R. S. Priest, London, 1611, pp. 29–30, 64, 156; also Chapters xx–xxi.

[3] Op. cit., pp. 70–1.

[4] Ibid., pp. 63–4.

[5] Ibid., pp. 6–7, also pp. 67–69.

[6] Ibid., p. 70.

[7] Ibid., p. 168.

[8] Ibid., Chapters xv, xxxiii–xxxiv; also p. 76.

[9] Ibid., Chapter xxxiv; also p. 87.

By such arguments the authority of the secular State and its claim to be a Christian State was defended. That the reasoning was mainly addressed to Catholics need not distract our attention from the fact that it could have been applied to any nonconformist by substituting 'congregation' or 'presbyter' for Pope. The significant fact is that its basic argument was Marsilian, and that we can gauge from it what the appeal to Marsilius in the sixteenth century really meant. It meant that the spiritual aspect of man's existence is completely divorced from the natural part of his life. Marsilius's teaching was propagated in order to foster this consciousness. Only when this is understood clearly can one see the serious conflict in which Hooker was involved when he was forced to borrow from Marsilius. His fundamental conviction was alien to this line of thought, for he believed with St. Thomas that nature and supernature are two integrated realms of being.

APPENDIX D

HOOKER AND LOCKE

LOCKE has often quoted the authority of Hooker and it is therefore taken for granted that Hooker was a forerunner of Locke's political theory.[1] But this is true only in a very limited sense. If one looks at the quotations, one will find that they are chiefly concerned with one aspect of Hooker's work, namely with what one might call the technology of constitutionalism. There is no doubt that in these points Hooker anticipated Locke; or rather, that Hooker represents the link between St. Thomas and Locke. There are subtle differences between the constitutionalism of Hooker and that of Locke. But they are in agreement as to the spirit, if not as to the letter, of the basic principles of constitutional government.[2]

The main quotations are in Locke's second Treatise. Locke quoted Hooker in support of the following views: No man can be judge in his own cause:[3] the ruler must be bound by law;[4] every citizen is subject to the law;[5] laws are available by consent, because the power to make them belongs to the whole society;[6]

---

[1] 'I have indeed myself heard him styled the Father of the Whigs.' Hoadly, *Works*, 1773, Vol. II, p. 253. Cp. Hallam, *Const. History*, 1827, Vol. I, p. 235, and Dowden, *Anglican and Puritan*, London, 1901, p. 85.

[2] The chief difference is that Hooker believed with St. Thomas that one cannot depose an unjust ruler, whereas Locke held that one could.

[3] Section 91.

[4] Section 94.

[5] Section 94.

[6] Section 134; to Hooker the notion of 'consent' is merely another expression for the fact that power belongs by nature to society. To Locke, the notion of 'consent' expresses his conviction that no man can be compelled to do a thing

the two foundations of society are man's natural inclination and
the tacit or explicit agreement as to a form of government;[1] and
finally: human law must agree with natural law.[2]

These principles concern only the technique of government;
they say nothing as to fundamental principles of political philosophy. Among these fundamental principles we find the main
difference between Hooker and Locke. To Hooker, for one, the
idea of a State was insolubly linked up with the idea of a Church.
He could not envisage that a purely secular institution, such as
the State, should be competent to make and administer all the
law that was required. He conceived of society as having a
material as well as a moral function, and it was therefore axio-
matic to him that the organ set up for its government should be
a dual organ: a secular and an ecclesiastical body. Locke, on the
other hand, looked upon the whole problem as a purely secular
problem which could be solved entirely in terms of natural
reason. Whatever moral factors there were involved could be
taken care of by natural morality.

This fundamental and far-reaching difference between Hooker
and Locke is reflected in their theories of natural law. Hooker, in
fact, stood at a turning-point in the history of natural law. He was
the last great representative of the medieval natural-law school.

The common core of all natural-law theories is expressed in the
statement of Ulpian that natural law is what human beings do by
instinct or what their nature impels them to do. Natural law is
the system of those rules which men will follow because they are
men, and as long as they are not interfered with or compelled to
act differently by another power. One's view as to the content of
natural law will therefore be determined by one's view of human

to which he has not consented. Hooker believed, with St. Thomas, that law is
the dictate of reason. If he stressed consent, he did it because he saw that that
was the practical way in which in England man exercised his natural power to
make laws for the social life for which he had a natural inclination: but not
because he thought that the right to compel obedience rested on consent or
contract. His theory of consent or contract does not mean that he is in agreement with either the Monarchomachi or Locke. For a further discussion of
this point see A. P. d'Entrèves, *Riccardo Hooker*, Torino, 1932, p. 89 ff.

[1] Section 135.
[2] Section 136.

nature. But an inquiry into human nature is very largely an inquiry into facts; and its results will depend on one's method of inquiry. Thus methodology, in the long run, determines one's view of both human nature and of natural law. It is clear therefore that there should always be a close correspondence between a thinker's theory of knowledge and his theory of natural law.

The medieval philosopher, using his own epistemological apparatus, which consisted of such methods of obtaining knowledge as revelation, reason and authority, in order to assess human nature, believed that man was made in the image of God. St. Thomas believed that he was not completely depraved but only handicapped by original sin. Human nature was held to contain a divine element which compelled it to seek knowledge of and communion with God; and all human efficacy was the analogy of divine efficacy. Whatever man did because he was human he did as an analogue of God. His natural propensities were those divine propensities which God allowed man to exercise on His behalf.

But when this epistemological apparatus came to be discarded and human nature made the subject of a purely empirical study, its needs began to appear in a different light. Without the help of theology or revelation, one had to take human nature as one found it in everyday experience: dominated by self-interest; ruled by worldly appetites; and here and there relieved by a sprinkling of rational enlightenment and brotherly affection. Hence the new law of nature laid down that men are working primarily for their own advantage. Whether one goes so far as to hold that *homo homini lupus* or whether one confines oneself to the observation that the orderly acquisition of property is the ultimate spring of human action, is irrelevant for our purposes. Such differences are due to the philosopher's temperament and the character of his general experiences. The important point is that both views are due to nothing but empirical observation of man. This was the new element in Hobbes and Locke. The first took such a drastic view of human nature that 'natural law' became the law of the jungle and was worthless as a norm of conduct or legislation.[1]

[1] It had to be replaced by positive law which thus became to him the very antithesis of natural law and the *only* norm of justice.

Locke took a milder view and thus could retain natural law as a standard of measurement.

The most important theory of natural law of the seventeenth century is based on the same empirical outlook. It is clear from Grotius's remark that natural law does not depend on God, that he too confined himself to empirical observation in his study of human nature. Thus he found that men were prompted by selfishness. They ought to realize, he concluded, that it is in their very best interest to do unto others as they would be done by. That the actual content of his natural law is so similar to St. Thomas's must not blind us to the all-important fact that its method of derivation, and hence the grounds for its validity, are entirely different.

Hooker stood at the turning-point in the history of the theory of natural law. He was the last great representative of a theologically conditioned theory of natural law. The growth of an empirical outlook, and the consequent narrowing of the field over which reason could rule supreme, opened a new chapter in the history of natural law. Hooker would have been unable to understand the reasoning of Locke.

ABBREVIATIONS

BF R. Pecock, *The Book of Faith.*

D   R. Pecock, *The Donet.*

E.H.R. *English Historical Review.*

F   R. Pecock, *The Folewer to the Donet.*

In   R. Hooker, *A Preface To them that seek (as they term it) the Reformation of the Laws and orders Ecclesiastical in the Church of England.*

MA *Francisci Mildapetti Navarreni ad Ever. Digbeium Anglum Admonitio de unica P. Rami Methodo.*

MD *Pro Mildapetti De unica Methodo Defensione contra Diplodophilum commentatio Gulielmi Tempelli.*

Re   R. Pecock, *The Repressor of over much blaming the Clergy.*

Ru   R. Pecock, *The Rule of Christian Religion.*

S.c.G. St. Thomas Aquinas, *Summa contra Gentiles.*

S.Th. St. Thomas Aquinas, *Summa Theologica.*

All references to Hooker's works are to the *Laws of Ecclesiastical Polity* unless stated otherwise.

INDEX

Alvarius Pelagius, 122, 123, 133–7; quotes Aristotle, 120; considers state the servant of the church, 142 n.

Antoninus, St., *Summa Theologica*, 137

Aquinas, St. Thomas, Hooker's debt to, 46, 50 ff., 63, 151, App. A; criticizes Plato, 47, 147; Hooker adapts terminology of, 49; on second causes, 57–8, 129, 197; and naturalism, 59, 98–9; on church and state, 81–2; reconciles Aristotle with Christianity, 94; and Marsilius, 98; as 'first Whig', 104; and Tudor Constitution, 110; defines place of grace, 118; misunderstood in fourteenth century, 119 ff.; a defence against Protestantism, 125; new heyday of, 145; his empiricism, 148; and acquisition of knowledge, 166; Christian humanism of, 170; his doctrine denied by Widdrington, 202; on human nature, 207

Aristotle, on end of state, 1; preferred by St. Thomas to Plato, 48; synonymous with reason, 50; and Hooker, 75, 83; on natural power of societies, 85 f.; and Tudor State, 89; and Thomism, 94; and Marsilius, 97, 100; on power in society, 103;

and sixteenth-century state, 113 ff.; decline of, in sixteenth century, 116; and revival of, 117, 124, 145 f.; quoted by Alvarius Pelagius, 120; regarded as dangerous in fourteenth century, 121 ff.; his influence on political theory during later Middle Ages, 122 n.; his influence in Oxford, 126; essence of his political theory, 127; and Giles of Rome, 138; opposed to Plato, 147 ff.; opposed by Ramus, 152; and by Temple, 156; defended by Digby, 157 ff.; opposed by Ficino, 168

Arnold, F. X., *Die Staatslehre d. Kardinal Bellarmin*, 125, 129

Arquilliere, H. X., *L'Augustinisme politique*, 8 n., 123 n., 130 n., 136 n.

Ascham, R., 59, 63, 65, 69; favours Ramus, 155

Augustine, St., on *lex aeterna*, 2; *Confessions*, 11 n.; and Protestantism, 25; and principles of Augustinian philosophy, 46 f.; criticized by St. Thomas, 47–8; rejected by Hooker, 48; his influence on political thought, 129 ff.; on the two Cities, 135 f.; climax of his influence on political thought, 145; tends towards first type of Christian

INDEX